CW00558141

First published in Great Britain in 2018 by
PEN & SWORD MILITARY
An imprint of
Pen & Sword Books Ltd
Yorkshire - Philadelphia

Copyright © Charles J. Esdaile and Mark Reed 2018

ISBN 978-1-5267-3795-3

The right of Charles J. Esdaile and Mark Reed to be identified as Authors of this work has been asserted by them in accordance with the Copyright, Designs and Patents Act 1988.

A CIP catalogue record for this book is available from the British Library

All rights reserved. No part of this book may be reproduced or transmitted in any form or by any means, electronic or mechanical including photocopying, recording or by any information storage and retrieval system, without permission from the Publisher in writing.

Typeset in INDIA by Geniies IT & Services Private Limited

Printed and bound by TJ International Ltd, Padstow, Cornwall

Pen & Sword Books Ltd incorporates the Imprints of Aviation, Atlas, Family History, Fiction, Maritime, Military, Discovery, Politics, History, Archaeology, Select, Wharncliffe Local History, Wharncliffe True Crime, Military Classics, Wharncliffe Transport, Leo Cooper, The Praetorian Press, Remember When, Seaforth Publishing and Frontline Publishing.

For a complete list of Pen & Sword titles please contact

PEN & SWORD BOOKS LTD
47 Church Street, Barnsley, South Yorkshire, S70 2AS, England
E-mail: enquiries@pen-and-sword.co.uk
Website: www.pen-and-sword.co.uk

Or

PEN & SWORD BOOKS
1950 Lawrence Rd, Havertown, PA 19083, USA
E-mail: Uspen-and-sword@casematepublishers.com
Website: www.penandswordbooks.com

Contents

For Gareth Glover, friend, fellow enthusiast and
tireless worker in the Peninsular, vineyard

List of Plates

Foreword

I am very excited to bring forth this unique Peninsular War diary of Ensign Charles Paget of the Fifty-Second Foot. This diary was given to me by my grandmother a few years after my grandfather passed away in 1969. I do not know how it came into my grandfather's possession; however, I do know he was an avid military history buff. Having recently retired, I decided to pursue a greater understanding of this diary which for years has been stored in my safety deposit box. I reached out to Charles Esdaile whom I found via a Google search to be quite the scholar on the Peninsular War. Charles was extremely excited to help me put context around this document. His diligent research resulted in the identification of the diary's author, Ensign Charles Paget, as well as many contextual footnotes relating to the campaign during which the diary was written. I am very grateful to Charles and for his unending enthusiasm on this project.

My grandfather, Luis Pérez, was very interested in all types of military history. Originally from Spain, the story has it that he crossed the Pyrenees Mountains and joined the US forces during the First World War. I do not know what unit he fought with or where he saw action since his military records were among the 16–18 million that burned in a 1973 fire at the National Personnel Records Center in St Louis. As a child, I remember him showing me his scar on his arm where a bullet had grazed him as well as another on his leg where a bullet was still lodged in his thigh. I also remember him showing me his gas mask, rifle and helmet in his suburban Chicago basement. Not long after he died in 1969, my grandmother unfortunately sold these items when she moved.

After the war, my grandfather emigrated to the United States and became a Spanish translator for a Chicago law firm. He was also very active in the 1930s raising money for the resistance against the Franco regime in Spain, volunteering at the Spanish consulate and working hard to represent the Spanish Republic's interests at the Chicago World Fair. Murkier yet, he was somehow involved in fundraising via the sale of art, and, in particular, Picasso's efforts to raise money by selling silk screen sketches, one of which was passed down to me from my mother. Given his diverse experiences, I can only imagine how my grandfather discovered this manuscript, but it is not impossible that he came across it in his attempt to resist Franco.

I think my grandfather would be very pleased to see this document being published, especially with the added content that Charles has put together. Through Charles' efforts, I am happy to see another facet of the Peninsular War come alive. Curators of history are important to our culture so that we have a record of events which we can not only enjoy, but draw upon for valuable insights. While wars are a dreadful part of our human history, it is greatly to be hoped that the continual effort to document terrible events of the sort described here will provide lessons for us in avoiding the same mistakes that brought us war, this being a pretext with which I believe my grandfather would absolutely agree. More than that, indeed, I am sure he would have been proud to fight alongside Charles Paget: if he was prepared to volunteer to fight Wilhelm II in 1918, it is difficult to see why he would not have volunteered to fight Napoleon in 1808.

Mark Reed, June 2018

Preface

It is not often that one gets an email as exciting as the one I got a few months ago. Completely out of the blue, I was being asked to examine a Peninsular War diary that had hitherto gone completely untranscribed, let alone published. As it happened, this turned out to cover the campaigns of Vimeiro and Corunna, and there followed months of hard labour of which by far the simplest part was the wearisome task of copying out the many thousands of words that constituted the diary and the various documents which I have chosen to support it. More complicated by far was the task of uncovering the identity of the author, and it was not without considerable pride that I eventually showed him to be Ensign Charles Paget, an obscure connection of the prominent Anglo-Irish family that produced not one but two of the generals who fought under Sir John Moore. As discussed elsewhere, however, though interesting enough, the diary is not the most eloquent of documents – indeed, many of its entries are very brief – and it was therefore necessary to add flesh to its bones by means of extensive annotations that drew upon a host of alternative accounts, and the inclusion of two parallel accounts of the campaigns in which Paget served. Finally, also to be found in its pages are substantial extracts covering important episodes in the narrative that were far too long to be incorporated into the footnotes. It is to be hoped that the result makes for interesting reading, for the work in effect places side-by-side examples of several different types of the literature generated in such large quantities by the officers and men who served in Portugal, Spain and the South of France in the six years between 1808 and 1814: setting aside the diary itself, we have several memoirs written after the event – in at least two cases long after the event – by men who had gone through the same experiences as Paget; examples of collections of correspondence; and, finally, two accounts written during the campaign and then published in often rather mannered form as collections of letters. All of these different literary types present different advantages and disadvantages in so far as the historian is concerned, and it is fascinating to see how see how they can produce very different versions of the same event. Also of great interest, meanwhile, is the fact that the regiment in which Paget served, namely the Fifty-Second Foot, is one of the most well known in Wellington's army, and yet also one that is rather ill-served in terms of the literature generated by its veterans: aside from Dobbs' memoir, which was published (and very likely written) in the author's old age, all that we have is a single diary that covers only the period 1811–12, a memoir that covers only the period 1813–14 and a rather sketchy collection of letters.

In addressing the task of readying the text for publication, a number of strategic decisions have necessarily been taken, most of these concerning matters of presentation. First of all, with the important exception of Corunna (properly La Coruña), the rather erratic renditions of Spanish and Portuguese names have in every case been changed to their modern forms, and, second of all, punctuation, too, has been modernised. Finally, in a few instances minor changes have also been introduced in the wording though readers may be assured that in no case has anything remotely approaching violence been done to the original text: in almost every case, the issue has simply been clarification.

What lends this work added poignancy is the 'back-story' of the diary. One of the most moving memories that I have from almost forty years of working on the Peninsular War concerns a lady from London who, equally out of the blue, wrote to me to enquire about a Spanish pamphlet describing the sack and destruction by fire of San Sebastián on 31 August 1813 that had been handed down from generation to generation in her family for as long as there was memory, and was regarded as one of its most treasured possessions. The text is a graphic tale of plunder, arson, rape and murder that reflects all too well the experiences of a city that was utterly laid waste by war. So far so good, but the question was why so strange an artefact had been cared for so lovingly for so long. There followed some digging of a similar sort to that engaged in for the current work, and, lo and behold, it transpired that the lady's great-great-great-great-great-great uncle, from whose great-grand-daughter the pamphlet had come down to the generations still alive today, had been a young officer in the King's German Legion who had actually fought at San Sebastián, the inference, of course, being that he passed on the pamphlet to his children with instructions that is should stand for ever as a reminder of the horrors of war. Just maybe we have something similar here: what Luis Pérez made of the diary we will never know, but the dark events it detailed are very likely to have struck a chord with both his sympathy with the Spanish Republic and his experiences in the First World War, and, like Mark, I sincerely hope that he would approve of the record of the horrors of war which the current work constitutes.

Last but not least, my debts are many. In particular, I am indebted to Mark Reed, for approaching me in respect of publishing the diary; to Rupert Harding and all at Pen & Sword for their unfailing enthusiasm and efficiency; to Gareth Glover – a worthy recipient of a dedication if ever there was one – for the extraordinary contribution which he has made to the literature of the Peninsular War and the Waterloo campaign and his great generosity in sharing his sources with me; to Catherine Macmanamon of the Sydney Jones Library for the patience with which she has accommodated my many demands for yet more books; to my students for their never failing devotion and moral support; to Ron McGuigan for his help in locating information on the career of Charles Paget after 1815; to Philip Haythornthwaite for his great generosity in respect of sourcing the illustrations and, above all, to my family for the patience with which they have endured yet another summer of me fighting battles in Spain when I should rather have been playing the role of husband and father.

Charles J. Esdaile, Liverpool, June 2018

Sir John Moore and the Corunna Campaign: A Reassessment

A Controversial Hero

Sir John Moore is often treated by historians of the British army and its operations with something approaching reverence, while to this day his name is revered in the 'military buff' community. In the foreword to a recent biography written by an amateur historian, then, we find the following:

> This work was written from the onset only with a view to obtaining the objective truth about Sir John's life. It is thus an attempt to rekindle the memory of this man of unassailable integrity and courage, and as a reminder that, in a world of corrupt and intriguing politicians, a man could, and still can, rise to the top of his profession without compromising his dignity or his integrity.[1]

Yet Moore is a far more complex figure than is often allowed, while there were sides to him that are often forgotten, just as it is possible to question some of the achievements which he is traditionally accorded, whether it is the role he played in the introduction of light infantry in the British army, or the manner in which he is supposed to have saved Spain from conquest in 1808. Above all, meanwhile, the general remains a figure who is deeply controversial, so much so, indeed, that he is one who is likely to elicit very different opinions for as long as historians continue to look at the Peninsular War. In consequence, the presentation of this hitherto unknown account of the operations of the British army in Spain and Portugal between August 1808 and January 1809 seems an opportune moment to attempt a re-assessment of his character.

Britain and the Peninsular War

Let us begin with some context. The story begins, of course, with the arrival in Britain of the astonishing news that Spain, an ally of France since 1796, had risen

---

1. R. Day, *The Life of Sir John Moore: Not a Drum was Heard* (Barnsley, 2001), p. iii.

in revolt against Napoleon. To say that this news was greeted with acclamation would be a great understatement. For the Portland administration – the highly vulnerable Tory government that held the reins of power at the time – nothing could be more welcome than the news that a fresh front had emerged in the struggle with Napoleon. Thus, the fact was that Britain was in a situation that was distinctly parlous, if not downright calamitous. Let us begin here with the economic situation. As is well known, in October 1806 Napoleon had initiated the so-called Continental Blockade. Over the course of time and by dint of changing circumstances, Britain was able to circumvent the effects of this measure by developing new markets and building up undercover links with the Continent, but in 1807 it was by no means clear that matters would work out so well. To make the situation worse, subject to the provisions of both the Blockade and the counter-measures put in place against it in the form of the so-called Orders-in-Council, the United States, which was not only the chief neutral state, but also a commercial operator of great importance, was so exercised at being caught between a dangerous Scylla and an even more dangerous Charybdis that on 22 December 1807 President Jefferson passed into law a total embargo on all trade with Britain and France alike. Hit by both a squeeze on exports and a general increase in the price of raw materials, indeed, many industries were in the grip of a severe slump. Matters being worsened still further by the actions of French commerce raiders and a poor harvest, the handloom weavers of Lancashire mounted an impressive campaign to petition Parliament for a minimum wage, while many northern merchants and manufacturers began to organise petitions for peace, prominent commercial figures who opposed the war including the Liverpool Member of Parliament, William Roscoe, and the brewing magnate Samuel Whitbread. Hand in hand with the demands of such men, meanwhile, went others for political change: in the general elections of 1807, for example, Westminster, then the most representative seat in the country, returned the popular demagogues Sir Francis Burdett and Lord Cochrane on a platform of electoral reform. Nor could such displays be disconnected from opposition to the war: Burdett was a leading light in the peace movement, while the massive strike that falling wages and ever increasing lay-offs eventually produced among the handloom weavers of Lancashire in May 1808 was accompanied by loud demands for an end to hostilities. For the time being there was no repetition of the rumours of a secret insurrectionary movement of the sort that had been heard in 1802 at the time of the so-called 'black lump' conspiracy in Yorkshire, but, for all that, the country cannot be said to have been wholly united behind the war effort. Between 1803 and 1805 there had been a genuine danger of invasion, and this had encouraged a strong degree of 'Church and King' loyalism. But by 1807 things were very different, there being many observers who could not see why Britain should fight on for, as they saw it, the interests of Austria, Russia and Prussia.

If the home front had been the limit of the government's problems, matters might not have been so serious, but this was not the case. On the contrary, the naval, military and diplomatic outlook could not have been more gloomy. Just as had been the case a century before in the days of Louis XIV, to beat France Britain needed Continental allies as, except in very special circumstances, on their own her land forces were simply too weak even to be able to maintain themselves against the French in mainland Europe let alone to win a decisive victory against them. In practice, this meant at least one and preferably two of Austria, Prussia and Russia, but in 1808 none of these powers was interested in an alliance with Britain: Austria was engaged in an important series of military reforms and would not be ready for a fresh clash with France for another year even if she could be persuaded to fight at all (something that was anything but certain: there was a strong party in the Habsburg court that opposed war with Napoleon under almost any circumstance); Prussia had been reduced to half her previous size following the war of 1806–7; and, since the Treaty of Tilsit of July 1807, Russia was a de facto ally of Napoleon. Even supposing that the Austrians and Prussians got into a position in which they could get back into the fight, it currently seemed highly unlikely that they would do so given Britain's failure to provide Alexander I and Frederick William III with an adequate degree of financial and logistical support in the campaigns of the previous two years. Only through mounting a substantial war effort on the Continent could Britain change this situation, and, until the opportunity that was now so suddenly afforded by events in Spain and Portugal, this was something she could not hope to do. Until then, all that she had on her side of the balance was Sicily and Sweden, and these were so weak that they were more a drain on her resources than a source of military strength.

Only at sea was Britain in a relatively comfortable situation – whether in terms of the number of her ships or the quality of her crews, her superiority in this respect, indeed, was overwhelming – but even here there were serious problems, some of which were potentially all but fatal. In the first place, in the early winter of 1807 Britain's operational capacity had been badly hit when a French army commanded by Jean Andoche Junot had marched into Lisbon following Napoleon's decision to invade Portugal, unrestricted access to the wonderful anchorage afforded by the Tagus estuary, not to mention the victualling resources available in the Portuguese capital, having been a priceless strategic asset (Portugal, of course, a long-standing British ally even though she was at this point neutral in the struggle with France). In the second place, unalloyed naval power had very strong diplomatic disadvantages in that, while the Royal Navy could sweep enemy trade from the sea, enforce the draconian provisions of the Orders-in-Council and facilitate the elimination of the French empire in the wider world, all these successes served only to lend weight to the constant refrain that Britain was only interested in, on the one hand, acquiring fresh markets and sources of raw materials for her booming industries, and, on the other, destroying foreign competition, the result being that every success in the wider world could be argued to postpone victory in the war as a whole, true though it is that it was precisely this maritime success that allowed Britain to pay the massive subsidies that sustained the final overthrow of Napoleon in the wars of 1813–14, not to mention support the Spanish insurgents. In this sense, in the long run British naval power was more of an advantage than a disadvantage, and all the more so as it was able to provide an effective answer to French commerce raiding, but there were still other issues in that, in the third place, its very existence could prove a serious distraction: in 1806–7, then, the so-called 'Ministry of All the Talents' had been led into a series of abortive expeditions against the Spanish colonies that form present-day Argentina and Uraguay – while in 1807 it had been naval supremacy that had led the Portland administration into launching the attack on Copenhagen that marked the very nadir of Britain's international standing in the Napoleonic Wars while at the same time dealing yet another blow to her chances of securing Continental allies.[2]

If the Royal Navy was a double-edged sword, it was a double-edged sword that was frighteningly prone to rust. In the first place, not only did ruling the waves represent an immense effort in itself, but it placed huge strains on the navy and was by no means cheap in terms of men and ships: as the years rolled by, many ships were lost to storms and shipwreck, while even Britain's copper-bottomed fleet needed a constant supply of fresh timber to keep it at sea and at the same time augment its strength. More and more, the most important source for this timber had become the Baltic and, especially, Sweden, while this region had also been a major source of iron, hemp and flax. Under the young Gustav Adolf IV, Sweden (which at this point also included Finland) had maintained friendly relations with Britain and since 1805 had been a firm ally. Yet with the Treaty of Tilsit, Swedish naval supplies – the very

---

2. The product of a combination of panic and false intelligence, the expedition to Denmark was a political and moral disaster that secured the relatively worthless prize of the Danish fleet – a force composed almost entirely of obsolescent vessels incapable of taking their place in a normal line of battle – at the cost of the destruction by fire of a large part of the city of Copenhagen, the loss, or so it was claimed at the time, of up to 2,000 civilian lives and a Danish alliance with Napoleon. See T. Munch-Petersen, *Defying Napoleon: how Britain bombarded Copenhagen and seized the Danish Fleet in 1807* (Stroud, 2007). Meanwhile, a general discussion of the strategic background may be found in C.J. Esdaile, *Napoleon's Wars* (London, 2007), pp. 254–300, while the travails of the Portland administration are covered by R. Muir, *Britain and the Defeat of Napoleon, 1807–1815* (London, 1996), pp. 21–31 and C.D. Hall, *British Strategy in the Napoleonic War, 1803–1815* (Manchester, 1992), pp. 153–69.

stuff of life as far as the Royal Navy was concerned – were suddenly desperately vulnerable, a lesson that was driven home very hard on 21 February 1808 when Alexander I sent his armies into Finland. Immediately, the Portland administration rushed into action, but it could achieve very little, no more, indeed, than helping to secure the coast of Sweden-proper from Russian invasion from the sea, this doing nothing whatsoever to save Finland from being completely over-run. As we shall see, this affair was to play a considerable part in the manner in which things worked out in Spain in 1808, but for the time being let us simply note that the Russian conquest was one more blow to Britain's tottering international prestige and, with it, something that would have been serious enough even had it not been accompanied by the threat to British naval power that has already been outlined.[3]

If the Portland administration welcomed the emissaries who started to arrive in London from the Spanish insurgents from the first week of June onwards, this was only to be expected: a friend in need being a friend indeed, scarcely had the news of the rebellion arrived than the Foreign Secretary, George Canning, was getting up in the House of Commons to announce that any enemy of Napoleon was a friend of Great Britain and would in consequence get the latter's full support. Very quickly, then, some liaison officers were dispatched to the various foci of revolt that appeared in Spain, together with an earnest of the support to come in the form of large amounts of money, while preparations were made to dispatch an expeditionary force to Spain in the form of a division that had been fitting out for an attack on present-day Venezuela – then yet another Spanish possession – under the command of the up-and-coming general Sir Arthur Wellesley (Wellesley was, of course, just back from winning an impressive series of victories in India, while he was also very closely connected with the Portland administration of whose ranks he was actually a member as Chief Secretary for Ireland).[4]

Right from the beginning, the decision to send help to Spain gripped the imagination of the British public. For this development there were a whole series

---

3. In practice, the impact of the loss of the Baltic, which was seemingly completed by the collapse of Swedish resistance in the spring of 1809 and the subsequent cession of Finland to Russia, was not nearly so great as might have been feared, not least because the Swedes, the Russians and even the Danes all refused completely to turn their backs on their economic interests at the behest of Napoleon. Yet this could not have been foreseen in 1808 and the very fact that a British squadron continued to be deployed there throughout the war suggests that concern in respect of the area was never far from the surface. See N.A.M. Rodger, *The Command of the Ocean: a Naval History of Britain, 1649–1815* (London, 2004), pp. 557–9.

4. For the response of the Portland administration to the Spanish uprising, see Muir, *Britain and the Defeat of Napoleon*, pp. 38–41.

of reasons. First of all, thanks to the efforts of a series of novelists, playwrights and travel-writers, the very country had a ring that was as exotic as it was exciting, the Spaniards being perceived as a nation in which old values of courage and honour had survived untrammelled by the highly mannered 'polite society' of the eighteenth century. Second of all, both sides of the political debate could unite in throwing their weight behind Wellesley's division in that the Tories could see the Spanish struggle in terms of an entire people rising in defence of the traditional values represented in this case by the Catholic Church and the Spanish monarch, while the Whigs – whose aversion to making war against Napoleon had temporarily been overcome by revulsion at the way the emperor had first invaded a defenceless neutral power and then turned on an equally defenceless ally – could revel in the vision of an entire people rising to reclaim liberties taken away from them by centuries of despotism. And, third of all, the struggle in Spain was perceived as being likely to be a mere military promenade in which a handful of British grenadiers would be more than sufficient to set a rapid seal upon the victory of the popular will, this happy vision being given graphic expression by the cartoonist James Gillray: in a print entitled 'Spanish patriots attacking French banditti: loyal Britons lending a lift', published on 15 August 1808, a horde of French troops are seen being overcome by a still more imposing horde of Spanish civilians commanded, or so it seems, by a variety of priests and nuns, the only British presence in the scene being a solitary British redcoat who is depicted in the act of bayoneting a miniscule French soldier.[5] Also worth considering in this respect, meanwhile, is a further Gillray cartoon in which a hapless Napoleon is seen being tossed in a bullring by an imposing *bravo* to the lusty applause of the monarchs of Europe![6]

The mood, then, was exultant, even ecstatic. Here, for example, are the recollections of the Conde de Toreno who, under his then title of the Vizconde de Matarrosa, was one of the first representatives of the insurrection to arrive in England:

> At the time the First Lord of the Treasury was the Duke of Portland, while serving under him were figures as renowned thereafter as Castlereagh,

---

5. 'Spanish patriots attacking French banditti: loyal Britons lending a lift'; accessed at http://www.npg.org.uk/collections/search/portrait/mw63006/Spanish-patriots-attacking-the-French-banditti---loyal-Britons-lending-a-lift, 6 August 2017. In testimony to the way Spaniards were perceived as being survivals of an older and nobler age, the opponents of the French are dressed in the style of the Spanish 'Golden Age' (i.e. the sixteenth century).
6. 'The Spanish bullfight or the Corsican *matador* in danger', accessed at http://www.npg.org.uk/collections/search/portrait/mw63332/The-Spanish-bull-fight---or---the-Corsican-matador-in-danger--, 6 August 2017.

Liverpool and Canning. They had as their guiding principle the ideas of Mr Pitt, of whom they had been the closest of allies. However, in so far as Spain was concerned, all the parties were of the same opinion: as was shown in the session of the House of Commons of 15 June, there was not, in fact, the slightest difference or dissension. To quote Mr Sheridan, a leading opposition figure celebrated both as a writer and orator, 'Will not the animation of the Spanish mind be excited by the knowledge that their cause is espoused, not by ministers alone, but by the parliament and the people of England? If there be a disposition in Spain to resent the insults and injuries, too enormous to be described by language, which they have endured from the tyrant of the earth, will not that disposition be roused to the most sublime exertion, by the assurance that their efforts will be cordially aided by a great and powerful nation? Sir, I think this a most important crisis. Never was anything so brave, so generous, so noble, as the conduct of the Asturians.' Both sides of the chamber applauded these eloquent words, eloquent words that expressed the common sentiment of all its members so very well. Neither Trafalgar nor the greatest victories obtained by the Royal Navy had ever given rise to either greater joy or more universal enthusiasm. With the national interest temporarily walking hand-in-hand with the dictates of justice and humanity, opinions that on other matters were utterly opposed to one another could come together for a moment and commingle in the common celebration of the Spanish insurrection and that in a manner that is difficult to describe. Just the news from Asturias was enough to have the most prodigious effect. The emissaries could not stir abroad, nor still less make the slightest journey, without cheers and applause breaking out on all sides . . . Among the extraordinary demonstrations [of joy] that their presence elicited, we might particularly cite the first occasion on which they attended the opera . . . the ovations which they attracted being so great that the performance had to be suspended for an hour.[7]

In testimony to Toreno's reference to the manner in which even men of progressive principles swung behind the notion of aid to Spain, let us here turn to the future Whig Prime Minister, Lord John Russell:

---

7. Conde de Toreno, *Historia del levantamiento, guerra y revolución de España*, ed. R. Hocquellet (Pamplona, 2008), pp. 108–9. Asturias was the first province to revolt against the French.

The second act of the great tournament of Europe was of a very different description [to that of the first, i.e. the French Revolutionary Wars]. Napoleon, flushed with success, pretended that peace never could be made between France and the ancient monarchies, and considered his own supremacy over all the states and nations of Europe as the only security for what he and others called the principles of 1789. This pretension alienated those in England . . . who had been quite willing to see France constitute herself as she pleased, and even enlarge her boundaries to a considerable extent. In 1805, Mr Fox, in office, conducted the negotiation which broke off, not merely, as he told his nephew, on the point actually in dispute, but on account of the evident insincerity of the French government. After this there remained nothing for those who were not disposed to allow England to be absorbed in the French empire but to resist and to persevere. The task seemed not only a difficult, but almost a hopeless one: no amount of subsidy, no coalition of powers, seemed likely to end otherwise than in such defeats as Austerlitz, Jena and Friedland. Happily, from an unexpected quarter appeared the dawn of better times. Napoleon invited the King of Spain and his heir apparent to Bayonne with the view of betraying and dethroning them. Many Spanish grandees bowed their necks beneath the yoke, but every Spanish peasant felt his own honour assailed in the persons of his unworthy, contemptible but still national sovereigns. The signal fire was lighted on every hill, the fame of independence blazed up in every bosom. Here was indeed a crisis in the affairs of Europe. The cause of national independence, which in the first portion of the war was defended by France, was now about to be upheld by the other nations of Europe. No matter how ignorant, how ill-armed, how ill-led the Spanish people might be, here was a nation animated by a real enthusiasm, ready to fight in the field of battle, in the town, in the village, in the farm-yard, and in the peasant's cottage for the sacred cause of national independence. It behoved England, therefore to welcome this reviving spirit, to expend her growing treasures, to employ her extensive credit, to dispatch her most skilful officers, to marshal her bravest troops in defence of this sacred cause.[8]

---

8. J. Russell, *Recollections and Suggestions, 1813–1873* (London, 1875), pp. 5–6. Eager to see what was going on for himself, Russell later travelled to Spain in the company of Lord and Lady Holland. Another enthusiast in this respect, and one still more extravagant, was the writer, Walter Savage Landor: 'I am going to Spain. In three days I shall have sailed. At Brighton one evening, I preached a crusade to two auditors. Inclination was not wanting, and in a few minutes everything was fixed. I am now

And, last but not least, herewith a sample of the views of the arch-Tory *Times*:

It is now three weeks . . . since Viscount Matarrosa and Don Diego de la Vega arrived in London. And yet what has been done? All we can speak of with certainty, exclusive of a few arms which have been sent, is that, exactly on this day fortnight, Sir Arthur Wellesley left England to take the command of an expedition send to be bound to Gibraltar, and by letters from Ireland we find he had not quitted Dublin on Sunday last. We verily believe that, ere now, Lord Chatham would have had troops on the Spanish territories. Every port is open for their reception; every tongue will greet their arrival. It is no hostile territory upon which they have to make good a landing, and which they durst not approach but in large bodies: Spain is, for the present, another Britain, and thousands, perhaps we may say millions, of heroes are ready to fight by their sides . . . There have been no fresh arrivals from that country, but more minute details are daily appearing which certainly justify, to some extent, the hopes we are so anxious to entertain. The following statement we give on the authority of a gentleman who, speaking of personal transactions and events which came under his observation, is entitled to full credit. 'In the provinces of Leon, Galicia, Andalusia, Castile and the Asturias, every man has turned out. I was confined in the city of Lugo . . . Two days before I quitted that place, 14,000 troops with fifty pieces of cannon marched through towards Madrid, and on the road we met 5,000 troops proceeding by forced marches; they uttered the loudest invectives against Bonaparte. The governor of Lugo informed me and other English officers that the province of Galicia had already enrolled 700,000 men. All the friars and monks wear ribbons with the motto "Viva Fernando VII". The English are most earnestly looked to for assistance.' Other anecdotes are also related which correspond in their result with this statement. In Catalonia we understand that General Ney had been induced to furnish the people with arms on assurances of their subserviency to the French interest.

---

about to express a wish at which your gentler and more benevolent soul will shudder: may every Frenchman out of France now perish! May the Spaniards not spare one! No calamities can chain them down from their cursed monkey tricks; no generosity can bring back to their remembrance that a little while since they mimicked, till they really thought themselves, free men. Detestable race, profaners of republicanism . . . Since the earth will not open to swallow them all up, may even kings partake in the glory of their extermination!' W.S. Landor to R.W. Southey, Falmouth, 8 August 1809, *cit.* J. Forster (ed.), *The Works and Life of Walter Savage Landor* (London, 1876), I, pp. 115–16.

He afterwards had reason to doubt the sincerity of the Catalonians, and resolved to take away the arms he had distributed. He succeeded in disarming 3,000 of them; the rest resisted and are now among the enemies of France.[9]

From Vimeiro to Corunna

Rarely, then, has a British army sailed to war buoyed by greater enthusiasm – the prospect of encountering the women of Spain, a species fabled both for their beauty and their sexual avidity, was of great assistance here! – and backed by more unanimous public support.[10] And still the excitement grew, for news began to arrive from Spain of a series of glorious victories: not only had French forces been beaten at Valencia and Zaragoza, but on 19 July an entire French army was compelled to surrender at the town of Bailén in Andalucía. Somewhat surprisingly, true, when Wellesley made landfall at Corunna, he was told that his troops were not needed in Spain, but a secondary insurrection had since broken out in Portugal and so he took his men there instead, while he had no hesitation in confirming the general impression that all was not just well but more than well. Thus:

> Since my arrival I have had frequent conversations with the Junta, and Mr Stuart, who arrived also yesterday, will send by this conveyance to Mr Canning an account of all the intelligence which we have received from them respecting the present situation of affairs in Spain. The general result, however, appears to me to be that the whole of the Spanish nation, with the exception of the provinces of Biscay and Navarre, and those in the neighbourhood of Madrid are in a state of insurrection against the French, that several French detachments in different parts of the country had been destroyed, viz. a corps under Lefebvre, which had been attacked four times near Zaragoza in Aragón particularly on the 16th and 24th June; a corps which I believe to have been under the command of Dupont, and [of which] it is said that Dupont was taken prisoner in an action fought between Andujar and La Carolina before the 23rd June; and two corps defeated in Catalonia before the 19th June, one on its march to Montserrat and the other to Zaragoza. The Catalonians have also got position of the fort of Figueras in the neighbourhood of Rosas, and have blockaded the French in Barcelona. As, however, the

9. *The Times*, 30 June 1808.
10. For a discussion of perceptions of Spanish women in the rest of Europe, see C.J. Esdaile, *Women in the Peninsular War* (Norman, Oklahoma, 2014), pp. 189–93.

communication . . . has been impeded by the march and position of the French armies, and particularly by their late success at Río Seco, to which I shall presently refer, the Junta have no official accounts of any of these actions, but they give credit to those they have received, copies of which will be transmitted to Mr Canning by Mr Stuart. He will also send the account which the Junta have received of the action at Río Seco. The army of Castile and Galicia united was posted in that place, which is in the province of Valladolid . . . It is stated that they intended to attack Marshal Bessières on the 16th, but he attacked them on the 14th. His infantry was at first defeated by the Spaniards with the loss of 7,000 men, but afterwards his cavalry fell upon the left wing of the Spanish army, which consisted of the peasants of Castile and defeated it. I understand that the Spanish army, which consisted of 50,000 men, lost about 7,000 men and two pieces of cannon, and that they had taken and still retain six pieces belonging to the French . . . I understand that the Junta were much alarmed when they received the account of this defeat, but the arrival of the money yesterday has entirely renewed their spirits, and I did not see either in them or in the inhabitants of this town [i.e. Corunna] any symptom either of alarm or [of] doubt of their final success. The capture of Santander by the French is not considered an event of any importance, and it is said here that a corps was actually on its march from the Asturias to retake that place. It is impossible to convey to you an idea of the sentiment which prevails here in favour of the Spanish cause. The difference between any two men is whether the one is a better or worse Spaniard, and the better Spaniard is the one who detests the French most heartily. I understand that there is actually no French party in the country, and, at all events, I am convinced that no man now dares to show that he is a friend to the French.[11]

In respect of all this, however, never has the phrase 'castles in Spain' seemed more apposite. It was not just that the supposed victories of the Patriots (as the

---

11. Sir A. Wellesley to Lord Castlereagh, 21 July 1808, in J. Gurwood (ed.), *The Dispatches of Field Marshal Lord Wellington during his Various Campaigns in India, Denmark, Portugal, Spain, the Low Countries and* France (new and enlarged edn, London, 1852), III, pp. 31–3. It does not take much knowledge of the events of 1808 to realise that the reports retailed by Wellesley were a farrago of exaggerations, half-truths and downright falsehoods even if one of said falsehoods – the story of the surrender of an entire French army in Andalucía – became true a month later, and, what is more, in exactly the same place that it was reported to have happened.

Spanish insurgents became known) had been much exaggerated, true though it was that this was the case.[12] Much more to the point was the fact that the whole Spanish uprising was a chimera. Of all the events of the French Wars, there is probably none that has been more misunderstood. Generally the revolt has been portrayed as the product of outraged patriotism: in brief, Napoleon had overthrown the Bourbon dynasty and sought to give Spain a new monarch in the person of his elder brother, Joseph. Such a view, however, is increasingly difficult to sustain. In both Spain and Portugal the risings were actually distinctly murky affairs that reflected many of the different tensions that were besetting the body politic. What appears to be the case, in fact, is that the various provincial risings – for there was no concerted uprising as such – were engineered by a variety of dissident groups. In Spain, in particular, the insurrection's leaders included disgruntled office-seekers, radicals eager to make a political revolution, prominent civilians resentful of the privileges of the military estate, discontented subaltern officers eager for promotion, conservative clerics horrified by Bourbon anti-clericalism, and members of the aristocracy opposed to the creeping advance of royal authority. As for the crowd, meanwhile, its motivation was as much material as it was ideological. There was intense loyalty to Ferdinand VII, the young prince placed on the throne by means of a military coup at Aranjuez in March 1808, true, but this stemmed not so much from who he was as from what he represented, the numerous enemies of the erstwhile royal favourite, Manuel de Godoy, having deliberately represented Ferdinand as a ruler who would as if by magic right all of Spain's ills, this vision being all the more appealing in view of the terrible conditions that were being endured by the bulk of the population (thanks in part to the alliance with France that had been in operation since 1796 and, in part, to sheer misfortune in the form of a series of harvest failures and epidemics of disease, Spain was experiencing a severe economic crisis). With the vast majority of those in political and military authority still men who owed their prominence to Godoy and the populace persuaded, first, that Napoleon's intervention was somehow the work of the favourite, and, second, that the French were bent on the wholesale massacre of the Spanish populace – the rising of the Dos de Mayo was commonly believed to have been an unprovoked attack on the people of Madrid – and it was from here but a short step to a great social convulsion.

In the circumstances, it might be tempting to assume that the Spanish rising, or rather revolution, was a re-run of events in France in 1789. This, however, was not the case. At the root of the trouble was the belief that those

---

12. For a detailed analysis of the gulf between report and reality, see C.J. Esdaile, *The Spanish Army in the Peninsular War* (Manchester, 1988), pp. 101–2.

in authority were traitors – it hardly assisted their cause that they had in most cases been urging the populace to remain quiet and accept whatever Napoleon might decree – and that it was therefore necessary to remove them. However, at the same time, they were also men of property and privilege, the consequence being, of course, that the rising became as much a traditional peasant protest as it did a movement against the French. Desperate to save themselves and restore order, the élites responded by rushing to assume the lead through the formation of a variety of new local governments. Taking the form of either juntas of notables or petty military dictatorships, these struggled desperately to restore the social hierarchy by directing the hostility of the populace back towards the French, in which respect they were also happy to avail themselves of the weapon of universal conscription. In short, the image of 'people's war' that has come down to us from Spain and Portugal conceals a reality that was much more complex. On the one hand, we see the full panoply of the *levée en masse* complete with mass armies and a sustained attempt at political mobilisation, and yet on the other we find widespread apathy, disaffection and resistance to conscription. Given, first, that it was the war in the Iberian peninsula that gave the English language the word 'guerrilla', and, second, that many historians have portrayed the indigenous aspects of the struggle very much in terms of an irregular conflict waged by bands of armed civilians, this revisionist approach may seem hard to swallow. However, the guerrillas thrown up by the conflict that now opened have themselves been subjected to a stringent re-evaluation, and this has in turn suggested not only that the phenomenon of popular resistance was far more the work of the political, military and social élite than has generally been imagined, but also that such popular engagement with the irregular struggle as did take place was the fruit of a great many factors other than patriotism.[13]

For the time being, however, the realisation that all was not well in terms of the manner in which the risings had been presented in Britain still lay in the future. Not least was this the case because the campaign went well enough. Wellesley beat the French at Roliça and Vimeiro, and Lisbon was liberated shortly afterwards. Admittedly, something of the shine was taken off this victory by Wellesley's supercession in the command by the uninspiring team constituted by Sir Hew Dalrymple and Sir Harry Burrard, the net result of which was Junot's escape from total humiliation by means of the highly controversial Convention of Sintra, but the speedy conclusion to which the campaign was brought did at least free the

---

13. The Spanish uprising is a topic of great complexity that simply cannot be done justice to in the space available in this introduction. For a more lengthy discussion, see C.J. Esdaile, *The Peninsular War: a New History* (London, 2002), pp. 37–61.

British army, now much reinforced, for operations in Spain, where the French had in the wake of the battle of Bailén fallen back to the line of the River Ebro.[14] In an operation whose details will be discussed at a later point, the army, which was now commanded by Sir John Moore, Dalrymple, Burrard and Wellesley having all alike been recalled to London to account for their conduct, moved into Spain and concentrated its forces at Salamanca, a further division of troops having in the meantime been sent to Corunna under the command of Sir David Baird from which port it eventually advanced to join Moore after a lengthy delay occasioned by quarrels with the Junta of Galicia. For various reasons, however, it was the beginning of December before Moore could even think of taking an active part in operations in Spain, and by then the situation had changed dramatically. Having heavily reinforced the 'Army of Spain', Napoleon had come to Spain himself and within a month every Spanish army was in a state of panic stricken flight and the French at the very gates of Madrid, Moore's troops only escaping the general rout because of their secluded position in western Spain.

The defeat of the Spanish armies obviously came as a terrible shock to Moore and his men, not least because they were now in terrible danger, but, as revealed in the documents which follow, what came as a still greater blow was the attitude which they encountered among the populace. To put it mildly, this was disappointing, indeed, completely bewildering. All too evidently, enthusiasm for the struggle was non-existent, and, unwilling to revisit the assumptions with which they had started the campaign, this they could only put down to the failure of the Patriot authorities in particular, and the ruling classes in general,

---

14. An interesting glimpse of the army's opinion of the Convention of Cintra is afforded by a letter written by General Sir Edward Paget to his mother from Ciudad Rodrigo on 13 November 1808. Thus: 'You seem, in truth, to be in a pretty state of uproar in England on account of this convention of which there is so much talk. I knew you would hear so much about it that I thought it would be charitable to spare you my opinions. But as you seem disposed to eat me for my silence, I must inform you that I consider it as the most fortunate convention that was ever entered into: but for it, we should still be pottering. As it is, the effect of the convention has been to place a man at our head in whom we all feel confidence. Had His Majesty's Ministers been disposed to sacrifice their prejudices to the public good, this convention would never have been heard of, and as a punishment for their want of patriotism, they are now compelled, in spite of their teeth, to appoint the very man to command whom they have done everything in their power to mortify.' *Cit.* E. Paget (ed.), *Letters and Memorials of General the Hon. Sir Edward Paget, G.C.B., collected and arranged by his daughter, Harriet Mary Paget* (London, 1898), p. 104. An officer who had served under Moore in Sweden, Paget was loyal to him to a fault. As we shall see, however, there was absolutely no substance to the idea that Moore had been deliberately denied the Peninsular command by the British government.

to provide adequate leadership, this being something that only increased their conviction that Spain as a state was politically, morally and ideologically bankrupt, not the least of the problems here being the manner in which the Catholic Church had supposedly constituted a massive stumbling block in the way of progress:

> Oppressed and outraged by the French, with a wild revenge hordes of enraged people rose in every quarter of the kingdom: their sudden and impetuous vengeance carried all before them; the veteran armies of France were destroyed; the usurper [was] driven from his assumed capital; and the cry of restitution resounded everywhere. This was the sympathetic act of a whole nation, and this was the fortunate moment for a virtuous nobility to have turned it to their country's advantage. Had some great spirit seized this conquering body and guided it with the singleness of aim which actuated the soul of Pelagio when, at the head of his zealous Asturians, he drove the invading Saracens, we should not now be shut up at Salamanca, nor would the flying Spaniards be seeking a temporary refuge in their dishonoured homes.[15]

This, however, was little short of nonsense. There were numerous problems with regard to the reconstitution of authority in Patriot Spain in the wake of the complete collapse of the state in the course of the uprising, and it was also true that, as many British observers pointed out, by no means all the parties concerned had acted either wisely or in the national interest. In this respect the views of the British diplomat, Sir George Jackson, are sensible enough:

> The more I see, the more I fear that the time is now gone by when we might have hoped for success, and that those precious moments which . . . might have been employed in following up the advantages the Patriots' cause certainly possessed two months ago . . . have been wasted in disputes and party intrigues, which are by no means ended by the establishment of a [central] junta. For the members of this junta – all pulling different ways and the measures opposed and secretly undermined by the Council of Castile on the one hand, while on the other they do not possess the confidence of the nation at large or authority sufficient to make themselves respected – have, as a body, neither the influence or the power necessary to enable them to act with

---

15. R.K. Porter, *Letters from Portugal and Spain written during the March of the British Troops under Sir John Moore* (London, 1809), p. 169.

that resolution and vigour which alone could bring to a satisfactory issue the present critical state of affairs. The nomination of their generals is, I think, a sufficient illustration of this. Every individual member of the Junta – a body formed, it must be remembered, of men who, although probably for the most part persons of the first prominence in their respective provinces, have been as little accustomed to deal with the great affairs of state as to see themselves invested with the means of patronage they now enjoy – has each his own particular friend or relative to push forward, and, as was to be expected, the first occasion that brought these men into public view has generally betrayed their incapacity. The clamour of the people – who have, after all, effected the revolution in this country – has compelled their removal, hence appointment after appointment has taken place, the natural consequence of which has been disunion among the members of the Junta and discontent among the troops, of whom it must in fairness be said that, when opposed to the enemy, they have uniformly fought with the greatest valour . . . The government make a great show of activity and all day long are closeted in council, yet in fact do little or nothing. If told that the enemy is advancing, instead of taking immediate steps to oppose him . . . they answer, 'Advancing? Impossible!', [and] then sit down to argue upon the possibility or impossibility of the fact, and in the meantime the enemy arrives at the gates.[16]

True enough though these comments were, they miss the point. In brief, to look for modern mass nationalism in a society that was still early-modern was simply out of the question: if Paget and his fellows could find no patriotism among the populace, the most important reason was that there simply *was* no patriotism among the populace. 'I know of no reinforcements anywhere', lamented Henry Paget. 'The game, therefore, is considered as completely up. Our government must have been most grossly received in regard to the situation of the Spanish armies, the resources of the country and the dispositions of the people. We do not discover any enthusiasm anywhere. The country appears to be in a state of complete apathy.'[17] When directly threatened in their own homes by French soldiers, as at Valencia and Zaragoza, the people might be galvanised into defending themselves, while they might, too, be persuaded to serve as the

16. Diary of Sir George Jackson, 17 November 1808, *cit*. Lady Jackson (ed.), *The Diaries and Letters of Sir George Jackson* (London, 1872), II, pp. 352–5, II, pp. 294–6.
17. *Cit*. Marquess of Anglesey, *One-Leg: the Life and Letters of Henry William Paget, First Marquess of Anglesey, K.G., 1768–1854* (London, 1961), p. 73.

sort of town militias observed by some British soldiers at Ciudad Rodrigo, but that was all. Meanwhile, even such regular troops as were got together were not an impressive sight. Landing at Corunna with Baird's division, for example, Captain Alexander Gordon later wrote: There were . . . in garrison . . . about 600 Patriots who mounted guards and shared fatigue duties with our infantry. These volunteers were wretchedly clothed and but indifferently armed, and their appearance was by no means calculated to impress an observer with a very high opinion of their prowess, but I was at this time sanguine in the cause and persuaded myself that these peasants possessed an invincible courage which would counterbalance every other deficiency.[18]

His confidence increasingly shaken, news of the French advance initially persuaded Moore that he should retreat into Portugal, and orders were actually sent out to this effect, though not before a series of bitter exchanges with the Junta Central – the provisional government that had been formed to head the uprising in September 1808 – and the British ambassador, John Hookham Frere. Fortunately for the British general's reputation, however, at the last moment news arrived that, against all expectations, the population of Madrid had resolved to defend itself, and thus it was that on 11 December the British troops who had been waiting at Salamanca found themselves marching north, the plan being that they would link up with Baird and attack Napoleon's communications with France somewhere in the vicinity of Valladolid. On receipt of intelligence giving detailed information on the whereabouts of the French forces, the plan of attack was changed, the aim now being to link up with the Spanish Army of the Left and hit the corps commanded by Marshal Soult at Burgos.[19] However, the end result was much the same: though Madrid surrendered on 4 December after what proved to be barely a show of resistance, news that the British army was operating against his flank caused the emperor to pull the bulk of his troops away from the capital and head north to, or so he hoped, inflict a decisive defeat on Moore. This he failed to achieve, of course, but even so the chief plank in what was to become the defence of Moore had been laid down, the general idea being that he had singlehandedly

---

18. H. Wylly (ed.), *A Cavalry Officer in the Corunna Campaign, 1808–1809: the Journal of Captain Gordon of the Fifteenth Hussars* (London, 1913), p. 21.

19. The 'Army of the Left' was the name given to the Spanish forces that had been operating in Santander and the Basque provinces. Now believed to be retreating westwards into the province of León, these had initially been under the command of an officer of Irish descent named Joaquín Blake y Joyes, but had recently been transferred into the hands of the Marqués de la Romana, a general whom the British were inclined to regard as something of a *protégé* on account of the fact that he had been the commander of the Spanish division that had been sent to help garrison Denmark in the autumn of 1807 and had just been rescued by the Royal Navy.

saved the Patriot cause by distracting the massive columns that had originally been intended to march on Cádiz and Lisbon. Meanwhile, having secured a minor victory at Sahagún de Campos, to the fury of his uncomprehending troops, Moore abandoned his offensive and retreated at full speed pursued by the corps of Marshal Soult and Marshal Ney. A successful rearguard action at Benevente dealt the oncoming French a bloody nose, but an encounter with La Romana's forces at Astorga destroyed any remaining notion the British general may have had of making a stand, the Spaniards proving to be in the last extremities of starvation and disease, and Moore continued to fall back at breakneck speed, pushing his men so hard that many units lost all order and dissolved into crowds of stragglers who harried the countryside unmercifully. Only a few units were unaffected, but chief among these were those belonging to the reserve division of Sir Edward Paget, it being this force that played the chief role in covering the retreat of the rest of the army as, for example, in the famous action at Cacabelos on 3 January. By the time that they reached the sea at Corunna, though well ahead of the pursuit, the British columns had lost over 5,000 men in dead, prisoners of and missing, while Moore had also been forced to abandon or destroy large quantities of supplies and materiel. Yet the combination of rest, hot food and the prospect of battle soon revived the troops, and, when the French finally attacked, they were driven off without too many difficulties, though the 600–800 casualties included a mortally wounded Sir John Moore: his shoulder shattered by a cannonball, he died in his lodgings in the city shortly after the fighting drew to a close.

The Creation of a Legend

Full of poignancy as it was, the British commander's death was the perfect launch-pad for a version of Sir John's life, and, indeed, vision of the man, that from the beginning bade fair to transform him into a story-book hero, and all the more so as he had fallen in the thick of the fighting while leading forward fresh troops in the defence of the hotly contested village of Elvina, it being very much with this Sir John Moore that the majority of readers will be most familiar. The construction of the Moore myth, for such it must be regarded, may be said to have begun hardly had the sound of the guns died away on the battlefield that cost him his life. Here, for example, is the official dispatch written by Sir John Hope in his capacity as the final commander on the battlefield of Corunna to Sir David Baird – with Moore's death now the overall commander of the expedition as a whole – while still on board ship on his way home to England:

> To you who are well acquainted with the excellent qualities of Lieutenant-General Sir John Moore, I need not expatiate on the loss his country

and the army have sustained by his death. His fall has deprived me of a valuable friend . . . but it is chiefly on public grounds that I most lament the blow. It will be the conversation of everyone who loved or respected his manly character that, after conducting the army through an arduous retreat with consummate firmness, he has terminated a career of distinguished honour by a death that has given the enemy additional reason to respect the name of a British soldier. Like the immortal Wolfe, he is snatched from his country at an early period of a life spent in her service; like Wolfe, his last moments were gilded by the prospect of success and cheered by the acclamations of victory; like Wolfe also, his memory will forever remain sacred in that country which he sincerely loved, and which he had so faithfully served.[20]

Also worth quoting here is the General Order which was issued by the Duke of York on 2 February 1809:

In a military character, obtained amidst the dangers of climate, the privations incident to service, and the sufferings of repeated wounds, it is difficult to select any one point as a preferable subject for praise. It exhibits, however, one feature so particularly characteristic of the man, and so important to the best interests of the service, that the commander-in-chief is pleased to mark it with his particular approbation. The life of Sir John Moore was spent among the troops. During the seasons of repose, his time was devoted to the care and instruction of the officers and soldiers. In war he courted service in every quarter of the globe. Regardless of personal considerations he esteemed that to which his country called him the post of honour, and by his undaunted spirit and unconquerable perseverance, he pointed the way to victory.[21]

Yet all this was but the military establishment, and, in particular, a Horse Guards that was very well disposed to Moore, closing ranks. From the beginning there were those who were not disposed to accept so roseate a view of the general. For obvious reasons, foremost among the critics were British diplomats and travellers who found themselves exposed to the fury engendered by Moore's decision to flee for the coast rather than continuing to wage war in the plains of central Spain. Cut off from events north of Madrid as they were – along with the provisional

20. J. Hope to D. Baird, 18 January 1809, *cit*. W.H. Wilkin, *The Life of Sir David Baird* (London, 1912), pp. 294–5.
21. *Cit*. B. Brownrigg, *The Life and Letters of Sir John Moore* (Oxford, 1922), p. 272.

Spanish government, they had almost universally been forced to flee to Seville when Napoleon took the capital – this came as a complete shock. As Sir George Jackson confided to his diary in several entries written between 1 and 5 February 1809, for example:

> Some imperfect accounts have reached us of the sad events in the north. How terrible that the resources of our country should be thus frittered away! How disgraceful that poor Romana should have been abandoned at Orense with the whole French force ready to pour down upon him as soon as they have completed the task of pursuing the English to their ships! Oh, my poor country . . . The further reports we have had of our calamities are so bad that we think that what yet remains to be known must be, in some degree, consolatory, if anything like consolation can be found in a disaster of such magnitude and extent as regards both the present and the future. We as yet know only of our own loss: surely the French must also have suffered greatly. A sad impression is produced here by these deplorable events; what must the feeling be in our own country . . . A more detailed account of the late deplorable events seems to justify the assertion that . . . we might, so far from allowing ourselves to be beaten, have claimed a victory . . . Moore, personally, appears to have behaved most nobly, but still there are two points I cannot comprehend: the one, what our armies were doing all that time marching and counter-marching in Salamanca; the other, how the French could have been allowed to pass . . . such defiles as those of Galicia, where one would have thought that the progress of a whole army might have been arrested by the merest handful of men.[22]

Jackson is clearly writing here more in sorrow than in anger, but the redoubtable political hostess, Lady Holland, a fervent hispanophile who had travelled to Spain with her husband in the belief that it would afford the edifying spectacle of a noble people bent on recovering its liberty, was downright furious:

> Romana, in the gentlest terms, ascribes the ruin and dispersion of his army to Sir John Moore having deceived him; he promised to defend the pass of Villafranca, and Romana accordingly made his movements with that object, but in this he was disappointed . . . He lost some of his best troops in consequence of co-operating as he expected with

---

22. *Cit.* Jackson (ed.), *Diaries and Letters of Sir George Jackson*, II, pp. 352–5.

Moore, but Moore disregarded the combination and left him to shift as he could, and, in consequence of Hope's division marching upon Vigo just before him, he had a corps consuming provisions in his front and a harassing enemy in his rear . . . Saavedra, the Minister, told Lord Holland that Sir David Baird's army, it had been settled at Madrid, should be landed at Santander, in consequence of which preparations were made at that place for their reception. It was to the strange choice of destination of the army that the delay arose at Coruña about their landing, and the subsequent delay of getting them forward. Whilst Moore was at Salamanca, Escalante and another officer of high rank were sent to him from the Junta in order to urge him to advance; they remained with him some days. He was cold, repulsive, scarcely civil to them, and not in the least disposed towards the cause he was employed in serving.[23]

With the British ambassador, John Hookham Frere, bitterly critical of Moore – desperate to get him to help defend Madrid, he had repeatedly crossed swords with him in the course of the campaign and at one point had even sought to get his subordinate generals to over-rule him via the intervention of a French émigré officer named Venault de Charmilly – controversy could not but spread to Britain, while it did not help that some of the survivors of Moore's army were more than

---

23. Earl of Ilchester (ed.), *The Spanish Journal of Elizabeth, Lady Holland* (London, 1910), pp. 266, 268. La Romana was, indeed, very bitter. Herewith the dispatch which he sent to the Junta Central at the end of the campaign: 'The English have seized . . . the mules and oxen that drew our army's artillery, munitions and baggage train; they have insulted and mistreated . . . our officers . . . They have stolen all the mules of the . . . inhabitants of Benevente and the *pueblos* of the Tierra de Campos, and have left a multitude of carts abandoned by the wayside, some of them broken down and others smashed up on purpose. They have without necessity killed and eaten the oxen that pulled these carts and have not paid their value. They have killed three magistrates and various other inhabitants. After allowing anyone who wanted to drink their fill without paying a penny, they have poured away all the wine in the cellars. They have not paid for the carts and animals that they have used to move their women and their immense baggage trains. In some *pueblos* the commissaries have refused to give receipts for the supplies made available to them by the justices, whilst in others they have arbitrarily reduced the sums that were asked of them. In a word the French themselves could not have found agents better calculated to whip up hate of the British than the army commanded by General Sir John Moore.' Marqués de la Romana to A. Cornel, 18 January 1809, Archivo Histórico Nacional, Sección de Estado, *legajo* 18, *carpeta* 8, ff. 32–4.

somewhat critical of his handling of the retreat to Corunna.[24] To quote Adam Neale, a surgeon who came out to Portugal with the same contingent of troops as Charles Paget and accompanied the army to Corunna:

> The campaign now terminated, many of our officers now speak very freely of the want of talent in the retreat as conducted by General Moore . . . It will be necessary for Sir John's friends to prove the absolute necessity of so much haste in order to [defend] his memory from some degree of blame: at least three fourths, if not four fifths, of the loss we have sustained is to be attributed to that cause . . . Many officers think that, after having retired to Villafranca del Bierzo, it was quite impossible for the French to get in our rear, and that a stand ought to have been made at that place.[25]

Although his views were not published till much later, one such critic was Captain Alexander Gordon of the Fifteenth Light Dragoons:

> I have frequently heard it asserted by the advocates of Sir John Moore that the plan traced out for him was so ill-conceived, and the points of debarkation and of action so injudiciously selected, that success was altogether unattainable, especially after the defeat and dispersion of all the Patriot forces. But, even if this be admitted, I am fully persuaded that the distresses the army encountered are chiefly to be attributed to the misconduct of its leader. It may appear invidious to reflect upon the

---

24. For a long account of this affair, see the pamphlet published by Venault de Charmilly himself in 1809, viz. P.F. Venault de Charmilly, *To the British Nation is presented by Colonel Venault de Charmilly, Knight of the Royal and Military Order of Saint Louis, the Narrative of his Transactions with the Right Honourable John Hookham Frere, His Britannic Majesty's Minister Plenitpotentiary and Lieutenant-General Sir John Moore, K.B., with the Suppressed Correspondence of Sir J. Moore, being a Refutation of the Calumnies invented against Him and proving that He was never acquainted with General Morla* (London, 1810). In this work Venault de Charmilly did not overtly denounce Moore's conduct of operations, but the implication was nonetheless that the general was mistaken in his refusal to march to the aid of Madrid, whilst he also accused him of prejudice, gross injustice and, in effect, conduct unbecoming a gentleman (in brief, incensed by the belief that Venault de Charmilly was party to Frere's ham-fisted attempt to mobilise his generals in favour of the cause of marching for Madrid, Moore in effect banished him from his army and refused to accept any further communication from him).

25. A. Neale, *Letters from Portugal and Spain comprising an Account of the Operations of the Armies under their Excellencies Sir Arthur Wellesley and Sir John Moore from the Landing of the Troops in Mondego Bay to the Battle of Corunna* (London, 1809), pp. 330–1.

character of an amiable and gallant officer whose death in the moment of victory has cast a veil of glory over the errors of his judgement, but it is only an act of justice towards the brave men he commanded to point out the causes of the misbehaviour which, unhappily, tarnished their fame.[26]

Rather less negative, but still far from wholly complimentary was another cavalryman in the person of Major Edwin Griffith, who, like Gordon, served in the Fifteenth Light Dragoons:

The province of Galicia is perhaps the strongest by nature and the easiest to be defended of any country on the face of the earth. Surrounded by mountains whose sides are almost inaccessible and height immense, it would hardly be possible even for infantry to enter it except by the passes, and in these passes there are positions where (like Thermopylae) a handful of men might arrest the progress of millions . . . Unhappily these advantages were neglected and, trusting more to celerity of movement than to the usual stratagems of war, Sir John subjected his army to the humiliating accusation of actually being driven into the sea by the French . . . During the whole of the retreat placed in the most arduous situation and harassed by continual reports of the most disagreeable nature, Sir John's presence of mind never forsook him . . . In action his post was always the post of danger, and, if the coolness for which he was remarkable on these occasions be a sign of courage, he was one of the bravest men that ever lived. Perhaps, indeed, he did commit some errors, but he has fully expiated them by the manner in which he terminated his career.[27]

---

26. Wylly (ed.), *Cavalry Officer in the Corunna Campaign*, pp. 208–9. Elsewhere Gordon is even more critical: 'Sir John Moore, although an officer of eminent bravery and of tried ability in subordinate commands, now that he was called upon to conduct a considerable force in circumstances of peculiar difficulty, proved lamentably deficient in those qualities of decision and firmness which he had so often displayed on former occasions, and which alone could have enabled him to extricate the army by some brilliant achievement from the perilous situation in which it had been placed by his own ill-advised measures and the disasters of our Spanish allies. At this juncture, however, he appeared to labour under a depression of spirits so different from his usual serene and cheerful disposition as to give a mournful expression to his countenance indicative of the greatest anxiety of mind, and it seemed either that his judgement was completely clouded or that he was under the influence of a spell which forced him to commit the gravest errors.' *Ibid.*, p. 169.

27. Journal of E. Griffith, *cit.* G. Glover (ed.), *From Corunna to Waterloo: the Letters and Journals of two Napoleonic Hussars, 1806–1816* (London, 2007), p. 89.

Had every soldier in the army kept his counsel, controversy would still have been inevitable. More than 6,000 men were missing; the army had lost much of its baggage and all its horses and draft animals; and enormous quantities of money, arms, ammunition, uniforms, footwear, equipment and supplies of every kind had been abandoned or destroyed. As if all this was not enough, there was also the condition of the troops. As Ensign Robert Blakeney of the Twenty-Eighth Foot recorded, this had an effect that was particularly powerful:

> Our appearance on landing was very unseemly, owing principally to the hurry attending our embarkation . . . Scarcely a regiment got on board the vessel which contained their baggage, and the consequence was that on quitting our ships we presented an appearance of much dirt and misery. The men were ragged, displaying torn garments of all colours, and the people of England, accustomed to witness the high order and unparalleled cleanliness of their national troops . . . and never having seen an army after the termination of a hard campaign, were horror struck and persuaded themselves that some awful calamity must have occurred. Their consternation was artfully wrought up to the highest pitch by the wily old soldiers who, fully aware of the advantage to be gained by this state of general excitement . . . recited in pathetic strain the most frightful accounts of their sufferings and hardships.[28]

The result was all too predictable, and all the more so as the rivalry between Pittites determined to fight Napoleon to the death and Whigs who saw no future in such a policy and were inclined to look with sympathetic eyes upon the French Revolution, did not make for reasoned discussion. As Blakeney continued:

> Interested persons at home profited by this state of universal ferment. One political party, eagerly catching at any circumstances which could tend to incriminate the other, highly exaggerated even those already incredible reports, while the other side, who felt that all the disasters attending the campaign properly rested with themselves joined in the cry and with mean political subterfuge endeavoured to throw the onus off their own shoulders on the breast of the silent, the unconscious, dead.[29]

---

28. J. Sturgis (ed.), *A Boy in the Peninsular War: the Services, Adventures and Experiences of Robert Blakeney, Subaltern in the Twenty-Eighth Regiment* (London, 1899), pp. 124–5.
29. *Ibid.*, p. 125.

Scarcely had the news of the battle of Corunna arrived in London, then, than the portrait artist, Thomas Lawrence, was writing to Joseph Farington that anger with Moore was 'common to the whole army, some few individual friends excepted'; that it was 'considered as fortunate for his reputation' that Moore had fallen; that it was now said not only that his talents had always been overrated, but also that they had 'proved to be greatly deficient when tasked by the command of a large army'; that the whole disaster had been the fruit of a combination of indecision and panic; and, finally, that, whereas Lord Nelson had always cheerfully accepted the resources he was given as the best that could be got together and set out to do the very best he could with them, Moore 'was always discontented, always complaining'.[30] Meanwhile, having originally expressed great confidence in Moore, the poet and writer, Robert Southey, now changed his views completely. Thus: 'Poor Sir John was too cautious a man. He waited in distrust of the Spaniards to see what course the war would take, instead of being on the spot to make it take the course he wished.'[31]

Already furious with Moore, anxious to put all the blame on him and well aware of his Whig politics – it did not help in this respect that they were under heavy attack from an Opposition that had scented blood and positively revelled in the idea of a massive French victory in northern Spain – the ministers of the Portland administration certainly colluded in this assault, while yet having no option but to go along with a parliamentary motion to erect a monument to Moore in St Paul's cathedral.[32] Various Tory newspapers, including *The Times*, published accounts of the campaign that were inclined to put the general in the wrong, while the debate that was held in the House of Commons on the campaign saw the Secretary of State for Foreign Affairs, George Canning, make a speech in which he blatantly damned him with faint praise and sought to imply that the fault for what at this point was still perceived as an outright disaster was his and his alone.[33] In later debates, meanwhile, Ministers continued to uphold Frere (a close friend of Canning), while they also dragged their feet in respect of the release of the letters the ambassador had sent Moore and the general orders that the British commander had issued to his army.[34] In short, to quote Blakeney again:

30. See C.M.A. Oman, *Sir John Moore* (London, 1953), pp. 606–7.
31. R. Southey to T. Southey, 10 January 1809, *cit.* C.C. Southey (ed.), *The Life and Correspondence of Robert Southey* (London, 1849–50), III, p. 209.
32. See D.W. Davies, *Sir John Moore's Peninsular Campaign, 1808–1809* (The Hague, 1974), p. 261.
33. Oman., *Sir John Moore*, pp. 608–17 *passim*.
34. *Ibid.*, pp. 620–1. An exception to the general rule here was the Secretary of State for War and the Colonies, Lord Castlereagh, who appears to have backed away from the general attack on Moore after becoming aware of the full details of the Venault de

A general outcry was got up against Sir John Moore. He was accused of being stupid, of being irresolute, of running away and of God knows what. His memory was assailed alike by those politically opposed to his party and by those who were once his supporters and who, although aware of his masculine genius, maintained their posts by basely resorting to calumny and deceit.[35]

Yet in all this Moore was not without his defenders. Other veterans of the campaign were fiercely supportive, the artist, Robert Ker Porter, for example, placing all the blame for the retreat and subsequent evacuation on the Spaniards in the account of the campaign that he published in the rather mannered form of a collection of letters, and penning a tribute to the general that was even more exaggerated than those we have already quoted. Thus:

Gallant Moore, low art thou laid. In blood has the rays of thy fame been sunk, but not extinguished. They shoot the brighter from thine ashes and settle on thy grave. Distant from thy native land, like the tomb of Achilles, it will hereafter become the pilgrimage of heroes to stand where thou art laid, and with brave regrets to muse upon thy valour and thy fate.[36]

Equally eager as a champion of the general, meanwhile, was his brother, the leading surgeon, James Moore, who within a year had published a detailed account of the campaign based on Moore's dispatches that was outspoken both in its condemnation of the government and the praise which it heaped upon him. Herewith, for example, the author's opening salvo:

Although the king and the British nation have loudly proclaimed their admiration of Sir John Moore, yet, like the great and the good of every

---

Charmilly affair. At all events, whilst he could have diverted much of the blame away from the Cabinet by pointing out that Moore had disobeyed his orders and marched on Salamanca when he should rather have been concentrating his troops in the safety of Galicia, he rather stayed completely silent on the matter, his dissatisfaction with Canning according to some accounts being one of the many reasons that led him to fight a duel with his former colleague later in the year. Cf. Davies, *Sir John Moore's Peninsular Campaign*, pp. 261–2.

35. Sturgis (ed.), *Boy in the Peninsular War*, p. 125.
36. Porter, *Letters from Portugal and Spain*, p. 310. For good measure, Porter also suggested that the decision to attack Soult was precipitated by, as he put it, 'urgent wishes from home that he would not retreat'. *Ibid.*, p. 194.

age, he has not escaped the insinuations of envy even after terminating an illustrious career by a most glorious death . . . Few private men have risen to so conspicuous a station as that filled by Sir John with fewer enemies. This was chiefly owing to his modest and unassuming manners, to firmness tempered with kindness towards those under his command, and to a conduct to all scrupulously just. He spent his life in the army, and his popularity, both among officers and soldiers, never was exceeded. But universal approbation never was attained by man, and it must be admitted that, with politicians, he was not sufficiently pliant to be always easily approved of by them.[37]

And, finally, Moore's Adjutant General, Sir Henry Clinton, published a stout defence of Moore's conduct in which he justified both the precipitate nature of the retreat and the failure to stand and fight in such positions as Lugo. For example:

When he had ascertained that Bonaparte had brought so large a force against him, he naturally expected that every effort of which his energetic mind was capable would be employed for the destruction of the British army. I know that the possibility of corps of the enemy marching by roads right and left of that by which the British army was retiring was strongly represented to Sir John at Astorga. He had not the means of ascertaining whether or not the enemy had actually detached corps upon those roads, and impressed, as I believe him to have been, with the probability of such an attempt, he felt it incumbent upon him to gain, as expeditiously as possible, that point of the road of his retreat where he would no longer be exposed to the danger of such a manoeuvre.[38]

In the face of this barrage, the government would probably have done better to maintain a dignified silence. However, its members' pride had been so injured that they appear to have lost all sense of proportion. What pushed them over the edge here was an ode to Moore of truly execrable quality written by one Monk Lewis that the management of the Drury Lane Theatre decided to include in its repertoire, and, indeed, in every sense to feature centre stage. Taking great offence at this, the Cabinet responded by having the Lord Chancellor ban any further

---

37. J.C. Moore, *A Narrative of the Campaign of the British Army in Spain commanded by His Excellency, Lieutenant-General Sir John Moore, K.B., etc., etc., etc., authenticated by Official Papers and Original Letters* (London, 1809), pp. 1–2.
38. H. Clinton, *A Few Remarks explanatory of the Motives which guided the Operations of the British Army during the late Campaign in Spain* (London, 1809), pp. 21–2.

performances after just three nights, the net result being that the Whigs were given the opportunity to return to the charge and attempt to pass a motion of censure. Defeated though this was, the government ended up looking quite ridiculous, the Whig orator, George Tierney, concluding the debate by observing that Castlereagh 'was not to be trusted with a corporal's guard'.[39]

At length, refuge being found in the line that by attacking the French in northern Spain, Moore had deprived Napoleon of the fruits of the victories of November and December 1808 – something, of course, that had not been apparent in the dark days of January 1809 – the controversy blew over, and Moore was left to rest in peace and at the same time to enjoy at least a modest share in the glory that accrued to Britain from the Peninsular War: in 1816 the planned monument to Moore was unveiled in St Paul's cathedral, while in 1819 a bronze statue of the general that cost £3,000 was erected in George Square in his native Glasgow. Infinitely more influential, meanwhile, was the publication in 1817 of Charles Wolfe's 'Burial of Sir John Moore', a poem that well into the twentieth century was to be etched into the memories of generations of British schoolchildren. Perhaps, too, it helped that there was a growing recognition that, as Neale had argued in the immediate wake of the campaign, the British commander never had much hope of achieving much in the way of glory. Thus:

> Sir John Moore was not a little unlucky in having to deal, first, with a madman in Sweden [see below], and then with a set of irresolute politicians and fanatics in Spain. It was next to impossible that he could escape from the dilemma in which he was placed without incurring from one party or other a certain degree of obloquy. He was placed in a position the most awfully responsible that any British commander had yet occupied. Commanding a divided force in the midst of a country to which, I may say, himself and the rest of his army were entirely strangers; in an open plain; surrounded by an enemy amply provided with cavalry; opposed to that man, too, who, from his superior fortune and his military genius,

---

39. Davies, *Sir John Moore's Peninsular Campaign*, pp. 264–5. What made this affair still more unfortunate was that Lewis made no real comment on the responsibility for what had occurred, but simply eulogised the personal qualities of Moore and the heroism of his army. For example: 'Lamented Moore: how loved, how graced wert thou! What air majestick dazzled on thy brow!' M. Lewis, *A Monody on the Death of Lieutenant-General Sir John Moore with Notes Historical and Political by Robert T. Paine, Esquire* (Boston, 1811), p. 20. It might be pointed out, meanwhile, that Lewis' utterly forgettable rhyming would probably never have seen the light of day in the United States, complete, be it said, with an introduction that savaged the Portland administration, had the government not intervened in so heavy-handed a fashion.

seems destined and fitted to direct all the nations of the Continent, it was next to impossible that he could justify all the sanguine expectations of his country. He had, therefore, but a choice of difficulties. Having made his election, he had to encounter the whole power of the enemy, brought against him from various points . . . Aware of the promise that Napoleon had made to the Parisians that he would 'present to them the remains of the gaily dressed English', he was therefore justified in expecting that every possible exertion would be used by that wonderful man to fullfil his promise, in attempting which, however, [the latter] has fortunately failed. The question, then, is narrowed to this point: was it necessary for our commander-in-chief to hurry his army by such severe forced marches through a country perhaps the strongest in Europe? If this necessity be proved, the character of Sir John Moore, distinguished as it already is for manly sense, patriotism, and an uncommon share of military knowledge, will be further ennobled, by the recollection that, having filled the most arduous of stations, he fell in the arms of victory after conducting a most difficult retreat pursued by the conqueror of Europe and the whole élite of the French army.[40]

Yet the issue of how Moore should have exercised his command continued to hang over his head. In the course of the 1820s, then, at least two accounts – those of Robert Southey and Lord Londonderry appeared – that were at the very least critical of Moore.

All but forgotten though it is, of these by far the more significant was Robert Southey's *History of the Peninsular War*. The first such work attempted on a major scale – the first volume appeared in 1823 – this was not written from a standard British perspective. In brief, established long-since as a major pillar of the literary

---

40. Neale, *Letters from Portugal and Spain*, pp. 332–4. In general, Neale is generous in his treatment of Moore. However, he does suggest that his psychological management of his army was seriously deficient. Herewith an extract from the letter he wrote on 30 December: 'The officers have begun to murmur at the rapidity of our retreat. Hitherto the greatest mystery has been sedulously thrown over all our proceedings which has not tended to conciliate the minds of either men or officers towards the measures of our commander-in-chief. A certain degree of secrecy is no doubt necessary and highly proper on many occasions, but too much of it is generally offensive to soldiers on service, and it would be, perhaps, better if Sir John Moore had steered more of a middle course in this respect . . . In the French army it has latterly been the fashion to act in a plan directly opposite: everyone [therefore] has some idea of the motives for his actions, and is therefore more prompt in doing whatever may contribute to the general good.' *Ibid.*, p. 290.

world, Southey was a somewhat conflictive figure. On the one hand, he was a firm
Tory who was an instinctive supporter of the Portland administration, and yet, on
the other, as a man who knew and loved Spain and Portugal and was fluent in Spanish
and Portuguese alike, he was probably Britain's foremost hispanophile. When he sat
down to consider the war, then, there was no question that he would approve of the
dispatch of the British army and, indeed, Moore's advance into Spain. Yet, whereas
by the time he was writing, there was a general consensus in Britain that the Spanish
contribution to the war had been much exaggerated – that the Spanish army had
been little short of a joke, that successive Spanish governments had been at best
incompetent, that the Spanish people had been utterly lacking in patriotism and
that even the much-vaunted guerrillas had been little short of brigands – Southey
was, rather, determined to take it seriously: a deep-seated Romantic, he could not
divest himself of the vision of a devotedly Catholic populace, whether Spanish or
Portuguese, heroically doing battle with the French invaders in support of God,
King and Fatherland.[41] Possessed of a perfect command of both Iberian languages
as Southey was, his work therefore drew heavily on the indigenous sources and gave
much prominence to such events as the battle of Bailén and the siege of Zaragoza.
In taking this line, however, it has to be said that Southey was not entirely judicious:
the Spanish people, he was convinced, were solidly behind the struggle, or, at worst,
would have been solidly behind the struggle if only their energies had been called
forth in adequate fashion, but the sources he made use of to further this conclusion
were without exception pamphlets and newspaper reports in the public domain that
formed part of what may be described as the official discourse: had he had access
to the archives, he would have quickly perceived that the reality of the situation
was quite different. With regard to the question of what Moore should have done
in the crisis of 1808, then, this led him to an unfortunate conclusion in that he was
convinced that Madrid could have been saved if only Moore had marched to its
relief. In fairness, this is never stated absolutely overtly, but the implication was
clear enough for anyone who cared to read it, while Southey was at the very least
openly critical of the general's spirit. Thus:

> [Sir John Moore] fell, as it had ever been his wish to do, in battle and
> in victory. No man was ever more beloved in private life, nor was there
> any general in the army so universally respected. All men thought him

---

41. With regard to Portugal, there was less hostility: the Portuguese army, after all, had
     eventually been brought to a pitch of efficiency sufficient to allow it to be integrated
     into the front line of Wellington's forces. Yet considerable cultural prejudice remained,
     the general assumption being that, if the Portuguese had done well in the war, it was
     only to the extent that they allowed themselves to be brought on by the British.

worthy of the chief command. Had he been less circumspect, had he looked more ardently forward and less anxiously around him, and on all sides and behind him, had he been more confident in himself and in his army, and impressed with less respect for the French generals, he would have been more equal to the difficulties of his situation. Despondency was the radical weakness of his mind. Personally he was as brave a man as ever met death in the field, but he wanted faith in British courage, and it is by faith miracles are wrought in war as well as in religion.[42]

Finally, as if all this was not enough, Southey also dealt with the issue of whether or not Moore's prerogatives had been interfered with, Frere coming off very well in this respect as well: far from the ambassador interfering gratuitously with his command, it transpired that Moore had rather turned to him for advice and stated very clearly that he considered the question of whether he should defend Madrid as being at least as much political as it was military.[43]

If this was damning enough, still more ferocious was the attack launched on Moore in 1828 by Castlereagh's half-brother, Lord Londonderry. The commander of the cavalry component of the column commanded by Sir John Hope, on 4 December Sir Charles Stewart, as he then was, rode on ahead of the troops to confer with Moore at Salamanca. Arriving in the city, the next day, he found, or so he said, a most gloomy scene. At the point that Stewart arrived, Moore was still insisting on a retreat into Portugal, preparatory, be it said to a complete withdrawal from the Peninsula (as even Moore's supporters were afterwards forced to admit, there was no question in his mind of making any attempt to defend even Lisbon, Portugal being, in his view at least, completely indefensible), and Stewart claims that not a word that either he or anyone else could say would sway him:

> The compliments usual on such occasions having passed, our conversation naturally took the turn to which the present situation of affairs, and the

---

42. R.W. Southey, *A History of the Peninsular War* (London, 1823–32), I, pp. 804–5. These opinions, meanwhile, received some support in the Tory press. Here, for example, is the *Quarterly Review*: 'Whoever peruses the lucid narrative of Mr Southey . . . will have no hesitation in pronouncing that . . . fully and freely as the historian must award to the memory of Sir John Moore the praise of upright and zealous intentions and unbounded personal gallantry . . . a tendency to believe in French invincibility thwarted his judgement and fettered his exertions, and that the rapidity and disorder of his retreat through a series of almost impregnable fastnesses which resulted from this unhappy opinion will ever be numbered among the misfortunes and errors of our first Spanish campaign.' *The Quarterly Review*, XXIII (April and July, 1823), p. 84.
43. Southey, *Peninsular War*, I, p. 762.

current situation of the army, were inclined to guide it. It was then that Sir John explicitly stated to me that he had come to a final determination to retreat. He had called the general officers together, he added for the purpose of acquainting them with his decision, as well as with the reasons which led to it, but he had neither requested their opinions nor demanded their judgement. He next entered, at great length, into the motives which swayed him, reasoning in conversation, as he reasoned in his letters, with a decided leaning to the gloomy side of the picture. He spoke warmly in condemnation of the Spanish government, and of the nation generally, and enlarged upon the absence of all right understanding among the generals . . . He expressed sincere regret that they had not marched as they ought to have done . . . to unite themselves with him, and declared that, with a force as yet uncollected, and having nothing but the remains of defeated units on his flanks, a choice of evils remained to him. The determination to which he had at last come, was not formed without extreme pain to himself, but the duty of preserving his army, situated as it now was, presented to his mind a consideration paramount to every other . . . Though I could not but deeply feel at such a declaration, I deemed it my respectful duty to say little in reply, further than by expressing my regret that so strong a necessity for the measure should exist, and my apprehension of its consequences to the cause. The slightest indication of a retrograde moment, exhibited at such a moment as this, would, I feared, produce fatal effects for Spain would fall, Portugal would fall and the whole of Europe would be once more at the feet of the enemy. Then what would become of Madrid, whose inhabitants were enduring the severest privations, chiefly with the hope of receiving aid from us, and of Castaños and Palafox and Blake, all of whom, on the same explicit understanding, were labouring to reassemble their troops . . . The feelings of regret under which I laboured were not, I soon found, confined to my own breast: they were shared by many in the army. Even the general's personal staff sought not to conceal their chagrin at the adoption of a system that seemed so unsatisfactory. General Hope having by this time joined, there were at Salamanca and the neighbourhood full 20,000 British troops in a state both from their equipment and discipline to oppose any French force of almost double the number. General Baird with a strong reinforcement, particularly in cavalry, was at Astorga, nor were there any impediments whatever in his way which should hinder him from arriving within six days at the furthest. But, should it be deemed unsafe to wait so long here, why not move towards him and concentrate the divisions behind the Duero, from whence offensive operations might be undertaken?

Anything, in short, was preferable to a retreat which, independently of the disgrace which it would bring upon the British arms, must expose Madrid to destruction and cause the certain annihilation of Castaños and Palafox's armies. Seldom did men, situated as we were, speak out so boldly against the measures of their chief. But murmurings and remonstrances were useless: the die was cast, and it could not be recalled.[44]

In support of his position, which broadly speaking coincided with that of John Hookham Frere, in another long passage Londonderry laid out the many factors which in his eyes rendered a march on Madrid at the very least a viable possibility. Should things go wrong, for example, there would be nothing to stop Moore retiring across the Tagus and retreating into southern Spain in company with the remains of the Spanish armies. Yet there was no reason to suppose that things would go wrong: Napoleon was in command, certainly, but even he was not unbeatable, while there was every reason to hope that the population of central Spain would throw off their lethargy as soon as a British army was active in their midst, the reason for the inactivity of which Moore proclaimed being not so much that they were lacking in patriotism, but rather that the region was so devoid of natural defences and open to penetration by the enemy that, without substantial outside help, even to essay resistance would have been suicidal. Had he chosen to do so, then, even without Baird's troops, Moore could have marched to Madrid's assistance at any time after Hope had got into touch with him, this being a move that would have been worth it even had it cost him half his army.[45]

There followed conclusions that were damning, indeed, even downright devastating, there being little doubt that twenty years earlier Londonderry had used his privileged access to the government to peddle similar views to the Cabinet:

Perhaps the British army has produced some abler men than Sir John Moore; it has certainly produced many who, in point of military talent, were and are quite his equals, but it cannot, and perhaps never could, boast of one more beloved, not by his personal friends alone, but by every individual that served under him. It would be affectation to deny that Sir John Moore, during his disastrous retreat, issued many orders in the highest degree painful to the feelings of honourable men who felt their conduct had not merited them. His warmest admirers have acknowledged this, and his best friends have lamented it, but, in all probability, no-one would have lamented it more

---

44. Marquess of Londonderry, *Narrative of the Peninsular War from 1808 to 1813* (London, 1828), I, pp. 178–81.

45. *Ibid.*, pp. 172–7.

heartily than himself had he lived to review, in a moment of calmness, the
general conduct of this campaign, for there never lived a man possessed of
a better heart, nor, in ordinary cases, of a clearer judgement . . . The truth
is that Sir John Moore, with many of the qualities necessary to constitute
a general, was deficient in that upon which, perhaps more than any other,
success in war must ever depend. He wanted confidence in himself; he was
afraid of responsibility; he under-rated the qualities of his own troops, and
greatly overestimated those of his adversary.[46]

To all intents and purposes, then, Londonderry was accusing Moore of both
treating his subordinates in an unjust fashion, and, still worse, moral cowardice.
Among the general's admirers such words could not but act as a red rag to a bull.
Hence, in part at least, the diametrically opposite views that were voiced in the
second of two great histories of the Peninsular War that appeared in the nineteenth
century in the shape of William Napier's *History of the War in the Peninsula and
the South of France*. Published in six volumes between 1828 and 1841, this was
hardly likely to take an objective view of Sir John Moore, Napier being not just
a fellow Whig, but also a veteran of the Peninsular War who had served in the
regiment which Moore had commanded and, in fact, obtained a company through
his patronage. Indeed, according to his biographer, it was precisely his devotion to
Moore's memory that led him to turn historian of the struggle. Thus: 'Doubting
seriously of his ability worthily to accomplish such a work . . . he remained long
in hesitation, and his scruples were only finally overcome by his burning desire
to vindicate the memory of his beloved chieftain from the unjust assertions with
which it had been assailed'.[47]

As might be expected, then, Napier's comments on the campaign of Sir John
Moore were vigorous indeed: the British army had been placed in an impossible
position by the irresponsibility of the Portland administration; there was no option
but to advance into Spain in the manner chosen; Frere had acted dishonourably
towards Moore and sought to press views upon him that would have led to disaster;
and, finally, the haste of the retreat across Galicia was unavoidable. Appended to
the account of Moore's death, meanwhile, was a panegyric more grandiloquent
than anything that had been seen hitherto:

Thus ended the career of Sir John Moore, a man whose uncommon
capacity was sustained by the purest virtue, and governed by a disinterested

---

46. *Ibid.*, pp. 234–5.
47. H.A. Bruce, *Life of Sir William Napier, K.C.B., Author of the History of the Peninsular
War* (London, 1864), p. 23.

patriotism more in keeping with the primitive than the luxurious age of a great nation. His tall graceful person, his dark, searching eyes, strongly defined forehead and singularly expressive mouth, indicated a noble disposition and a refined understanding. The lofty sentiments of honour habitual to his mind were adorned by a subtle playful wit, which gave him in conversation an ascendancy he always preserved by the decisive vigour of his actions. He maintained the right with a vehemence bordering upon fierceness and every important transaction in which he was engaged increased his reputation for talent and confirmed his character as a stern enemy to vice, a steadfast friend to merit, a just and faithful servant of his country. The honest loved him, the dishonest feared him . . . If glory be a distinction, for such a man death is not a leveller.[48]

Once again, Moore did not lack for other defenders: in 1833, for example, James Moore returned to the charge with a substantial biography which laid much stress on the claim that the advance to Sahagún had saved Spain and Portugal from complete conquest and concluded by defining the British commander as 'the general of an army who, in the midst of danger, deliberated calmly, resolved wisely and acted intrepidly'.[49] Equally, two years earlier in a narrative of the Peninsular War he published that was half history and half personal memoir, Andrew Leith-Hay, in 1808 a young captain who had served as a liaison officer with the Spanish forces in northern Spain, refused even to engage with the campaign against Moore, writing: 'It is neither my intention nor my wish to enter into the controversial opinions so often delivered on the conduct of [Sir John Moore's] last campaign further than to state a firm conviction that his talents, his energies [and] his motives are far above the reach of calumny, more particularly when clothed in all the grovelling and subservient infamy of party purpose.'[50] Finally, periodically there continued to appear accounts by admiring veterans, one such being the one written by Charles Steevens of the Twentieth Foot, an officer whose memories we shall examine in detail at a later date, and was positively fierce in his defence of his erstwhile commander:

---

48. W. Napier, *History of the War in the Peninsula and in the South of France from the Year 1807 to the Year 1814* (new edn, rev. by C.J. Esdaile; London, 1880), I, pp. 333–4.

49. J.C. Moore, *The Life of Lieutenant-General Sir John Moore, K.B.* (London, 1833–4), II, p. 231.

50. A. Leith-Hay, *A Narrative of the Peninsular War* (London, 1831), p. 126. Despite his unwillingness to comment on the campaign, Leith-Hay does provide one useful piece of information in that he seems to imply that the detour that took Sir John Hope almost all the way to Madrid before he finally found a road leading to Salamanca was his work rather than that of Moore.

It was well-known that many Spaniards who were enemies to their own country frequently gave the French information which was detrimental to our cause. What commander could therefore stay in a country like this? If Sir John Moore had received greater reinforcements, and at an early period, it was thought that he might have kept his ground, and the result would have been far different to what it was, but Sir John was unsupported in all ways . . . He was . . . a very clever man and a good general, but he never had a force sufficient to cope with the enemy, and the Spaniards behaved in such a dastardly manner, running away to their homes – particularly after we had commenced our retreat – instead of harassing the enemy to the utmost of their power, so that, being left to ourselves, our force was nothing in point of numbers when compared to that of the French, [and] we were therefore obliged to get out of the country.[51]

However, such was the reverence that was attached to Napier that it was all but superfluous for anyone else to take up the cudgels on the general's behalf. That said, criticism was by no means entirely silent. As early as 1832, for example George Gleig, a veteran of the Peninsular War who, as Chaplain General of the British army, went on to write not just a personal memoir of his experience of the struggle, but also an adulatory biography of the Duke of Wellington, produced an analysis of Moore's conduct that accused him of mistake after mistake, whether it was the failure to keep his army together during the march on Salamanca, the abandonment of the passes of the mountains of Galicia without a fight or the killing pace which was set in the course of the retreat. More than that, indeed, his conclusion was that Moore was not a great general at all. Thus:

To sum all up in a few words, a candid history of Sir John Moore's active life leads to the conclusion that, with almost every accomplishment necessary to the formation of a military mind, he was not at home in the guidance of an independent army. Brave, sagacious, active, cool and collected in danger, and well-versed in the minor details of his profession, no man has ever excited more lofty expectations while ascending to a station of command. Yet the conduct of his army in Spain did not justify these expectations, nor place him in the foremost rank of British generals. Whence did this arise? We answer, without hesitation, that his failure – for failure it was – must be attributed partly to a diffidence of his own

---

51. C. Steevens, *Reminiscences of my Military Life*, ed. H. Steevens (Winchester, 1878), p. 78.

powers for which there was no just cause, and partly to the absence of
those powers of calculation on the exercise of which the events of war
mainly depend. Experience of command might have removed these
defects . . . but, as it is, we are left to think of him with respect, perhaps
with admiration, though strongly tinctured with pity.[52]

In 1859 came a further intervention in the debate in the form of a life of Canning
written by his private secretary, Augustus Stapleton. That Stapleton was biased
goes without saying – throughout its length, the work is deeply loyal to its subject
– but his views are nonetheless an interesting addition to the criticism to which
Moore could be subjected. Thus:

Very opposite opinions prevailed as to the parties on whom to rest the
blame for the failure of [the] expedition . . . Mr Frere's conduct was
censored as presumptuous, and such as would certainly have led to the
defeat or surrender of the army had it been adopted by the commander.
How far these views are correct, others may undertake to determine, but
they were not shared by Mr Canning. He always thought that Mr Frere's
advice was wise, and that Sir John might have accomplished more than
he did had it not been for his misgivings as to the advisableness of the
undertaking which, too strongly, from the outset, influenced his mind. In
some respects Mr Frere certainly formed an erroneous estimate of what
the Spaniards would do, but, on the other hand, a more decided course
on the part of the general might have roused them to more vigorous
efforts than they actually made.[53]

While the link is never made explicitly, this passage is best read in connection with
an earlier one that casts still more aspersions on Moore. In brief, Stapleton asked,
what could be expected from a general who considered success to be impossible
right from the beginning? As for proof that this was so, Stapleton pointed to the
confrontation that had taken place between Moore and Castlereagh in London on
the former's return from Denmark in July 1808. All accounts agree that this was a
stormy occasion, but Stapleton goes one step further:

After [Sir John] . . . had taken his leave and actually closed the door,
he re-opened it and said to Lord Castlereagh, 'Remember, my Lord,

52. G.R. Gleig, *Lives of the Most Eminent British Military Commanders* (London, 1832),
    III, p. 356.
53. A. Stapleton, *George Canning and his Times* (London, 1859), pp. 163–4.

I protest against the expedition and foretell its failure.' Having thus disburdened his mind, he instantly withdrew, left the office and proceeded to Portsmouth to take command of the expedition.[54]

Finally, some thirteen years later the issue was revived yet again, this time by the Frere family. Damned by Moore's opponents and to all intents and purposes disowned by the government, which replaced him in the summer of 1809 by Lord Wellesley, John Hookham Frere had not come out well from the scandal, and in 1872 his nephew, Henry Bartle Edward Frere, a distinguished diplomat and colonial administrator, took advantage of the publication of a collection of his uncle's poems and articles to mount a staunch defence of his conduct whose centrepiece was the claim not so much that Moore had refused to accede to his pleas to march to the aid of Madrid, but rather that, at the moment when he despaired of the Spaniards and took the later reversed decision to retire from Salamanca, he had resolved on a retreat on Lisbon rather than on Astorga, a position from which he could in theory have continued to intervene in the campaign. If the campaign had been a success at all, then, it was only because Moore had ultimately followed the ambassador's advice:

> If we look only to the experience of Moore's campaign, it is clear that, as far as the general was swayed by the envoy's advice to advance so as to threaten the French communications and then to retreat on Galicia rather than Portugal, the campaign was a great success, and the cost, heavy as it was, was not out of proportion to the results. It was no fault of the envoy's that the loss was not further reduced by earlier and more complete preparations on the line of the retreat to Corunna.[55]

Nor was this all. On the contrary, it was further suggested that, albeit through no fault of his own, Moore was completely unsuited to the demands of his position:

> For an English general . . . to conduct active operations in Spain . . . meant to carry on war in a country with the language of which few . . . even of the best educated and accomplished of the officers had the slightest acquaintance, to disarm the hostility of a proud, jealous, sensitive and high spirited race, to avoid affronting the prejudices of an uneducated populace, or the bigotry of a fanatical and all-powerful

---

54. *Ibid.*, pp. 159–60.
55. H.B.E. Frere, 'Memoir [of John Hookham Frere]' in W.E. and H.B.E. Frere (eds), *The Works of John Hookham Frere in Verse and Prose* (London, 1872), p. cix.

priesthood, to draw supplies of money and food from a country where internal commerce was nearly extinct and which was almost destitute of roads passable by wheeled carriages, to depend on a maritime base of operations many hundreds of miles distant, and to use as auxiliaries the armies of a people possessed indeed of many soldier-like qualities but unaccustomed to united and systematic subordination . . . Most of the superior officers of Napoleon's army had acquired, more or less, by long experience in foreign war, the art of performing some portions as such a task as this, but it is no exaggeration to say that, at the commencement of the Peninsular War, it was impossible for any English general, with merely European experience, to have learned such a lesson . . . Moore had not in this respect been more fortunate than his contemporaries. He undertook the charge of the expedition as a matter of duty, with a sad foreboding of the certainty of failure, and nothing in his previous experience gave him much help in overcoming the peculiar difficulties of his position.[56]

By no means lacking in substance though they were, these attacks could not make much impression on the prevailing mood: such was the dominance of Napier that Moore's position remained unassailable, his admission into the pantheon of Victorian heroism being symbolised by the publication of G.A. Henty's adventure novel, *With Moore at Corunna*, in 1898 (a prolific writer who was intensely conventional in his attitudes, Henty specialised in tales of derring-do aimed squarely at the officers and imperial administrators of the future, and, as such, was hardly likely to extol a figure who could in anyway be regarded as being controversial).[57] At the same time, too, as more and more Peninsular diaries and

---

56. *Ibid.*, pp. cxii–cxiii. Reading this, it will be wondered how Wellington was able to operate so successfully despite being confronted by exactly the same problems as Moore. The answer, of course, is his Indian experience: as has often been pointed out, the campaigns of 1799–1803 afforded him an insight into the demands of coalition warfare in a difficult physical environment that stood him in good stead in Spain and Portugal.

57. Henty was not the only historical novelist to heap praise upon Sir John Moore at this time. On the contrary, in 1904 there appeared Herbert Strang's *The Light Brigade in Spain or the Last Fight of Sir John Moore*, a dramatised account of the retreat that stressed the manner in which the advance to Sahagún had saved the Allied cause by throwing the French into confusion and reviving the faltering cause of Spanish resistance. Hardly surprisingly, the appearance of this work was the occasion for still more hymns of praise. To quote the foreword contributed by Lieutenant Colonel Willoughby Verner, the then official historian of the Light Brigade: 'The story deals with a period full of interest to Englishmen. Napoleon, having over-run Spain with 250,000 men, swept away and defeated all the Spanish armies and occupied Madrid,

memoirs appeared so the balance of opinion continued to tilt in Moore's favour. Not the least of these fresh voices was that of Robert Blakeney, whose memoirs appeared in 1899. Thus: 'Like a staunch general of the empire, Sir John Moore terminated his splendid career in maintaining his honour and crushing his foes.'[58] Only with the publication of the first volume of Sir Charles Oman's seminal *History of the Peninsular War* in 1901 was a challenge made in a forum prestigious enough for it to be taken seriously. Forced constantly to justify his endeavours by the mere existence of Napier's work, from the beginning Oman could not but seek to show that his work was new, that it made, in fact, an original contribution to the historiography. In part, proof that this was so came from a much more considered and detailed approach to the Spanish and Portuguese aspects of the struggle than the deeply anglocentric Napier had ever been prepared to accord them. But in part, too, we see a desire to challenge Napier on every occasion that the latter presented a chink in his armour, one such being, of course, the campaign of Sir John Moore. In the end, Oman admitted, it had been a case of all being well that ended well: the French were diverted from the operations against Portugal and southern Spain that might have swept Napoleon to victory, while Moore's much tried army won a great victory and got away to England. However, it had truly been the proverbial 'near-run thing', the British commander having committed a series of errors that

---

had set his host in motion to re-occupy Portugal and complete the subjugation of Andalucía. At this critical point in the history of Spain, Sir John Moore, who had landed in the Peninsula with a small British army only about 30,000-strong, conceived the bold project of marching on Salamanca, and thus threatening Napoleon's line of communications with France . . . The effect was almost magical. Napoleon was compelled instantly to stay the march of his immense armies, whilst at the head of 80,000 of his finest troops, he hurled himself on the intrepid Moore. The latter, thus assailed by overwhelming numbers, was forced to order a retreat on his base at Corunna, a movement which he conducted successfully despite the privations of a rapid march in mid-winter through a desolate and mountainous country with insufficient transport and inadequate staff arrangements. Thrice he turned at bay and thrice he severely handled his pursuers. Finally, at Corunna, having embarked his sick and wounded, he fought the memorable battle of that name and inflicted on the French such heavy losses that his army was enabled to re-embark and sailed for England with but little further molestation. The gallant Moore himself was mortally wounded and died the same night, [but] the effects of the Corunna campaign were to paralyse the emperor's plans for nigh three months, during which time the Spaniards rallied and regained confidence, and the war took a wholly different turn'. H. Strang, *The Light Brigade in Spain or the Last Fight of Sir John Moore* (London, 1904), p. 9.

58. Sturgis (ed.), *Boy in the Peninsular War*, p. 123.

came close to producing a major disaster. In this respect, lengthy though it is, the following passage is worth quoting in full:

> When we turn to the weeks that preceded the advance from Salamanca, and that followed the departure from Astorga, it is only a very blind admirer of Moore who will contend that everything was arranged and ordered for the best. That the army, which began to arrive at Salamanca on November 13, did not begin to make a forward move until December 12 is a fact which admits of explanation but not of excuse. The main governing fact of its activity was not, as Moore was always urging, the disasters of the Spaniards, but the misdirection of the British cavalry and artillery on the roundabout route by Elvas, Talavera and Escorial. For this the British general was personally responsible: we have already shown that he had good reasons for distrusting the erroneous reports on the roads of Portugal which were sent in to him, and that he should not have believed them. He ought to have marched on Almeida with his troops distributed between the three available roads, and should have had a compact force of all arms concentrated at Salamanca by November 15. Even without Baird he could then have exercised some influence on the course of events. As it was, he condemned himself . . . to a month of futile waiting while the fate of the campaign was being settled 150 miles away . . . So much must be said of Moore's earlier faults. Of his later ones, committed after his departure from Astorga, almost as much might be made. His long hesitation as to whether he should have marched on Vigo or on Corunna was inexcusable: at Astorga his mind should have been made up, and the Vigo road . . . should have been left out of consideration. By failing to make up his mind and taking useless half-measures, Moore deprived himself of the services of Robert Craufurd and 3,500 of the best soldiers of the army . . . Still more open to criticism is the headlong pace at which Moore conducted the last stages of the retreat . . . All this hurry was unnecessary: whenever the rearguard turned to face the French, Soult was forced to wait for many hours before he could even begin an attempt to evict it . . . The general drove his men beyond their strength when he might, at the cost of a few rearguard skirmishes, have given them four or five days more in which to accomplish their retreat.[59]

---

59. C. Oman, *A History of the Peninsular War* (Oxford, 1902–30), I, pp. 598–601.

In writing thus, Oman was careful to pull his punches: on a personal level, Moore, he wrote, was a veritable paragon – 'Few men have been better loved by those who knew him best . . . Handsome, courteous, just and benevolent, unsparing to himself, considerate to his subordinates, he won all hearts.'[60] But he also argued that the speed of the retreat was the product of the 'excessive sense of responsibility' engendered by the knowledge that the consequences of a serious defeat would be so severe that Britain could be knocked out of the war.[61] Yet, coupled as it was with a distinct suggestion that excessive concern for the safety of his army had been coupled by excessive concern for the safety of his reputation, the attack was a body blow which caused outrage among Moore's admirers. The response, then, was not long in coming. In 1904, then, just three years after the publication of Oman's first volume, Sir J.F. Maurice, a strong supporter of military reform who was much influenced by Moore's activities at Shorncliffe Camp, published an important work that had not hitherto appeared in print in the form of Moore's diary. This was not as helpful in respect of the campaign of 1808 as might have been desired – hardly surprisingly, the text comes to an abrupt end at Sahagún – but it did contain considerable material on Moore's experiences at Salamanca that provided much ammunition for anyone wishing to paint a picture of the general as the long-suffering victim of the incompetence of the British government and the Spaniards alike. As editor, meanwhile, seemingly in part driven by a strong belief that military matters should not be written about by a mere civilian, Maurice launched a furious attack on Oman. This, however, was so extreme in tone and, indeed, so unconvincing, that it can scarcely be read without a feeling that the author was protesting a little too much. To quote the *English Historical Review*:

> [Maurice] has rightly thought to supplement the Peninsular entries by a long review of the campaign. Many parts of it are valuable, and we are grateful to him for it, but one cannot help regretting a certain want of measure and judgement in his handling of the subject. He begins by saying he has no thought of 'defending Moore': his intention is to show that Moore's march into Spain 'was the boldest, the most successful and the most brilliant stroke of war of all time'. With this object, it would have been better to go straight forward, showing what Moore did, why and with what result. But General Maurice wanders off into controversy, and deals with criticisms that have been made, especially those of Professor Oman, at much length and with unnecessary warmth. One may agree with every step of his argument in vindication of Moore, and yet stop short of his

---

60. *Ibid.*, pp. 601–2.
61. *Ibid.*, p. 601.

conclusion . . . In connection with this, General Maurice makes some remarks about the incident at Benavente which can only be described as extravagant. Napoleon had failed to intercept Moore . . . That he was irritated at his failure, and wished to have no further personal share in an inglorious stern chase, may be taken for granted, but to suggest that he brought on war with Austria to cover his shame, thereby imperilling his whole scheme of Spanish conquest, is fantastic.[62]

As Moore might have told Maurice, then, a cool head is always an asset on the battlefield. Yet Oman's strictures nonetheless fell by the wayside: the centennial celebrations in January 1909, which included a commemorative service in St Paul's, the unveiling of fresh memorials at Shorncliffe Camp and neighbouring Sandgate and a wreath-laying ceremony in Glasgow, the latter complete with heavy snow, seemingly went ahead without a qualm. At the same time the following year saw the appearance of what looks very like an Establishment counter-blast in the form of Volume VI of Sir John Fortescue's massive *History of the British Army*. The royal family's personal librarian and archivist, Fortescue was possessed by a loathing of politicians that was almost pathological and was therefore happy to second the violent denunciations which Napier, albeit from a very different standpoint, had heaped upon the succession of Tory administrations that had ruled Britain in the Peninsular War: in brief, Canning, Castlereagh, Perceval, Liverpool and the rest were universally portrayed as being selfish, penny-pinching incompetents who were more motivated by party interest than the national good. For Fortescue to have sided with anyone but Moore in his assessment of the situation was therefore unthinkable, and, while always maintaining the most gentlemanly of facades, he therefore clashed violently with Oman when his work reached the Peninsular War. The result was all too predictable. On the one hand, then, we have a positive paean of praise, and, on the other, a lengthy apologium whose basic line is that everything that had gone wrong was the fault of somebody else, that Moore was in an impossible situation and that every decision taken by the general was eminently defensible given the context of the moment, even if hindsight afterwards showed it to be incorrect:

> Moore's intellect . . . dwarfed that of many a statesman, so-called, and his remarkable insight and sagacity never failed him, whether in Ireland or the Mediterranean, in Egypt or in Spain . . . He was perfectly pure, perfectly gentle, perfectly honest, perfectly fearless, perfectly true . . . No

---

62. E.M. Lloyd, review of J.F. Maurice (ed.), *The Diary of Sir John Moore* (London, 1904), in *English Historical Review*, XIX, No. 75 (July, 1904), pp. 603–4.

man possessed a more irresistible faculty for winning hearts: all ranks of the army adored him from the private to the general . . . It remains to examine into Moore's action, to enquire how far he did what was best to be done, whether he might have done it better and whether he could have accomplished more . . . One critic [i.e. Oman] does indeed assert that Moore should have dragged his artillery over the mountains of Portugal instead of sending it round by Madrid and he ought to have had a compact force of all arms by Salamanca by the 15th of November . . . in which case, even without Baird, he could have exercised some influence. Passing over the fact that the artillery could not have travelled over any road except that which it actually took, I confess that I cannot see how an advance on Tudela or upon Madrid could possibly have mended matters. It would have been of no advantage to Moore to entangle himself with the Spaniards and he would have been obliged to beat a precipitate retreat with diminished chances of escape . . . On receiving the news of Tudela he decided that his presence in northern Spain was useless and that it was his duty to retreat to Portugal . . . Beyond all question he was right for his army could do little where it was . . . Was he therefore wrong when, upon what was, after all, false intelligence, he reversed his decision and determined to advance against Napoleon's communications? Judged purely from a military standpoint, he was wrong and he knew that he was wrong. The movement was in fact dictated wholly by political considerations, and it may be doubted whether, but for his peculiar relations with Castlereagh and the government, he would have undertaken it. But his position was more than ordinarily difficult. The public had no more devoted, conscientious servant than Moore and yet a cursed fate had constantly thrown him into collision with Ministers. Since, after first treating him shamefully, they had then committed to him a most important command, he was more than usually anxious to justify their confidence in him by the best and most loyal service, and yet the same fate pursued him and set him at variance with the government's most trusted agent, Frere. To the government, therefore, he sacrificed, as he thought, his military reputation.[63]

Just how far short these remarks succeeded as a defence of Moore's conduct will be left to the reader to decide on the basis of what follows, but there is more besides.

---

63. J.W. Fortescue, *A History of the British Army* (London, 1899–1930), VI, pp. 398–400, 411–12.

Here, for example, is Fortescue's response to the misbehaviour of the soldiery and the criticism to which Moore was subjected by many veterans of the campaign:

In reality the whole of the army's misconduct was due to one thing, and to one thing only, that the troops in their ignorance wished to advance whereas the general meant to retire. Moore, from the very nature of the case and from no fault of his own, was bound to retreat, sooner or later, on pain of utter destruction, and the army, which felt confident of its mettle and powers was therefore bound to be ill-tempered. Its ill-temper found innumerable voices, the loudest of which was that of Charles Stewart, who, over and above the criticism to be found in his memoirs, wrote privately to his brother Castlereagh that he would rather have sacrificed half the army than turned back without striking a blow for Spain. It is time to dismiss all such nonsense as this, together with the foolish criticisms of Moore which are based upon it.[64]

If Lord Londonderry ever made such a remark – and it has to be said that Fortescue does not provide even the barest hint of a footnote in this respect – then he was clearly very foolish, just as it would have been equally foolish for Moore to have continued with his attack on Soult once he knew that Napoleon had turned the bulk of his forces upon him, let alone to have suddenly doubled back on his tracks and hurled himself upon the French somewhere in the wilds of Galicia. However, as we have seen, not one of Moore's critics takes such a line, their argument being rather that the British commander conducted the retreat at an utterly breakneck speed that put the army under a strain that was quite intolerable when the nature of the terrain was such as to have allowed the withdrawal to be conducted at a much more measured pace. As the new generalissimo of Moore's cause, Fortescue therefore left much to be desired, but this did not prevent other champions from coming forward to fight for the general. Let us here first turn to Beatrice Brownrigg's 1923 work, *The Life and Letters of Sir John Moore*, this generally adopting a moderate tone and seeking to avoid the polemics that had so marred Maurice's work. Yet the author was the great-grand-daughter of the officer who in 1808 had held the post of Quartermaster General at the Horseguards, Sir Robert Brownrigg, and was evidently extremely proud of this connection – in her preface she tells us that she had originally embarked on the biography as a means of acquainting her son with Moore's character – and, as such, is scarcely an impartial witness. In consequence, her account acquits Moore of allegations of indecision and faint-heartedness,

---

64. *Ibid.*, p. 409.

glosses over the curious arrangements made for the march into Spain, engages in the usual stigmatisation of Frere, of whom it is said that his 'ignorance of the Spanish character and methods of government was only equalled by his ignorance and conceit', follows Maurice in maintaining the impossibility of making any stand on the road to Corunna, and, finally, says nothing about the extreme demands which Moore made of his army: if Oman, perhaps, is guilty of hindsight in playing down the danger posed by the French pursuit, it would nonetheless have behoved Brownrigg at least to address the charge. As for Canning, he very much emerges as the villain of the piece, and the man who, more than anyone else, was responsible for creating the impression that Moore was solely responsible for the disaster, if, indeed, disaster it was.[65] In fact, if men such as Canning undermined Moore's reputation after his death, they were also the root cause of the indecision which he had seemingly displayed at Salamanca, not to mention the patent want of enthusiasm with which he was often supposed to have embarked on the campaign. Thus:

> Southey's suggestion that the constitution of Moore's mind led him to look at the dark, rather than the hopeful, aspect of things is a misinterpretation of Moore's occasional despair at the inability or wilful blindness of Ministers to understand that military operations and campaigns required something more elaborate in the way of preparation and organization than reckless orders flung at the commander in the field to achieve some political end of which he was entirely ignorant.[66]

Though Brownrigg's work was certainly an advance on that of Maurice and, indeed, Napier, it was not long before it had been superseded by the discovery of fresh documentary materials. In consequence, conscious, perhaps of her father's role in opening Moore's character up to fresh discussion, in 1953, Carola Oman published the most substantial biography of the general to date in the form of the 700-page *Sir John Moore*. Greeted by the warmest of reviews on the part of military historians, this was, and still remains, the fullest statement of the case for the defence – 'the impossibility of J.H. Frere and the political agility of Canning are fully illustrated', exulted one enthusiast – but in fact the work adds little that is new to the historical canon.[67] Even though the author did do something to flesh out the hitherto rather bare bones of Canning's attempts to exonerate the Portland

---

65. Brownrigg, *Sir John Moore*, pp. 206–75.
66. *Ibid.*, pp. x–xi.
67. T. McGuffie, review of C.M.A. Oman, *Sir John Moore* (London, 1953), in *English Historical Review*, LXIX, No. 272 (July, 1954), p. 456.

administration of all blame for the general's misfortunes, while at the same time providing a reasonable explanation of Moore's decision to split the army into three columns as it advanced into Spain, albeit one that does not entirely acquit the general of the charge of culpable negligence, the general's most recent biographer is scathing in her assessment: the book, she claimed, was 'more fiction than fact, often reporting things which do not appear in any of the original sources and thus can only come from the author's imagination'.[68]

Reflection and Reassessment

By the middle years of the twentieth century, then, Moore's place in the British historiography of the Peninsular War seemed to be absolutely assured, while it was continually reinforced by the efforts, whether direct or indirect, of popularisers such as Christopher Hibbert, Roger Parkinson and Michael Glover. In 1974, however, there at last appeared a work that took a more critical line in the form of D.W. Davies' *Sir John Moore's Peninsular Campaign, 1808–1809* (The Hague, 1974). Not least because its rather odd place of publication rendered it unlikely to be much noticed among British readers of popular military history, this cannot in itself be said to have had much of an impact. That said, it remains an important work that might otherwise have shifted the debate away from such traditional bones of contention as the roads Moore made use of when he led his army to Salamanca. Thus, to Davies, this issue mattered not a whit:

> Actually, the choice or roads had no effect on any subsequent action or possible action of the campaign. Nothing good or bad, disastrous or brilliant, resulted from sending the army by the Lisbon–Madrid highway. None of Moore's four columns moving into Spain suffered a casualty from a Frenchman, and, indeed, with the exception of a French patrol fleetingly glimpsed by one of Hope's patrols, no British soldier even saw a Frenchman. After his arrival at Salamanca Moore had no

---

68. J. Macdonald, *Sir John Moore: the Making of a Controversial Hero* (Barnsley, 2016), p. 254. Given this criticism, not to mention the title of her book, Macdonald might have been expected to approach her subject in a more critical manner than Carola Oman, but this, alas, is not the case. Far from accepting the numerous criticisms made of Moore's generalship, she rather chose to sweep them aside as 'nit-picking by those who do not want to lay the blame where serious consultation of the available original documents shows that blame to lie: in the inexperience and poor judgement of the British government where the Spanish nation and its leaders were concerned and the intransigence and unwarranted boastfulness of the Spanish generals who failed to back up their promises.' *Ibid.*, p. 251.

possible objective for an advance until Napoleon . . . bypassed the British army and so left his supply lines open to attack . . . By that time the army was reunited and ready to move. No delay had been experienced, no opportunity had been lost.[69]

If the issue was not the routes that should have been followed to the frontier, then, wherein did the problem really lie? The answer, perhaps, is surprising. In brief: what mattered was rather the fact that Moore had advanced directly into Spain at all, Davies demonstrating that several of his senior staff officers preferred the idea of a move by sea to the north coast of Spain, and that the Duke of York – a very strong patron of the general – was positively alarmed at the prospect. Given that the Cabinet had originally been in favour of a descent on the north coast (the area usually mentioned was Asturias), and that it had subsequently only modified this to the extent of suggesting that Moore should transfer his army to Galicia, it followed that it was not Canning that was the sinner after all.[70]

Though he is no particular admirer of Canning, a vain and rather silly man whose conduct in the wake of the campaign wrecked the Portland administration and carried with it the very strong risk of handing power to the Whigs (in brief, convinced that the Cabinet was too weak to survive for any length of time, Canning intrigued against Castlereagh in an attempt to have him replaced in a reshuffle, the latter being so incensed that he challenged the Foreign Secretary to a duel), this theme has been picked up by the current author. We come here to a chapter that was written in conjunction with the Australian historian Rory Muir some thirty years ago on the topic of the workings of civil-military relations in Britain at the level of government and high command in the Napoleonic period. The relationship between the Portland administration and Sir John Moore having been selected for

---

69. Davies, *Sir John Moore's Peninsular Campaign*, pp. 267–8.
70. For a summary of Davies' views in this respect, cf. *ibid.*, pp. 62–5. It does have to be asked, of course, whether a move to Galicia was genuinely practicable, not least because of the onset of the autumn's usual quota of gales and the fact that much of the available shipping was being used to convey Junot's army to France, but the fact remains that the move to Salamanca was undertaken entirely on Moore's own responsibility, and that, if Moore's army could march to Salamanca, it could just as easily march to Santiago. Whether the Portland administration was wise to offer aid to Spain is another matter, and there is a strong case for arguing that, militarily speaking, the dispatch of a British army to the Peninsula was from the start a genuinely risky proposition, but to have turned down the Spanish emissaries when they arrived in London or even to have fobbed them off with mere promises of finance would have been a diplomatic disaster of the first order that would have made Britain's chances of obtaining Continental allies even more unlikely.

the purposes of the chapter concerned as an important case study, this opened the way for a detailed examination of the campaign of December 1808–January 1809. The result, alas, did not make for easy reading. While the traditional view of Moore as the kindliest and most sensitive of commanders may have held good in so far as his subordinates were concerned, it was shown that in other areas the picture was not nearly so roseate. Such was the situation in Spain and Portugal that what the British army sent to the Peninsula required was a commander of the utmost tact and diplomacy with a good record of inter-acting with foreign statesmen and generals, and, for that matter, British diplomats, but that is precisely what it did not receive. On the contrary, an examination of Moore's career prior to the outbreak of the Peninsular War suggests at the very least that he was a difficult subordinate, as well as one who had very little tolerance of foreigners and British diplomats alike: appointed second-in-command in Sicily in 1806, for example, he had the next year to be brought home on account of his scorn for the Sicilian government and repeated quarrels with the British ambassador and his commanding officer, Sir Charles Fox, alike. Needless to say, given that Moore was already feeling very poorly treated by the fortunes of war – early wounds had denied him much share of such credit as was going from both the campaign in Holland in 1799 and the invasion of Egypt in 1801 – this did not go down well, while any chance that he might be mollified by being offered command of the division that was sent to succour Sweden in its war against Russia in March 1808 was dissipated by the fact that relations between Moore and the Swedes broke down to such an extent that at one point he was put under house-arrest by the Swedish monarch, Gustav IV. Convinced that he had deliberately been put in an impossible situation by a Tory government bent on ruining his reputation, the general returned to London in a state of fury, while his mood was not improved by wholly unfounded suggestions from friends at the Horseguards to the effect that he had been denied the command in the Peninsula because he was not a friend of the Ministry. With the Portland administration no better pleased with Moore than Moore was with the Portland administration – many of the problems with the Swedes were rather unjustly held to be the fruit of the general's own obstreperousness – the result was a stormy confrontation with Castlereagh whose culminating moment may or may not have been the dramatic warning chronicled by Stapleton (there is, in fact, some circumstantial evidence to the effect that this particular detail was invented or, at least, much exaggerated).[71]

With relations so bad between Moore and the London government, in ordinary circumstances he would in all probability never have been selected for the

---

71. For all this, see R. Muir and C.J. Esdaile, 'Strategic planning in a time of small government: the war against Revolutionary and Napoleonic France, 1793–1815', in C. Woolgar (ed.), *Wellington Studies, I* (Southampton, 1996), pp. 48–71.

command when this became available in the wake of the controversy unleashed by the Convention of Sintra. However, the circumstances were not ordinary. Refusing to allow him to accede to the command would have alienated Horseguards and with it much of the army, but, more to the point, Moore was on the spot, a spot, moreover, that demanded that action should be initiated in the shortest possible time. Though Canning, especially, seems to have been most unhappy, it therefore fell to the Scottish general to take things forward. As to what happened next, inclined though the current author might be to sympathise with Davies' revisionism in a general sense, the claim that Moore should never have marched on Salamanca, but rather obeyed the orders that he had been given – 'orders', it should be noted, rather than the 'option' written of by some historians – to take his troops to the frontiers of Galicia seems unfair: given that that much of the army was already deep in the interior by the time that Moore took over the command, and given, too, both the advanced season of the year and the need to get his troops into Spain as quickly as possible, the British commander does not appear to have acted so unreasonably in this respect. What mattered, then, was how the move was made, and here there was, Davies' views notwithstanding, considerable cause for blame: like it or not, Moore accepted the utterly incredible idea – the fruit of faulty intelligence gathering and assimilation on the part of his predecessor, General Dalrymple – that there was no road suitable for artillery and cavalry between Lisbon and Almeida (the logical route for any troops heading for Salamanca) and that despite the fact that Almeida was one of the most important fortresses in Portugal. That being the case, although being deeply worried by its implications, he failed to countermand the decision that had been taken prior to his assumption of the command, then, that all the cavalry and artillery, together with a small force of infantry, should be sent to Spain via the main Lisbon–Madrid highway, this meaning that it would cross the frontier far to the south at Elvas. Thus far, the fault was beyond doubt Moore's: he both could and should have had the information on the roads to Almeida checked out immediately and, had he done so, would have been in time to bring back the cavalry and artillery without too much delay. Yet, the fault was not all Moore's: given that there were two roads leading north from the Lisbon–Madrid highway that could be used to reach Salamanca, the one starting from Badajoz and running up through Alcántara through the Sierra de Gata to Ciudad Rodrigo, and the other starting much further east at Almaraz and striking northwards via Plasencia and Baños through the Sierra de Gredos, it might have been expected that the commander of the column sent on the southern route, Sir John Hope, would have checked them out in the course of his advance. These roads, true, were not of the best, and it is conceivable that, given the season of the year, they may have been rendered still more difficult by snow and ice, but we know from later events that in ordinary circumstances they were adequate for the passage of large bodies of troops, complete with cavalry and artillery. Like the roads from Lisbon to Almeida, then, they should have been reconnoitred, but, in so far as can be ascertained, no attempt was made to do so. Hope, a commander who displayed much carelessness when he returned to the Peninsula in the autumn of 1813 as commander of the First Division, therefore continuing his plodding progress all the way to Navalcarnero before finally turning back towards Salamanca via El Escorial and the main highway leading from Madrid to the northwest.[72]

Davies, then, is wrong. It was not the decision to march on Salamanca that was at fault, but rather the culpable laxity of Moore and his subordinate commanders. Excuse may be found in the pressure under which the British commander found himself to get the army on the move, but, in the end, it is difficult to write of the issue with patience: after all, because of it, Moore found himself for some weeks not only quite incapable of intervening in the campaign, but also exposed to a serious risk of destruction. We here come to the darkest part of the story. Moore was placed as he was placed though nobody's fault but his own, while, had he followed the government's orders, he would, in the first place, have been perfectly safe, and, in the second, in all probability, just as well placed to act against Napoleon's communications as actually turned out to be the case. In this situation, the honourable course would have been to accept personal responsibility for his misfortunes, but this he absolutely failed to do, instead writing a series of letters to such figures as Sir James Willoughby Gordon and Sir David Baird in which he complained bitterly that the army had been sent too far forward and that too much attention had been paid to the liaison officers who had been sent to the various provincial juntas in the summer of 1808, their reports having been, or so he claimed, wildly misleading and over-optimistic.[73]

---

72. The best analysis by far of the decisions that led to the loss of Sir John Hope's column for such a long time, not to mention the manner in which it came within an ace of being snapped up by Napoleon as he fell on Madrid, is to be found in Oman, who also denounces Napier's efforts to safeguard Moore from blame as but 'ingenious and eloquent casuistry', cf. Oman, *Peninsular War*, I, pp. 493–7. The most useful source for the march of Sir John Hope's column makes no mention of the roads across the Sierra de Gata and the Sierra de Gredos, but, with reference to the question of whether or not the mountain passes were blocked, it does say that from a couple of days before the troops reached the frontier 'every appearance in the sky was for the continuation of a long period of sunshine and drought', Londonderry, *Narrative of the Peninsular War*, p. 149.

73. Esdaile and Muir, 'Civil–military relations', pp. 76–7. The charge against the liaison officers is difficult to sustain: a few of them, true, did behave irresponsibly in terms of ill-judged attempts to back one Spanish general or another as potential commanders-in-chief, but, if anything, their reports tended toward pessimism, this probably being the reason that led Castlereagh to suggest concentrating the army in Galicia.

Still worse, meanwhile, his criticisms of his political superiors do not appear to have been particularly guarded, quickly becoming, as they did, the veritable gossip of the army. To quote a Hanoverian exile who had enlisted as a commissary named Auguste Schaumann:

> Everybody pities General Moore and the critical position in which he has been placed by the stubborn attitude of the British ministry, which continues to give a wholly sympathetic hearing to the lies and insinuations of the Spanish junta and Mr Frere, the British government's representative on that body [sic]. As the result, in the first place, of his fatally compromising mission to Sweden, whence, owing to the mad demands of the Swedish king he was obliged to withdraw; secondly, of the difficult command which has been given to him here; and, thirdly, of the fact that the dispatches from the Spaniards receive more credence than our own, General Moore is said to be very much at loggerheads with Lord Castlereagh.[74]

This episode is scarcely pleasant to relate, but the evidence is irrefutable. Thin-skinned, highly strung, obsessed with his reputation and increasingly paranoid, by 1808 Moore was also deeply frustrated: he had been denied glory in Holland, he had been denied glory in Egypt, he had been denied glory in Sweden and now it looked as if he was to be denied glory in Spain as well. As before, this last was not his fault, but he had yet committed a serious error of judgement that had placed his army in the deepest jeopardy. That he should have responded by seeking to shrug off the blame for misfortune on to the shoulders of his political superiors is understandable, perhaps, but it was scarcely the response of a hero.

---

74. E. Ludovici, *On the Road with Wellington: the Diary of a War Commissary* (London, 1924), p. 85. In confirmation of the manner in which Moore's differences with the government we have the following comment from Adam Neale: 'Everything has fallen out as disastrous and perplexing as possible for Sir John Moore . . . There is scarcely an officer of feeling who does not sympathise with him in the very difficult and critical position in which he is placed. The unpleasant circumstances surrounding his return from Sweden, his personal quarrel with Lord C. before he sailed for Portugal (a circumstance notorious here, and much talked of, the sensibility of his character, his high sense of honour, and, above all the warm glow of patriotism that warms his breast, makes Sir John an object of the liveliest interest in all those around him. No British general, perhaps, was ever placed in a more arduous and embarrassing situation.' Neale, *Letters from Portugal and Spain*, pp. 247–8.

Some Conclusions

What, then, are we left with? First of all, of course, whatever mistakes he may have made in the course of the campaign, Moore had in the end struck a most effective blow against Napoleon and, in the process, ensured that the French were denied the only chance they ever had to end the Peninsular War without the disadvantage of having to engage in a long-drawn-out conflict, while it is difficult to see how the British army could have been used in a more effective fashion than was actually the case: an advance to the Ebro would beyond doubt have led to complete disaster; an attempt to confront Napoleon while he was still descending on Madrid would probably have led to the evacuation of Lisbon; and an attempt to concentrate the army not at Salamanca but on the frontiers of Galicia would have achieved no more than was actually the case, and might have taken even longer to effect. Second of all, there is no reason to deny Moore's claims to be regarded as a serious military reformer who had a profound impact on the history of the British army. Third of all, it is quite clear that Moore was every inch the considerate, generous commander who was so idolised by William Napier and so many of the other men who served under him. And, finally, fourth of all, no one can doubt Moore's physical courage: his leadership on the battlefield that saw him fall mortally wounded was genuinely inspiring. Yet paragon of all the virtues Moore was not. Analysis of his diary and correspondence paints a picture of a vain and petulant figure and difficult subordinate who was contemptuous of politicians, felt that his career had been blighted and shared the disdain for foreigners that was typical of his compatriots: Sicilians, Swedes and Spaniards were all successive targets of his scorn. It was not a happy mixture, and Britain could think herself fortunate that it had not been productive of a serious military disaster.

The Diary of Ensign Charles Paget, July 1808–January 1809

Introduction

Charles Paget, alas, is not an officer about whom we know a great deal. Thus far, not a single reference to him has been found in any of the numerous diaries, memoirs and collections of correspondence generated by the British forces that fought in the Peninsular War, and we would not be able to tie the current manuscript to him at all were it not for the fact its author notes that in September 1808 he transferred from the Second Battalion of the Fifty-Second Regiment of Foot to the First Battalion of the same regiment. As the extraordinary Challis index – essentially an alphabetical list of every single officer of the British army (some 9,000) who served in the Peninsular War compiled in his spare time by a veteran of the First World War named Lionel Challis in the period 1920–50 – reveals, only three officers made this change in the autumn of 1808 and two of them – Captain William Chetwynd and Major Henry Ridewood – are simply too senior to fit with the rather callow youth revealed in these pages.[1] What clinches the identification, meanwhile, is the fact that the author had a brother named John who was an officer serving with the crew of HMS *Ville de Paris*, there being evidence from naval records that a Lieutenant John Paget was appointed to the crew of that ship in July 1808.

To return to Charles Paget, according to his death notice in the London *Standard*, he was born in 1791. Beyond that, the obvious place to start is the entry in the Challis index. This states that he was commissioned, by purchase, as an ensign in the Second Battalion of the Fifty-Second Regiment of Foot on 1 February 1808, and, having fought at the battle of Vimeiro, was transferred to the First Battalion of that same regiment in September of the same year. Evacuated to England with the rest of Moore' army in the wake of the battle of Corunna, having

---

1. The Challis index is a remarkable resource whose elaboration in the days before computers and databases is a marvel rivalled only by the lists prepared by the French historian Martinien of all the French officers killed or wounded in the Napoleonic Wars. Available in full on the 'Napoleon Series' website at http://www.napoleon-series.org/research/biographies/GreatBritain/Challis/c_ChallisIntro.html, it has been used extensively in the annotation of Paget's text.

been promoted to the rank of lieutenant (seemingly without purchase), he next served in the abortive Walcheren expedition. There follows a break in his record of active service of some two years – something which suggests that he fell victim to the malaria which struck down so many of the troops sent to Walcheren – and he did not rejoin his battalion (now once again deployed to the Peninsula) until October 1813, instead being employed in recruitment activities at home. Hardly had he got back to the 2/52nd, however, than he purchased a captaincy in the Royal York Rangers, a colonial battalion reputedly largely recruited from condemned prisoners that was permanently stationed in the West Indies, though he did not leave for his new post until the beginning of 1814 as his record shows that he fought with the Fifty-Second at the battles of the Nivelle and the Nive (indeed, given that, as we shall see, he served in the Royal York Rangers for a very short time, he may not have even have gone to the West Indies, the acquisition of a captaincy in that regiment having simply been a device to help him secure advancement more quickly). Thereafter there is nothing except the bare fact that in 1847 he was still alive to claim his Military General Service Medal (the decoration issued after a long campaign driven by the sense of injustice generated by the Waterloo Medal to all those who had fought in the Napoleonic Wars), and such further information as we have comes from the pages of the *London Gazette*, this source revealing that after barely a year he had exchanged into the Thirty-First Foot. After this came a few months in the Ninetieth Foot in the winter of 1820–1 before he finally came to rest in the Second Dragoon Guards the following spring. To add anything else to the story, we have to return Paget's death notice. This paints a picture of a man who had succeeded in achieving his position in life, for his death notice shows that his address at the time of his passing away on 29 August 1849 at the age of 58 was highly fashionable: Sussex Gardens, a pleasant Bayswater avenue lined with substantial Georgian terraces just off Hyde Park; assuming that Charles Paget was indeed somehow a member of the family, the Pagets had evidently looked after their own, and one hopes that his widow, Frances, who outlived him by some nineteen years, therefore enjoyed a comfortable old age.[2]

We have, then, the bare bones of a military career, but there is much else that can be learned about Paget from the pages of his diary. First and foremost here is the fact that he was evidently a connection of the influential Paget family, a prominent Anglo-Irish clan from whose ranks sprang both Henry Paget (the Earl of Uxbridge of Waterloo fame) and Sir Edward Paget, the commanders, respectively, of Sir John

---

2.   Paget's wife, whom he married on 9 February 1826, was Frances Edwards, the third daughter of William Edwards of New Broad Street, London. Together with the information on the outline of Charles Paget's career in the years after 1814, the author owes this information to the independent researcher Ron McGuigan.

Moore's cavalry and reserve divisions. That said, it has been impossible to establish wherein lay the link, though one possibility is that he was an illegitimate son of either the generals' father, Henry Bayley-Paget, First Earl of Uxbridge, or one of his numerous progeny, several of whom are known to have been less than lily-white in this respect (the most famous of the scandals that resulted was Henry Paget's elopement with the wife of Wellington's younger brother, Henry Wellesley): with Charles Paget born in 1791, the dates fit well enough, while it was fairly common for such by-blows who were lucky enough to be acknowledged to take the name of the father. Meanwhile, the idea that he was some sort of 'poor relation' is reinforced by the set of pistols whose second-rate nature he repeatedly laments and the fact that he had no birding-piece to take with him when he was invited to go fowling.[3]

What, meanwhile, of Paget the man (or rather boy: he was, after all, but 17 in 1808). What comes over from his writing first of all is that he was not the most reflective or intellectual of young men: his English is at best pedestrian, sometimes clumsy even, while his diary entries are often frustratingly brief and generally as

---

3. There is, alas, no mention of any suitable candidate in the selections from the Paget family's private correspondence published by Eden Paget and Lord Hylton: this may mean nothing, but it could also again suggest a connection tolerated and even treated kindly, but kept at arm's length. See Paget (ed.), *Letters and Memorials of General Sir Edward Paget* and Lord Hylton (ed.), *The Paget Brothers, 1790–1840* (London, 1918). Charles Paget, too, does not appear in the Marquess of Anglesey's biography of Henry Paget: at the time of his birth in 1791, the future Lord Uxbridge was engaged in a highly scandalous affair with a married woman, but there seems to have been no issue from this union. Anglesey, *One Leg*, pp. 38–40. It may be thought, meanwhile, that Paget's transfer in 1813 to the Royal York Rangers is something else that suggests a certain lack of money (the cost of a captaincy in such a unit would for obvious reasons have been much less than it was in a more respectable regiment). However, this is not necessarily the case. To quote Ron McGuigan, 'Rules of purchase dictated that the offer to purchase went in the regiment first before it was offered outside of the regiment if the offer was passed or no one was on the regimental purchase list. An offer outside of the regiment was to be made to the most senior officer in the army at large on the purchase list looking to purchase … It could [therefore] be that Paget, having the funds, agreed to purchase a commission in an unfashionable regiment where it was likely he would be offered the commission given its status and location. Also [the York Rangers] being a single battalion regiment, he had a better chance of further promotion due to deaths, exchanges, etc. as he moved up in regimental seniority.' Private email from Ron McGuigan, dated 14 August 2017. In short, whilst we will never know for certain, by securing a captaincy in an unfashionable regiment, Paget was not so much responding to economic circumstance as greasing the wheels of his career. Whatever the truth here, one thing is certain in that a transfer to the Royal York Rangers represented a handy way of escaping the rigours of campaigning in the Pyrenees.

much concerned with recording the events of his social life as they are with those of the campaign (in fairness, though, he does make reference on several occasions to keeping a sketchbook, even if his efforts, by his own account, were less than impressive). At the same time the impression of a certain ineptitude is strengthened by a series of mishaps, including, not least, somehow managing to break his sword, though he was also clearly someone to whom mishaps happened on a more regular basis than might have been felt to be fair, the loss of all his sketches due to the carelessness of a camp-follower being one such example. As for his pastimes, keeping a diary and dabbling in sketching aside, they are absolutely what one might expect in an officer of the British army in the early nineteenth century: drinking, smoking, shooting and (somewhat dutifully one suspects) seeing the sights of the areas through which he passed. Just as conventional, meanwhile, are his attitudes: deeply anti-Catholic, he reveals prejudices that were only too prevalent among the officers who served in Spain and Portugal. Withal, however, there can be discerned a certain plodding earnestness, it being this that led him on several occasions to transcribe lengthy orders of the day, presumably with a view to fixing them in his memory. All in all, then, in the context of the time, at least, he comes over as an engaging figure, albeit a somewhat hapless one: certainly, he does not seem to have lacked for friends.

Moving on, we come to the issue of the units which Paget served in. As is well known, the Fifty-Second Foot, or Oxfordshire Regiment, was one of the two units chosen for conversion into one of the British army's first light-infantry regiments in 1803. As such it is strongly associated with Sir John Moore as it was under his tutelage that the transformation was effected, the other regiment involved being the Forty-Third Foot, or Monmouthshire Regiment (also forming part of the experiment was the Ninety-Fifth Regiment of Foot, but this was a different matter as it had never been a line regiment, rather owing its origins to a new unit entitled the Experimental Corps of Riflemen that was formed in 1800). Despite the appellation, however, the Fifty-Second had no more association with Oxfordshire than any other English regiment did with the county after which it was named, recruits rather being drawn from wherever they could be found, including, in very large measure the Catholic peasantry of Ireland (the officer corps had equally strong Irish connections, though in this case the connection was rather with the Protestant community: setting aside Paget himself, among the officers mentioned in the text alone, the Dobbs brothers and Forbes Champagné all came from this source).[4] What distinguished the regiment was therefore above all its light-infantry

4.   We know little about the soldiers who made up the Fifty-Second at the time which Paget's diary covers. However, one man whose story has come down to us is one Patrick Kelly, 'a great drunkard and so slovenly a soldier that he was continually getting in

status. Though it wore red rather than the dark green favoured by rifle units, every man in the regiment was trained to fight as a skirmisher – hence the absence of both grenadier and light companies and the universal wearing of a green plume on the shako – and this implied a much higher level of training and with it a much greater emphasis on individual initiative and personal responsibility, it being precisely these qualities that Moore had attempted to instil at Shorncliffe Camp. In theory, too, the stress on corporal punishment was lessened and efforts made to bring in a system of rewards designed to appeal to men's pride and sense of achievement. How far this was successful, it is difficult to say, but what cannot be denied is that the regiment had an excellent reputation in the Napoleonic Wars, both of its battalions eventually serving in the crack Light Division.

In the campaigns of Vimeiro and Corunna, the Light Division was, of course, still a thing of the future, the various brigades that Paget served with therefore being somewhat less illustrious assemblies. Landing in the Peninsula with the Second Battalion of the Fifty-Second, Paget was initially a member of the brigade of Brigadier General Robert Anstruther, this consisting in addition of the Second Battalions of the Ninth and Forty-Third Regiments of Foot and the Ninety-Seventh Regiment of Foot (a single battalion unit).[5] By switching to the First Battalion of

---

disgrace' who appears actually to have deserted during the Corunna campaign, and, when arrested by a Spanish mayor and sent back under guard to Wellington's army in the summer of 1809 claimed to have been fighting at the siege of Zaragoza, and, not just that, but to have amused the beleaguered garrison by dancing Irish jigs on the very parapets of the city while the enemy, as he put it, 'blazed away' at him. Reprieved from execution by firing squad, he served with the regiment throughout the Peninsular War, and in general fought bravely enough, albeit not without further incident in that in 1814 he was flogged for breaking into a house in a French village in which he was billeted. Such a man was always likely to come to a bad end, and in the event he died in suspicious circumstances in Dublin in 1822 – the verdict was officially accidental death, but there was some circumstantial evidence that he had actually been murdered – yet he was not just an example of one of the king's proverbial hard bargains: on the contrary, the years after 1814 saw him undergo a religious conversion and turn himself into something of a model soldier. For all this, see W. Leeke, *The History of Lord Seaton's Regiment (the Fifty-Second Light Infantry) at the Battle of Waterloo together with Various Incidents connected with that Regiment, not only at Waterloo, but also in at Paris and in the North of France and for Several Years Afterwards, to which are appended many of the Author's Reminiscences of his Military and Clerical Careers during a Period of More than Fifty Years* (London, 1866), I, pp. 334–8.

5. An officer who had served with great credit in the Egyptian campaign of 1801, Anstruther was destined to die of what was almost certainly pneumonia shortly after the British army's arrival at Corunna. As a mark of the high esteem he enjoyed, it was decided to lay Sir John Moore to rest beside him. An account of his passing is given by Adam Neale, a surgeon who had accompanied his brigade from England: 'As to the

the Fifty-Second, Paget should then in theory have entered a different formation, but his new battalion, which had been in Sweden with John Moore, had never been brigaded with other units, a state of affairs which was now remedied by uniting it with the First Battalion of the Twentieth Regiment and a detachment (three companies only), of the First Battalion of Ninety-Fifth, this force being placed under Anstruther, whose old command was now given to William Beresford. Such, then were the units with which Charles Paget marched to Salamanca, and, indeed, Corunna, though by that time the First Battalion of the Ninety-Fifth had been brought up to full strength. Where there were further changes was at the level of the division: when Moore established a divisional structure in October, the division that Anstruther's brigade was placed in also numbered that of Karl Alten (the First and Second Light Battalions of the King's German Legion), but when Baird and Moore finally succeeded in uniting their forces at Mayorga a further re-organisation saw Alten's brigade replaced by that of Moore Disney consisting of the First Battalion of the Twenty-Eighth Foot and the First Battalion of the Ninety-First Foot, the two rifle battalions being reassigned as a separate flank brigade.[6]

Finally, there is the journal itself. Though generally conventional in style and layout, it does possess one oddity in that it is effectively two manuscripts, the one contained in a single notebook, and the other jotted down on a series of scraps of paper. For the most part written in conditions that were reasonably conducive to keeping a journal – one thinks here of the long voyage from England and the many

---

illness and death of General Anstruther . . . I first saw him on the evening of the 10th at Betanzos. He was evidently labouring under inflammation of the lungs, but was relieved by letting blood. On visiting him early on the following morning, he was no better and I was alarmed to find that he had hardly any recollection of what had passed the preceding evening. He had been advised to travel in a carriage to Corunna. That conveyance, however, could not be procured, and he was obliged to ride on horseback . . . He informed the gentlemen about him that he had been for twenty-two hours on horseback during which time he had tasted nothing except a bit of ship's biscuit and a drop of rum and that, at length, quite worn out with fatigue, he had thrown himself down in a field and slept for about an hour in the rain: to this circumstance he attributed his illness . . . After his ride to Corunna on the 11th, he was much worse. He was again bled without his symptoms being alleviated. The disease ran its course very speedily, uninterrupted by any of the remedies employed . . . and on the night of the 14th he was no more . . . In common with the rest of the army, I deplore his death: he was by all allowed to be a worthy officer and a worthy upright man.' Neale, *Letters from Portugal and Spain*, pp. 343–4.

6. For all this, see R. McGuigan, 'The British army in Portugal and Spain, June 1808-April 1809, Part III: Sir John Moore's army', http://www.napoleon-series.org/military/battles/1808/Peninsula/BritishArmy/c_britarmy3.html#additional, accessed 7 August 2017.

weeks spent in inactivity in first Lisbon and later Salamanca – the first part of the text is by far the more accessible: the hand is clear and regular and the lines well spaced. By contrast, exactly covering and written during the campaign of Sir John Moore, the second part of the journal has proved far less easy to transcribe: at least twice as dense as that of the preceding section, the writing is often difficult to decipher. At the same time, to the question of accessibility can be added that of reliability: so far as it is possible to tell, the entries in the first part were for the most part completed on a daily basis, whereas there is some evidence that the second part was written up in arrears, and possibly without reference to the contents of the notebook, this being something that might explain the differences between the two accounts given of the three days (10–12 December) when there is an overlap between the two.

Part 1: 16 July 1808–12 December 1808

July 16th
Embarked at Ramsgate at five o'clock p.m. Arrived in the Downs at four o'clock next morning.

July 17th
Clear weather; wind westerly. Took my first watch.

July 18th
The Forty-Third Regiment arrived in the Downs. Went ashore and to the play in the evening.

July 19th
The Ninth Regiment's second battalion arrived. Dined at [the] Three Kings.

July 20th
Orders arrived to be convoyed by the *Saint Albans* (sixty-four, Captain Austen).[7] Wind contrary.

July 21st
Went to Ramsgate; came back the same evening with my brother, John.

July 22nd

---

7.   The Captain Austen referred to here is Francis Austen, the younger brother of the novelist, Jane Austen.

Blue Peter hoisted. Got under way at three o'clock with twenty-two sail of transports forming the Light Brigade under General Anstruther.

July 23rd

Calm and fine; wind south-westerly. Orders received for all masters to repair on board the *Saint Albans*. Sealed orders given which, in case of separation, desired us to repair either Weymouth, [the Downs], Dungeness, Plymouth or Falmouth. Passed Beachy Head, Brighton, etc, etc!

July 24th

Very little wind; south-westerly. Signal made to moor. Anchored in fifteen-fathom water off the Isle of Wight.

July 25th

Wind north-westerly. Rain in the night with lightning. Unmoored. Squally; signal made to tack. Going at five knots an hour.

July 26th

Wind westerly and squally. Signal made to anchor; brought to off Saint Alban's head. Sent ashore fifty opthalmia men. Weighed again; anchored in Weymouth Roads.

August 18th

Observed from the fleet a large fire on shore which was kept up during the night, and another opposite to it, apparently two or three miles distant. Men inspected preparatory to disembarkation: flints, etc., in good order and ammunition served out (sixty rounds per man).

August 19th

At ten a.m. signal hoisted for landing the troops. Orders: 'No man to land except those fit for the most active service, and those with a shirt and a pair of socks folded in their greatcoats. Landed in the *Saint Albans*' long-boat. Several apples, pears, etc., given us by the Portuguese.[8] At three o'clock formed on the beach

---

8.   The troops had to be landed on open beaches that were continually pounded by heavy Atlantic rollers, this making disembarkation an adventure in itself. Auguste Schaumann, for example, landed on 28 August in company with a regiment of cavalry: 'What a teaming multitude there was on the beach. I sat down on my portmanteau and watched the troops landing. It was funny to see a boat coming in through the breakers with its load of horses . . . They would all dash helter-skelter out of the reeling vessel

and marched up the heights by companies. Brigade formed by divisions in an Indian-corn field, which was marched over the previous day by the French, bayonets, pouches, etc., being found. Greatcoats put on and each man desired to sleep on his firelock in his respective place and officers to stay by their companies. Found a striking difference between a comfortable bed and the open fields. A friar present who blessed our undertakings.[9]

August 20th

Under arms at two o'clock in the morning. Marched over a very delightful country covered with myrtles, aloes, etc. Saw several cottages which the French had plundered. Weather excessively hot and no water, that in our canteens being excessively warm, which obliged nearly 300 men to quit the ranks. Fifteen miles' march. At five o'clock came up with Sir Arthur Wellesley's army, but with difficulty, some French cavalry having endeavoured to outflank us, which was frustrated by the Fortieth Regiment being sent to our assistance. No dinner, neither washed. Halted amongst the furze between the Ninth (Second Battalion) and Ninety-Seventh Regiments.[10]

August 21st

Under arms at two o'clock. Shots heard from the _____; enemy _____. As it grew later, the firing increased and the pickets were slowly withdrawing before those of the enemy. Brigade wheeled into line and marched to the top of the height, formed obliquely in the rear of each other. Distinctly perceived the French columns manoeuvring on the opposite hills and their riflemen (dressed in long white frocks) being detached from them to the _____ and woods. The enemy began a kind of independent fire on our lines when the general sent to us to

---

into the surf while the hussars . . . had to thank their lucky stars that they were not pulled overboard with them . . . As soon as they reached the shore they galloped wildly along it, to and fro, snorting, panting, neighing and biting and kicking one another to the great danger of all those gathered on the beach . . . The tumult on the shore was interesting. There were soldiers, horses, sailors; officers, both military and naval; shouting and directing the landing; guns, wagons (some of which were being fitted together), mountains of ship's biscuit, haversacks, trusses of hay, barrels of meat and rum; tents, some of which were already put up . . . The rocks and the sand were so burning with the heat of the sun that everybody went about barefooted and paddled in the surf from time to time to cool themselves. Fresh . . . water was not to be had and we suffered terribly from thirst.' Ludovici, *On the Road with Wellington*, pp. 2–3.

9. The detritus encountered by Paget had been left behind by French troops fleeing from the defeat inflicted on them at Roliça by Wellesley on 17 August.

10. The distance the brigade marched on 20 August was nearer to 5 miles than 15. Meanwhile, the reference to French cavalry on the loose is somewhat puzzling as the troops of General Junot were still on the march from Lisbon at this point.

'remember Egypt'.[11] Several men wounded fell out, Captain Ewart and Lieutenant Bell; five men of the Ninety-Seventh knocked down by a cannon ball, one killed.[12] Men became impatient to fire being now in the thick of it. The infantry of the enemy gained ground on the right when three of our companies were ordered to the valley to oppose them. Reserved our fire till the enemy drew nearer when it was opened with double fury. After three rounds we observed them running in all directions, upon which three cheers were genially given and the advance sounded. When below, the companies extended and each had its separate duty.[13] The Forty-Third, Fiftieth, etc., making a most gallant charge on the left, the ground was covered with dead and dying Frenchmen, knapsacks, shoes in quantity, papers, etc., etc.[14] Got a vast deal of silk [and] cotton pocket handkerchiefs, snuff-box, etc, etc., from the knapsacks of the French. Plainly perceived their columns forming on the hills which were absolutely hindered from retreating by the immense baggage

---

11. As the 2/52nd had not served in Egypt, it can be assumed that this was simply a generic exhortation, the Egyptian campaign of 1801, setting aside the minor affair at Maida in July 1806, having been the last occasion on which British and French troops had engaged one another in battle.

12. The Ewart mentioned here is Captain John Ewart and the Bell Lieutenant John Bell; in both cases, their wounds appear to have been fairly slight. The son of a diplomat, Ewart was born in 1786 and was commissioned in the Fifty-Second in November 1803, meanwhile, and kept a diary that was published by Gareth Glover as *The Peninsular-War Diary of Captain John Frederick Ewart, Fifty-Second Light Infantry* (Godmanchester, 2010). In the current context, he is of particular interest because, like Paget, he transferred to the Royal York Rangers. As the date of his move to that unit was September 1812 (i.e. over a year before Paget made the same move), it is impossible not to wonder whether it was at his suggestion that Paget chose that unit.

13. The only other account of the battle that has been located from Paget's battalion is that of Lieutenant Charles Kinloch, and this, alas, is little more instructive. Thus: 'We were exactly in the nick of time for the action of the 21st . . . It commenced about eight in the morning and continued for three hours when they thought it high time to [take] the right about . . . We had only 300 men in the field, [for], most unluckily, a brig with 200 of our men aboard had parted [from the] convoy some days before we disembarked and did not join us till the day after . . . We had two officers wounded and about forty eight men killed or wounded.' *Cit.* G. Glover (ed.), *'A Hellish Business': the Letters of Captain Charles Kinloch, Fifty-Second Light Infantry, 1806–1816* (Godmanchester, 2007), p. 28.

14. In the chapter of his *Forward into Battle: Fighting Tactics from Waterloo to Vietnam* (Chichester, 1981) dealing with the Napoleonic period, the late Paddy Griffith made much use of the charge of the Fiftieth Foot as evidence of his thesis that British infantry habitually relied on shock action when confronted by French attacks in column, firing only a single volley and then advancing with the bayonet. However, Paget specifically refers to the 2/52nd firing three volleys before going on the attack: evidently, then, practice varied from one unit to another.

and plunder in their rear as the prisoners told us after. The retreat sounded and the sight of the dying and the dead was most awful: blood, horses, wheels, etc., scattered throughout the hills. Our missing killed and wounded amounted to forty; those of the enemy must have been twenty times that number. Returned to our old ground. It was rumoured throughout the army that Sir AW wished to pursue the enemy but [that] it was not allowed by Sir HB who arrived during the engagement.[15]

15. Anstruther's brigade played a leading role in the battle of Vimeiro. Placed by chance alongside the brigade of General Fane on a low hill that shielded the village of Vimeiro, it found itself facing the full weight of Junot's first attack, and helped beat off two successive French assaults. Unfortunately, personal accounts from other units of the brigade are few and far between, while those that exist are no more revealing than those of Paget and Kinloch. Here, for example, is that of Private Anthony Hamilton of the Second Battalion of the Forty-Third Foot on the last French attack: 'A column, strongly supported by artillery, was . . . sent forward to gain possession of the village of Vimeiro. Here our regiment . . . was posted close by the road that entered the village. The enemy advanced upon us with determination and valour, but after a desperate struggle on our part were driven back with great slaughter. It was not only a hot day, but a hot fight, and one of our men of the name of MacArthur, who stood by me, having opened his mouth to catch a little fresh air, a bullet from the enemy at that moment entered it obliquely, which he never perceived until I told him his neck was covered with blood. He, however, kept the field until the battle was over. No further attempt was made by the enemy on our position, and they retired, leaving seven pieces of artillery and a great number of prisoners in our possession.' A. Hamilton, *Hamilton's Campaign with Moore and Wellington during the Peninsular War* (Troy, New York, 1847), p. 14. Also nearby was Lieutenant Colonel John Cameron of the 2/9th: 'About nine o'clock in the morning the light troops in front were . . . driven in by a rapid advance of the enemy's columns. Immediately our troops . . . took up their position in the following order of formation. The 2/9th on the extreme right; the 2/52nd in column on their left a little advanced; the 97th in line, their left extending as far as the windmill on the hill, and, to the left of the windmill, the 2/43rd in column. The enemy took not a moment in occupying the pinewood and the vineyards on the right . . . on which the 9th formed line, each company giving its fire in succession as it came up. The fire was kept up until the enemy had abandoned the pinewood, some little time before which three companies of the Fifty-Second were sent in pursuit . . . The 2/43rd were very hotly engaged with the enemy on the left of the windmill and behaved with great spirit.' *Cit.* G. Glover (ed.), *The Letters of Lieutenant-Colonel Sir John Cameron, First Battalion, Ninth Regiment of Foot, 1808–14* (Godmanchester, 2013), pp. 13–14. For a clearer view of the situation (and, indeed, one that, read carefully, closely corroborates Paget's account), we must turn elsewhere. Captain Jonathan Leach, for example, was serving in the Second Battalion of the Ninety-Fifth Regiment in Fane's brigade. 'We were posted in a large pine wood . . . About eight o'clock in the morning . . . a cloud of light troops, supported by a heavy column of infantry, entered the wood, and, assailing the pickets with great impetuosity, obliged us to fall back for support on the

August 22nd

Flag of truce arrived and an armistice concluded for forty-eight hours. A false alarm: under arms at daybreak. Went to the convent [*sic*: actually the parish church] at Vimeiro, which was made the hospital, and the windmill where the artillery was posted, which was made the receptacle for the wounded soldiers who were lying in all directions, covered with blood and the flies tormenting them and swarming round their [wounds], being without any medical assistance. Ordered to take three days provisions.[16]

Ninety-Seventh Regiment. As soon as we had got clear of the front of the Ninety-Seventh . . . that regiment poured in such a well-directed fire that it staggered the resolution of the hostile column, which declined to close . . . with them. About the same time the second battalion of the Fifty-Second, advancing through the wood, took the French in flank, and drove them before them in confusion. On the pickets being driven in, I joined my own brigade, which was on the left of the Ninety-Seventh. Here the business was beginning to assume a serious aspect. Some heavy masses of infantry, preceded by a swarm of light troops, were advancing with great resolution . . . against the brigade on which our battalion was posted. In spite of the deadly fire which several hundred riflemen kept up on them, they continued to press forward . . . until the old Fiftieth Regiment received them with a destructive volley, following it instantly with a most brilliant . . . charge with the bayonet.' J. Leach, *Rough Sketches in the Life of an Old Soldier* (London, 1831), pp. 50–1. Finally, there is the long and detailed account in the memoirs of George Landmann of the Royal Engineers and that of the surgeon, Adam Neale: too long to quote from here, they are included in full as appendices.

16. By comparison with many other Napoleonic battles, losses at Vimeiro were not excessive: in all, British casualties came to 135 dead, 334 wounded and 51 missing (mostly prisoners), while, not counting the 350 men taken prisoner, the number of French left on the field was in the region of 1,500. However, the usual horrors were much worsened by the behaviour of the local inhabitants: 'Here I beheld for the first time a sight even more horrible – the peasantry prowling about, more ferocious than beast and birds of prey, finishing the work of death and carrying away whatever they thought worthy of their grasp . . . No fallen Frenchman that showed the least signs of life was spared. They even seemed pleased with mangling the dead bodies. When light failed them, they kindled a great fire and remained around it all night, shouting like as many savages. My sickened fancy felt the same as if it were witnessing a feast of cannibals.' Anon., *Journal of a Soldier of the Seventy-First, or Glasgow Regiment, Highland Light Infantry, from 1806 to 1815* (Edinburgh, 1819), pp. 61–2. Meanwhile, the hospital visited by Paget is described in detail by Private John Harris of the Ninety-Fifth: 'The scene . . . was somewhat singular. Two long tables had been procured from some houses near, and were placed end-to-end-amongst the graves and upon them were laid the men whose limbs it was found necessary to amputate. Both French and English were constantly lifted on and off these tables. As soon as the operation was performed upon one lot, they were carried off and those in waiting hoisted up: the surgeons with their sleeves turned

August 23rd

At break of day began our march: eight miles through a most hilly country covered with firs [*sic*: actually pines] and vineyards.[17] Halted and took our position which from the kettles and half-dressed victuals that we found there, [I] suppose that the French had just quitted. Got some melons, honey, etc., and found the boards of a cottage torn up by the French to look for plunder.[18]

---

up and arms covered with blood looking like butchers in the shambles. I saw as I passed at least twenty legs lying on the ground, many of them being clothed in the long black gaiters of the infantry of the line. The surgeons had plenty of work on hand . . . and not having time to take off the clothes of the wounded, they merely ripped the seams and turned the cloth back, proceeding with the operation as fast as they could. Many of the wounded came straggling into this churchyard in search of assistance by themselves. I saw one man, faint with loss of blood, staggering along, and turned to assist him. He was severely wounded in the head, his face being completely encrusted with the blood which had flowed . . . and had now dried. One eyeball was knocked out of the socket and hung down upon his cheek. Another man . . . had been … propped against a grave mound. He seemed very badly hurt. The men who had carried him into the churchyard had placed his cap filled with fragments of biscuit close beside his head, and, as he lay, he occasionally turned his head towards it and munched it. As I was about to leave the churchyard, Dr Ridgeway, one of the surgeons, called me back to assist in holding a man he was endeavouring to operate upon. "Come and help me with this man", he said, "or I shall be all day in cutting a ball out of his shoulder." The patient's name was Doubter, an Irishman. He disliked the doctor's efforts, and writhed and twisted so much during the operation that it was with difficulty Dr Ridgeway could perform it. He found it necessary to cut very deep, and Doubter made a terrible outcry at every fresh incision. "Oh doctor dear" he said, "it's murdering me you are! Blood and 'ounds! I shall die! I shall die! For the love of the Lord, don't cut me all to pieces!" Doubter was not altogether wrong for, although he survived the operation, he died shortly afterwards from the effect of his wounds.' C. Hibbert (ed.), *The Recollections of Rifleman Harris* (London, 1970), pp. 41–2.

17. Other observers are less prosaic. James Ormsby, for example, was a chaplain attached to the army's headquarters. 'The hills were flung in graceful and picturesque confusion: at the base [they were] covered with cork trees and on the sides and summits with fir [i.e. pine]. It wanted only water to be completely beautiful, but this deficiency was not very long felt for in the afternoon torrents of rain similar to those of the preceding night fell for such a continuance that I withdrew my objection.' J.W. Ormsby, *An Account of the Operations of the British Army and of the State and Sentiments of the People of Portugal and Spain during the Campaigns of the Years 1808 and 1809* (London, 1809), I, p. 35.

18. Though brief, the campaign of Vimeiro had nevertheless gone hard on the civilian population. In the castle at Mafra, for example, 'the horse dung left by the French stood houses high, while the walls were blackened with the fire from the bivouacs' Ludovici, *On the Road with Wellington*, p. 31.

August 24th

Men ordered to wash their shirts and stockings. Washed myself and [my] flannel waistcoat in a bye-ditch. Got a fowl, some Indian corn and a quantity of grapes.

August 25th

Sir John Moore arrived this morning, inspected the troops, shook hands with me and asked after my friend, Captain Robinson.[19] Two flags of truce arrived and some conditions [were] proposed.[20]

August 26th

Dreadful thunderstorm and some lightning about the camp the whole of the day, so much so that during the night the rain fell in such torrents that out huts were beat down upon us. The drops were so big that 'twas impossible to light fires to dry our clothes, and [I] was obliged to go on outlying picket with a wet shirt, etc., etc. Eleven French deserters arrived in the camp. Orders for half of the army to march on the following day.

August 27th

Very wet. Part of the army marched to Torres Vedras (a part remained under Sir John Moore), a tolerable town and everything very dear. Reports of a convention being agreed upon, but the terms totally unknown.[21]

---

19. If the reference is to an officer present with the expedition, the man after whom Moore asked was Captain Peter Robinson of the Twentieth Foot.
20. The behaviour described here on the part of Sir John Moore is entirely in character. Prickly, egotistic and highly strung though he was, Moore was unfailingly charming and considerate when it came to dealing with subordinates and was renowned for his command of names and faces. One man who recorded a personal interview with him was the commissary Auguste Schaumann: 'The commander-in-chief, Sir John Moore, arrived and summoned me to speak with him. He was a refined, somewhat pallid and interesting looking man with a *je ne sais quoi* of melancholy in his expression. He was grave but courteous, and asked me how everything was going, what I had thought of the provisioning and spirit of the Portuguese . . . and what were the methods of victualling the regiment in these parts.' Ludovici, *On the Road with Wellington*, p. 55.
21. The convention referred to was, of course, the notorious convention of Sintra. As we have seen, the journal expresses some regret in respect of the failure to pursue the French on 21 August, but appears much less exercised when it came to the idea of negotiating with Junot once the opportunity was lost.

August 28th

Walked to Torres Vedras and bought some soap, lemons, needles and thread, etc. Two ducks for a dollar and a half. Hedges chiefly of myrtle, geranium and aloes.[22] A shocking noise from the Portuguese cars [i.e. carts].[23]

August 29th

Marched a league beyond Torres Vedras and slept in a cart shed in some straw. Got a quantity of grapes, apples and Indian corn. Weather exceptionally hot, and unpleasant marching from the dust.

August 30th

Marched at break of day and towards evening halted in a farmyard, which I left to forage, and was lucky enough to get some potatoes, onions and cabbage which were made up with some beef for the dinner of the mess.

August 31st

Halting day spent in resting, mending my kit and getting fruit.

---

22. Clearly, Paget did not think the local fauna worthy of notice. Other observers, however, paid it greater attention. For example: 'All the peasants' gardens were surrounded by hedges of aloe. One hedge . . . had an aloe plant in full bloom. A stem as thick as my arm had shot out from the centre of the plant to a height of five or six feet, and, like a candelabra, bore clusters of bloom on its branches. The stem looked as if it had been made of leaves rolled together and was so hard that the staff-sergeant of . . . had some difficulty in cutting it off with his sword.' Ludovici, *On the Road with Wellington*, p. 19.

23. Many soldiers who fought in the Peninsular War complained of the noise that emanated from the bullock carts that made up the bulk of the transport available in the Peninsula. In brief, the problem was that the wheels did not rotate by themselves, but were rather fixed to the axle tree. Herewith the recollections of Auguste Schaumann: 'Today fifty Portuguese bullock carts came down on to the beach to fetch victuals for the army, and with great interest we contemplated these vehicles which in their primitiveness seemed to be exactly like those which had been found by the ancient conquerors of Iberia. They consisted of rough planks nailed on to a massive pole or shaft. At right angles to the shaft, and under the planks, two blocks of semi-rounded wood were fixed having a hole in the centre, and through these holes the axle was fitted. It was a live axle fixed firmly to the wheels. As these axles are never greased, they make such a terrible squeaking and creaking that the scratching of a knife on a pewter plate is like the sweet sound of a flute beside them. And when a number of these carts are moving together, it is enough to drive one quite mad.' *Ibid.*, p. 9.

September 1st

Marched three leagues further and halted at Cheleiros under a stone work. Got some wine from the village.[24]

September 2nd

Bathed and wrote letters to England. Lost my canteen.

September 3rd, 4th, 5th

Remained on the heights.

September 6th

Encamped on a hill close by the delightful village of Pertusaco [?], having a delightful prospect of Sintra, the rock of Lisbon, Fort São Julião and Belem with the British fleet at the mouth of the Tagus.

September 7th

Walked to Fort São Julião which is west of Lisbon twelve miles. It is famous for its immense strength, being situated on a strong rock which commands the entrance of the Tagus. It has a vast quantity of guns and is defended on the left by a strong mortar battery. The interior is composed of small houses and shops and [is] garrisoned by some Portuguese soldiers, and the Third Regiment or Buffs. Returning home, lunched with an American and a friar, on some fish smothered with oil and fresh vinegar and a bottle of bad red wine.[25]

September 8th

Bathed in the Tagus after which we went to a coffee house somewhat resembling a stable, being out in the open air and the ground covered with straw. Paid two dollars for dining on fish and oil.

September 9th

Dundas and self went on board a brig to buy provisions and shoes.[26] Bathed and observed the French flag flying on Fort Belem.

---

24. A Portuguese league was equivalent to something over 4 miles, and a Spanish one to about a mile less. What the 'stone work' referred to here was is unclear. The usual meaning would be some sort of fortification, but, if Cheleiros had a castle, no trace of such a feature has survived.
25. Given the context, the American mentioned in this entry was almost certainly a Brazilian rather than a citizen of the United States.
26. Paget's companion was Ensign Thomas Dundas who not only survived the war unscathed, but did not die until 1860.

September 10th

Remained at Pertusaco. Orders to receive a month's pay.

September 11th

Went to Belem in a boat with _____. [It] was garrisoned by French soldiers who behaved in a most respectful manner and said they had not received pay for several days. Went over the fort and afterwards dined at a hotel with two Portuguese officers. Returned to camp in the morning.

September 12th

Mounted in-lying picket. The Russian fleet sailed out of the Tagus under Russian colours.[27] Our transports arrived except the *Robert*.

September 13th

Went on board the *Robert* and the *Alfred* (74). Dined at Belem and walked to Lisbon: the cannons pointed down the streets in case the Portuguese should rise on the French who are a soldier-like and respectful set of men.[28]

---

27. The Russian fleet mentioned here was a squadron that had been deployed to the Mediterranean in 1805 to help defend Naples against the French. Commanded by Admiral Dmitri Senyavin, in the wake of the Treaty of Tilsit of July the previous year it had been ordered to return home, but had been caught at Lisbon by the British blockade that had been imposed in response to Junot's occupation of the city in October 1807. Much to the French commander's fury, Senyavin refused point-blank to give him any assistance in the face of Wellesley's disembarkation, this being an action that won him very generous terms in the convention that he eventually signed with the British naval commander, Admiral Cotton: in brief, the ships were taken over by British crews and impounded for the duration of the war and the officers and men repatriated to their home country.

28. At this point the situation in Lisbon was somewhat confused in that, not being prisoners of war, Junot's troops remained at liberty. Among the lower classes, this undoubtedly caused much unrest and all the more so as they were perceived to be under British protection. To quote Joseph Sinclair of the Seventy-First Foot: 'We remained in camp until the day the French were to embark. We were then marched in to protect them from the inhabitants, but, notwithstanding all we could do, it was not in our power to prevent some of their sick from being murdered. The Portuguese were so much enraged at our interference . . . that it was unsafe for two or three soldiers to be seen alone. The French had given the Portuguese much cause to hate them, and the latter are not a people who can quickly forgive an injury or let slip any means of revenge, however base.' Anon., *Soldier of the Seventy-First*, p. 50. Still worse, meanwhile, as Leach notes, there was considerable fraternisation between the British and the French. Thus: 'The best possible understanding existed between the soldiers of the two armies who were to be seen drinking, carousing, shaking hands

September 14th

Superintended the landing of the baggage. Got my portmanteau to camp and walked to Aives [?].

September 15th

French sailed out of the Tagus. Junot embarked 25,000 men, 5,000 disabled.[29]

September 16th

Walked to Fort São Julião and copied these lines from the walls of a dungeon which were written by a Frenchman confined therein: 'Le charmant objet que j'adore, brûlent des meme feux dont je suis enflammé, mais je sens que je l'aime encore, mille fois plus, que je m'en suis aimé.'[30] After having reconnoitred the above room, went to the grand mortar battery.

---

and walking arm-in-arm around Lisbon.' Leach, *Rough Sketches*, p. 56. By no means all the French troops behaved as well as Paget implies, however: Harris complained of being on two occasions menaced by enemy soldiers resentful of their defeat, while Captain John Patterson of the Fiftieth Foot claimed that he was actually shot at by a sentry. See Hibbert (ed.), *Recollections of Rifleman Harris*, pp. 44–6; J. Patterson, *The Adventures of Captain John Patterson, with Notices of the Officers, etc., of the Fiftieth or Queen's Regiment, from 1807 to 1831* (London, 1837), p. 53. One of the oddities of the journal is Paget's failure to say much about Lisbon when it was somewhere that clearly made a great impression on other members of the British army. To take just one example, Ormsby wrote approvingly of the 'numerous and splendid' public buildings, the enormous Praça do Comercio on the waterfront and the new streets laid out by the Marquis of Pombal in the wake of the terrible earthquake of 1755 that connected it with the rival Praça do Rossio, remarking of the houses that lined the latter that they were of such uniformity that 'the side of a street has more the appearance of a palace than of a continuity of buildings', while yet complaining bitterly of the 'abominable filth' that reigned elsewhere, not to mention the large numbers of churches and convents. Ormsby, *Operations of the British Army*, I, pp. 99–108 *passim*. For an interesting discussion of the impact which Lisbon had on the British army, see G. Daly, 'A dirty, indolent and priest-ridden city: British soldiers in Lisbon during the Peninsular War, 1808–1813', *History*, XCIV, No. 316 (October, 2009), pp. 461–82.

29. The departure of the French was marked by wild celebrations. For example, 'When the embarkation was completed and the national flag of Portugal once again waved on the citadel and forts in place of the tricolour, there was such a combination of *vivas*, sky-rockets, ringing of bells, singing, dancing, screeching, crying, laughing [and] old and young embracing in the streets, added to the curses and execrations uttered by the populace against their late masters, as must render every attempt at description hopeless.' Leach, *Rough Sketches*, pp. 56–7.

30. 'The charming object of my adoration burns with the same flames that consume me, but I sense that I still love her one thousand times more than she loves me.'

September 17th

Marched at a quarter before eight in the morning to Queluz with the Ninth and Forty-Third Foot where [there] is a grand palace fitted out superbly by Junot.[31] Outlying picket this night in a windmill two miles from the camp.

September 18th

Headquarters 16th September 1808

General Order. The following letter has been received by Lieutenant-General Sir Harry Burrard from Lord Castlereagh, Secretary of State of the Foreign Department. 'Downing Street, 1 September 1808. I received from Captain Campbell, *aide de camp* to Sir Arthur Wellesley, your dispatch of the 24th inst. Enclosing the report to you from that general of the signal victory obtained by His Majesty's forces under his orders when attacked at Vimeiro by the whole French force in Portugal commanded by General Junot in person. Having laid the same before his Majesty, I am directed by His Majesty to inform you [that you] will signify to Lieutenant-General Sir Arthur Wellesley that the dispositions made by him to receive the enemy, and the skill and valour displayed by him in effecting their total defeat, has afforded His Majesty the highest gratification. The conduct of Major-General Spencer and of the other general officers, who so ably executed the orders they received, and displayed so many instances of judgement and valour is highly honourable to themselves and acceptable to His Majesty. You will be pleased to communicate the satisfaction His Majesty feels in the deliberate and steady bravery with which his troops distinguished themselves, reflecting at once the great honour, upon the character and discipline of his army, by which qualities alone success in war can prematurely be obtained [rather] than hoped for. The delicacy and honourable forbearance which determined you, though present in the action, not to interfere with the arrangements previously made by Sir Arthur Wellesley and their prospect of execution, are being _____ by His Majesty with approbation. I have the honour to be, etc., etc., Castlereagh.'

Relieved pickets at day break and lost ourselves in the fog. Went to Lisbon and bought several trinkets. Got from a Portuguese all Junot's proclamations. Visited the opera in the evening: at our entrance they played 'God save the King!' and the flags of England, Spain and Portugal were displayed in the

---

31. The palace at Queluz was certainly grand and was also made use of by Junot as his headquarters, but it was not in any sense fitted out by him.

centre; one dollar entrance. Went to the playhouse and returned to the camp that night.[32]

September 19th

Sir Arthur Wellesley embarked for England. Orders for the tents to be paved. Went to Queluz and a concert in the evening of the Prince Regent's band.

September 20th

Went to Lisbon. Dined at Moore's hotel, went to the play and returned in the morning.

September 21st

Received orders to join the First Battalion encamped near Belem.

September 22nd

Went to Pertusaco with my servant to get my luggage for the First Battalion, but, on returning home, [we] lost ourselves in the fog and were obliged to sleep under an old windmill, having got some chocolate and fish at a neighbouring hut.

September 23rd

Settled my accounts with the paymaster up to the 24th inst. Tinted some sketches.

September 24th

Heard of the First Battalion going to Elvas. Two hundred miles from Aldea Gallega: at a great loss how to dispose of my baggage.

September 25th

Joined the First Battalion which was under orders to march on the 27th; officers only allowed to carry twenty-five pounds weight with them, and one mule being allowed for a captain and two subalterns. Went to Lisbon with Dundas and bought a brace of pistols and a pair of shoes.

---

32. Another member of the army who visited the opera was James Ormsby: 'The opera-house is built in the Doric order and is a very elegant piece of architecture. Within, it is fitted up like our King's Theatre but is not quite so large . . . The orchestra is amply filled and of itself is an ample inducement for lovers of music to frequent the house.' Ormsby, *Operations of the British Army*, I, p. 143.

September 26th

Rose at eight o'clock and took a boat to Belem. Got completely wet through attempting to join the camp, it pouring a deluge of rain.[33] Orders to march at twelve o'clock next day: men to carry four days' provisions, one day not cooked, and tents to be struck at seven in the morning.

September 27th

Marched at twelve o'clock through Buenos Aires [and] Belem to Lisbon. Embarked in the Portuguese boats but from their ignorance of the river ran aground several times, and, although it was but fifteen miles they had to go, we did not reach it till eight o'clock at night, when we billeted the men, and afterward got some fish, bacon and a quince to eat. Slept with Sheddon in a straw bed.[34]

September 28th

Marched at quarter before five in the morning, twenty-four miles over a vast, extensive and hilly country. Bad roads and loose sand occasioned numbers of our men to fall out of the ranks; numbers of wagons broke down. Washed my shirt and stockings in a little ditch full of bullrushes, and laid me down to sleep about ten o'clock on the bare floor of a house without a roof. Scarcely got a wink of sleep being tormented to death by bugs and fleas; covered with pimples the following morning.[35]

---

33. The autumn rains were the subject of much comment. Amongst the many British observers was Robert Porter, a celebrated artist who had attached himself to Moore's command to record the glories of the campaign for posterity and wrote a series of letters to a friend in England in which he described it in considerable detail: 'Rain here is not like the rain with you. Compared with us, the heaviest showers descend on your heads like dew, but here ... the rain pours down in floods like torrents from a waterfall.' Porter, *Letters from Portugal and Spain*, p. 55.
34. Paget's companion was Lieutenant John Sheddon.
35. This part of the manuscript is rather muddled, but in what he clearly intended to be a footnote, the author provides some further details of events at about this time. Thus: 'I forgot to mention having fallen in with a French deserter and a young man who was taken prisoner on the 21st August. The former enlisted in the Fifty-Second and gave me a sketch of the French service. He marched from Paris with Junot, and [of] the amazing difficulties he since underwent, he told me nearly thus, that for five successive days they lived on nothing but the small kernel of the cork tree; that Junot, when the troops were being daily harassed by fatigue and ready to starve ... said, "Soldiers! Push on! There is plenty of wine, bread and eatables in the village before you", [whereupon] they went and [found] not a mouthful to be got; [that] they marched daily thirty-six miles at least; [that] the surgeons went around the army in the morning when [it was] sleeping to feel the pulses of the men to see if dead or alive; [that] every day they

September 29ᵗʰ

Marched twelve miles to a village where there was a handsome palace fitted up for
the Prince-Regent: it contains several beautiful paintings and no fewer than forty
privies. It had formerly been occupied by the French as the walls were written over
in the French language.³⁶

September 30ᵗʰ

Marched at six o'clock a.m. over a lovely country with mountains in the distance.
Halted twice from the heat. The roads getting better, sixteen miles' march this day
to a nice town called Montemor-o-Novo. Heard that we were not all to go to Elvas,
but only a party of 200 men, two captains, two field officers and six subalterns,
and that the rest were all to be billeted in separate houses. About twelve o'clock
we got to Montemor and procured two convents for the regiment. The monks
were to live in their cells and have their keys: these gentlemen seemed particularly
fond of the soldiers' wives. Procured my billet which was . . . though not good, I
thought a blessing, it consisting of a good table, bed on the floor, eight chairs, two
pots de chambre, one dish and leaden _____, one window, etc. My landlady seemed

---

threw (?) away sixty souls from hunger and weariness; [that] those also who lagged on
the march were cut down or tortured by Junot; and that [beside] the difficulties he
[had] experienced then, he now had a bed of roses. He also added that Junot would
undoubtedly be beheaded when he saw the emperor. The young man, Mr Wales, who
was taken prisoner, was treated well, dined with Junot, and was taken by a Frenchman
who he took for a Portuguese. Mr Wales is of the _____.'

36. Perhaps finding more time on his hands than he expected, Paget provides a much
longer account of his doings on 29 September immediately after the first entry. Thus:
'We had this day to march twelve miles to a town the name of which I forget. The
country continues still flat and sandy; likewise, quantities of fruits and shrubs, [like]
bay leaf and fennel; firs [i.e. pines] innumerable. Halted twice and refreshed ourselves
with a clear spring of water. About two we came to the town and billeted the men in a
palace made for the Prince Regent in the hunting season, an amazing beautiful place.
The French had lived in it before, and the natives made us to understand that they
had committed more depredations in this part of Portugal than anywhere else. Indeed,
[this] was very visible, boards [i.e. panelling,] and paintings, etc., being daubed and
written over in the French language. They also tore the earrings from the women's
ears and _____, and committed their brutal lusts [in] some of the neighbouring
convents. The officers occupied the higher rooms of the palace of which there are
an innumerable number, likewise upwards of forty necessaries, the first of which I
have seen in Portugal. I therefore conclude that princes merely use them; however,
I determined to do them the honour. This evening got some sugar-plums and some
coffee, but, from no covering and the hardness of the boards, [I] could not sleep much.
I have now been in Portugal sixty-four days, seven of which I have lain down without
my clothes.'

a tolerable good old dame: she had two pretty daughters and some little brats; the old man devilish sulky, however. I went to bed after buying two fowls for three *reis*, and slept most soundly; luckily, no fleas.[37]

September 31st

Parade at one quarter before five between the two convents, and immense deal of duty, two captains to each convent and four subs [i.e. subalterns] besides two of the day, etc. Seven men flogged this morning, mostly for drunkenness and quarrelling [over] who should carry the camp-kettles. The party for Elvas chosen out: report says they are to protect the French from this to Gallega Nova, and the xxth regiment and the Queen's [to] protect them here.[38] General Paget, whose brigade [*sic*: actually division] we are in, remains here.[39] Many flying reports: some say we stay here for three days and thus the winter and some a month. However, report is a common liar, as yet I have found it. I will now give a slight sketch of the English and the Portuguese. The latter are a malicious bad set. They will cry out 'viva' as you pass, but would see you hung before they'd spare a piece of bread, [and] are excessively stingy, mean and cowardly [so] that in the dark you may be poignarded in a moment, though they have a respect for English officers, who were at first looked up to as demi-gods, especially, and English sailors, whom they

37. In general, living conditions in Portugal came as a great shock to Moore's army. For example, 'Lisbon, like almost every other continental capital, appears to an Englishman to lack even common comforts. Not an inn is to be found in which you could pass the night without undergoing the tortures of a hell, almost as bad to me as flames and brimstone. I made an attempt to lodge in one, but, had I been destined to pass my nocturnal hours in the worst hovel in England or to have put up in this place, I should have preferred the former. It would be impossible in all Great Britain to find a habitation so ruinous, so ill-furnished, so filthy and so infested with vermin.' Porter, *Letters from Portugal and Spain*, pp. 39–40.
38. The situation referred to here arose from the circumstances in the wake of the Convention of Sintra. In brief, Junot had only maintained two garrisons outside Lisbon, these being situated at the fortresses of Almeida and Elvas. These, of course, had not heard of the convention for some time, and even then they refused to leave the safety of their fortifications until British troops had arrived to escort them to the coast. 'The Queen's' is a reference to the Fiftieth, or Queen's Own, Regiment of Foot.
39. The author slips up here, for he and his fellows were in the division of General Paget, their brigade commander rather being Robert Anstruther. As for the divisional commander, this was Sir Edward Paget (1775–1849), a veteran of the campaigns in Flanders and Egypt who was to lose his right arm at the battle of Oporto in May 1809 and be taken prisoner by the French during the retreat from Burgos in 1812. His brother, Sir Henry Paget, commanded Moore's cavalry and was responsible for the victory at Sahagún, later winning fame at Waterloo as the Earl of Uxbridge.

suppose almost invincible. They like dress and finery much and the first thing they demand is your rank. An English officer once in Lisbon was nearly stabbed by a Portuguese, but from our men being there the natives nearly killed him. Often have I begged for a piece of bread for myself or a man and the Portuguese will not give it. They are all very dirty, one house out of ten on an average being free of lice; these houses are chiefly of lath and plaster. Very little cultivation, and their pots are thrown out in the open streets, which is so offensive in Lisbon that a pocket handkerchief is absolutely necessary.[40] In a word, the nation has, as well as I can justly judge, all the bad qualities of Spain without a single good one. The latter are generous and brave, the former excessively stingy and cowardly. A shell at the battle I saw burst over a troop of cavalry's heads, and they immediately, shameful to say for England's allies, turned their backs and ran. However, so it is, and, was it not for the French crossing Spain to enter this country, they must and would have Portugal, as the inhabitants of this country would be as happy with the French as with us was it not for their priests who rule.[41]

---

40. Complaints in respect of conditions in Portugal are legion. Here, for example, is Robert Porter: 'On a nearer approach to Lisbon . . . the cleanliness which the external whiteness of the houses shining in the sun leads one to expect vanishes, and the miserably plastered dwellings present themselves in their true colours, bespattered with dirt of every description and rendered almost intolerable by the accumulated filth and the raging heat which draws their honours reeking up to heaven. On disembarking I landed some distance from the suburbs. The foul imagination of Dean Swift himself could not prefigure the scene that presented itself: a chaos of nastiness, poverty and wretchedness lay on every side. Rags or nakedness seemed the condition of every person who approached me, except now and then I saw a man enveloped in a mass of cloak in no better state, hung in . . . folds about him, leaving to the fancy the animated filth it concealed.' Porter, *Letters from Portugal and Spain*, pp. 6–10.

41. Though the same sentiment was widely voiced elsewhere, including, not least, by the French, Paget is completely mistaken in believing that the Church was the mainstay of the Portuguese uprising: in Oporto, certainly, it was the archbishop that came to the fore, but, as in Spain, the clergy was deeply divided in its response to Napoleonic occupation. That said, he was far from alone in holding the Portuguese to be lacking in backbone. To quote Ormsby once again, 'It must, indeed, be an uncommon crisis which could rouse the lower orders of the natives from their lethargy. I know not that I have yet seen anything which has struck me with so much surprise as the extreme and constant idleness of the populace. The number of huge fellows stretching their lazy length upon the ground is barely credible . . . To confess the truth . . . a distrust and jealousy of us pervade the public mind . . . Certainly, their joy was unbounded at the extermination of the French, but it by no means follows that, because they hate them, they should love us, and, had their plunderers and oppressors conducted themselves with more moderation . . . I am persuaded they would have been hailed as the deliverers of Portugal from an odious government, and that any proffers of assistance

October 1ˢᵗ

Mounted picket this day. Stayed at the convent in an old, dirty cell. Got bitten terribly by the vermin, mostly flies, etc.

October 2ⁿᵈ

The French marched in here from Elvas escorted by the Second [Battalion of the] Queen's Regiment. They were a very raffish set, the men seemingly much fatigued and ready to sell everything: a very handsome double-barrelled fowling piece was sold for twenty dollars; horses, etc., equally cheap. Our men escorted them three miles from Montemor o Novo where they encamped for the night in a wood of fir [i.e. pine] trees.

---

from us would have been indignantly rejected . . . Notwithstanding all their offences, there is a strong French party at this moment in Lisbon . . . Too many are dazzled by their conquests and duped by their promises. The inherent love of change operates most powerfully and they flatter themselves with the vain hope of regeneration from the tyrant of mankind.' Ormsby, *Operations of the British Army*, I, pp. 123, 171–2. Porter, meanwhile, is just as scathing: 'Men and seasons are sadly altered with the Portuguese since the time of their royal Juans, Alfonsos and Sebastians, and, having been long out of practice in victories, no wonder when the battle comes they should be a little shy of arms. Notwithstanding I offer an excuse for the late supineness of the once valiant Lusitorians [*sic*], I cannot but be seriously surprised that it should exist. Surely the people had every stimulative to make a glorious effort . . . yet all was not sufficient to arouse the glorious spirit of the country. The people murmured but bore it . . . I am yet young in my knowledge of this nation, but I doubt whether anything like the glorious fire which now blazes throughout Spain would ever have burst forth in its sister kingdom. The iron rule and insinuations of the French acted like a charm upon the Portuguese. They seemed as if caught in a trap, and, hopeless of release, resigned to their fate . . . Our friends here do not seem to wear their hearts precisely in the right place: I see no symptoms of gratitude, much less of magnificent hospitality. The characteristics of the people appear to be haughtiness, envy and revenge, qualities which seldom fail to bring forth the monster cruelty. The lower ranks are well known for their love of taking unto themselves many things which are the property of others, a failing which is father and mother to another, the very spirit of lying. Were we to seek a reason for these faults, I should find it in their perverted religion, moral indolence and exclusive preference for the spirit of their own countrymen . . . It has [also] been a growing evil with Portugal the assistance she has always sought in her wars from foreign powers . . . This practice lowered the martial spirit even of the nobles.' Porter, *Letters from Portugal and Spain*, pp. 16–38 *passim*. Of course, no such 'glorious fire' was raging in Spain either, but that was something of which every member of the British army from Sir John Moore down had yet to be apprised.

October 3rd

Marched at three o'clock this morning; twelve miles which is equal to three Portuguese leagues; country hilly and many men fell out from the heat. Got billeted this night in a tolerable house: my landlord was very obliging and had three beautiful daughters who amused me much. Spoke to Mr Hutchinson. Found myself much fatigued and very weak. Alas, the Lisbon beauties, what tricks they play upon us!

October 4th

Marched at three o'clock this day, a march of twenty-four miles which at this time I was not well-calculated to perform. Halted two hours on the road and arrived at Estremoz about two o'clock, where I got two bad billets, and luckily got a third, much better. My landlord consisted of a grocer and an old hag of a landlady. I was shown up to a garret: six chairs, a table and an image which they worshipped. It held in its hands roses and a little child meant, I suppose, to represent our Blessed Saviour. Underneath was a smaller waxen figure to represent Him in swaddling clothes, these and several other images in a glass case which the family daily adored. Thus was profaned the second commandment in all the smaller houses of Portugal: either a cross or an image is adored, in higher families a man nailed to a wooden cross. Oh, the superstition and ignorance of these poor souls! It is to be allotted to the monks who keep them in this state of ignorance.[42]

---

42. Iberia's Catholicism was something on which British observers never ceased to pour scorn: 'During the public rejoicings for the departure of the French I visited [the ancient cathedral and the . . . convent at Buenos Aires] . . . None of these consecrated structures, as public buildings, have any claim to admiration . . . Imagine a mob of . . . figures [supposed] to represent saints and Virgin Marys dressed in gothic habits, stiff sacks and fine brocaded petticoats gazing at you with bedaubed faces and lighted up on all sides with long and glimmering candles. These, with one hundred [other] objects . . . call forth any ideas but those of religious awe and respect . . . Processions and ceremonies are passing to and fro without end. No day escapes but what you witness whole trains of monks, accompanied by swarms of idle people, traversing the streets in every direction. Independent of these personages, groups of singers bearing baskets, and begging in couples, interrupt your walks.' Porter, *Letters from Portugal and Spain*, pp. 25–46 *passim*. Here too is the Anglican clergyman James Ormsby: 'Images and paintings of our saviour, the Virgin and the numerous saints, erected upon the walls and enclosed in a large glass lantern with a lamp perpetually burning arrest the attention almost every fifty yards you go. To these an obeisance is offered, an ejaculatory prayer repeated and the sign of the cross made at proper intervals. These images are of stone or painted wood and executed in the vilest manner imaginable.' Ormsby, *Operations of the British Army*, I, p. 133.

Sir John Moore: though much loved by his subordinates, Moore was a difficult and egotistical individual whose relations with civilian diplomats and politicians were invariably very poor.

Sir Henry Paget: the commander of Moore's cavalry, Paget performed well in the retreat to Corunna and went on to lose a leg at Waterloo.

Sir Edward Paget: conceivably Charles Paget's father, had a record of bad luck in the Peninsula, losing an arm at Oporto and then being taken prisoner in the retreat from Salamanca in November 1812.

An officer of the Fifty-Second Foot: as was common in Wellington's army, a substantial minority of the Fifty-Second's officers were drawn from the Protestant ascendancy in Ireland.

A private of the Fifty-Second Foot: even in well-disciplined regiments, few British soldiers came close to achieving this level of sartorial splendour by the time they reached Corunna.

The battle of Vimeiro: an easier fight than many of Wellington's Peninsular victories, Vimeiro cost fewer than 750 British casualties.

Lisbon: Charles Paget says little about Lisbon, but most of Wellington's solders were horrified by its dirt and poverty; when the Fifty-Second set off to travel by river to Abrantes, it embarked at the quay in the foreground.

The main street in Alcántara: poverty-stricken and remote, Alcántara was not the best of introductions to Spain.

The Puente de Alcántara viewed from the south bank: originally built by the Romans, in 1809 it was the site of a sharp fight between a French division and the Loyal Lusitanian Legion of Sir Robert Wilson.

The Puerta de la Colada at Ciudad Rodrigo: having crossed the River Agueda via the town's Roman bridge, Paget's battalion filed into the city via this mediaeval gateway and barbican.

The Roman bridge at Salamanca, as sketched by the artist Robert Porter: many British soldiers were deeply impressed by the city's architecture.

The Calle Veracruz: little changed from the days of the Peninsular War, the Calle Veracruz was the main road into Salamanca from the bridge over the River Tormes.

The Roman bridge at Salamanca today: now reserved for pedestrians, in 1808 it was part of a busy highway.

The house made use of as his headquarters by Sir John Moore at Astorga: when Napoleon entered the city shortly after the British departure it was used by him as well.

A typical street scene in Astorga: the chaos that gripped the city as British and Spanish troops alike competed for food and shelter, both of them equally scarce, can easily be imagined.

The town hall and *plaza mayor* at Astorga: magnificent though it was, the former is not mentioned in any British account of the retreat to Corunna.

The Puerto de Manzanal: situated between Astorga and Bembibre and rising to a height of over 3,900ft, the Puerto de Manzanal was the first major obstacle that faced Moore's army in the course of its retreat.

The Puente de Constantino: situated west of Nogales (today As Nogais) on the road from Bembibre to Lugo, the Puente de Constantino was the scene of a fierce rearguard action on 5 January 1809.

A typical Spanish ox-cart: it was in a vehicle of this sort that Charles Paget was brought into Corunna at the end of the retreat.

A distant view of Corunna: the evacuation of Moore's forces went smoothly enough, but nearly 1,000 lives were lost to shipwreck on the voyage back to England.

October 5th

Not being well, rested myself this day.

October 6th

Reduced to the necessity of speaking to the surgeon and writing different things.

October 7th

Went out with my pistols [and] found them to be very bad ones. Mounted picket this night at the convent: the monks behaved very civil and gave me sweetmeats, etc.

October 8th

Went off picket this evening: convent all clean and in good order. Went to see the nunnery and had a peep at the old Lady Abbess; way of speaking most curious and sending messages.[43] Slept in my new lodgings: got sadly bit by the fleas.

October 9th

Was late for divine service today. A mess [was] formed by the officers of the regiment. Weather rather cold though clear and fine. Various reports relating to Spain and the shameful capitulation of the British general.[44] Went to see the castle of Estremoz in which is an amazing collection of old arms taken in the battles with the French [*sic:* the battles referred to had rather been waged against the Spaniards in the wars of the seventeenth and eighteenth centuries].

October 10th

Monday. I forgot yesterday to mention the Portuguese ceremony of the Host. They got the permission of General Paget to have 200 men, six subalterns and two captains to attend their ceremony called 'Te Deum'. 'Twas something like the Lisbon one only not so grand. It passed the monastery at three o'clock consisting of fifty men with candles five feet high in large purple habits, after which was an image bearing a cross as large as life supported by six or eight monks each having golden candle-stick and candle. I could not make the people understand I wished to know who this image was, but have since heard it was a great Portuguese general

---

43. The syntax is garbled here. What the author means, of course, is that, if the Lady Abbess' manner of speech was most curious, so was the method used for passing messages in to the convent from the outside world (usually a tray that revolved in a slot in a door or grating).

44. Whereas this reads as if it is a reference to a capitulation on the part of some British general, the author is rather referring to the convention signed by Dalrymple.

who saved his country; as it proceeded, every person knelt and prayed before it. After this followed quantities of men, women and children with crosses, etc.; and then came the Host, which is a kind of wafer shut up in a little box covered by a golden canopy and supported by friars; to this mighty wafer, all was adoration and respect. The procession was out for an hour and stopped at Major-General Paget's who avoided it by taking a ride. Heard of Sir John Moore having command of the whole army in Portugal. Orders for the regiments to be well stocked with shoes and to march sixty-four miles a week to keep in practice.

October 11th

The regiment marched six leagues this morning, which is twenty-four miles, for practice. Stayed at home writing this day as letters for England were ordered to be sent to the orderly room of the convent of the right wing.

October 12th

The regiment ordered to be inspected by General Paget tomorrow. Orders that the Ninety-Seventh Regiment should be attached to the Reserve till further orders. His Majesty has been pleased to make several promotions: Captain Grant to be major in the Second Battalion. Orders also that the regiment will send immediately returns of their want of ammunition. Lieutenant Laye of the First Battalion was tried by a general court martial at Queluz for disobedience to his captain.[45] The court was of the opinion that the officer was not guilty and do therefore honourably acquit him. Two soldiers sentenced to be hung for stealing a cross and two watches out of the house of Jailus [?], men of the Ninth, Second Battalion. Spirits to be served out to the men in bad weather. Officers to received 200 days *bât* and forage money from the Deputy Commissary-General at _____ Sir Harry Burrard having received His Majesty's command to place a large part of the army in Portugal under Sir John Moore to be employed in a separate service. The following regiments compose the corps to be so employed and they are hereby directed to receive their orders from Sir John Moore accordingly: two Staff Corps; Eighteenth Light Dragoons; Third [Battalion], KGL; Fourth, First Battalion; Fifth, Sixth; Ninth; Twentieth, Twenty-Eighth; Thirty-Second; Thirty-Sixth; Thirty-Eighth; Fortieth; Forty-Second; Forty-Third; Fifty-Second, First Battalion; Fifty-Second, Second Battalion; Sixtieth; Seventy-First; Seventy-Ninth; Ninety-First; Ninety-Second; Ninety-Fifth, First Battalion; Ninety-Fifth, Second Battalion; First Light Dragoons, KGL; Second Light Dragoons, KGL. These are divided

---

45. The officer court-martialled was a Lieutenant Thomas Laye: nothing else is known of him other than the fact that he retired from the army in 1810.

into their respective brigades: we again compose General Anstruther's. Officers to furnish themselves with horses for baggage.

October 13th

Fired my pistols today and hit once at six paces' distance out of twenty-four times. Weather as usual remarkably cool and fine. Inspected by General Paget. At four o'clock this evening went and talked to my old friends the nuns and took three sketches. The party from Gallega Nova arrived yesterday after having marched it in the same number of days as they before accomplished it.

October 14th

General Orders

From the general orders of the 11th inst. The commanding officers cannot permit any woman with child, that hath a child or that is not stout and equal to fatigue in the long march which is about to take place and who he strongly recommends the rest of the women to accept of the present opportunity of returning to England in the manner of their proceeding to Lisbon and their support there till a good opportunity offers of their going to England will hereafter be pointed out.[46] On their arrival in England they will receive their usual allowance to carry them to their respective homes. The commanding officers will therefore send in by tattoo this evening the names of those who remain behind and of those who accompany the regiment. Companies to be inspected by the commanding officer for immediate and active service tomorrow at one o'clock. Men to be completed in white gaiters. Spent the whole of this day in writing to England: weather very fair and cool.

---

46. When battalions went on campaign, the wives of the rank and file were balloted and six per company allowed to embark with the troops along with their children, the purpose of this arrangement being to provide the troops with the rudiments of the support services possessed by contemporary armies: thus, in exchange for half rations for themselves and quarter rations for their children, in addition to caring for their husbands, the women concerned were expected to launder and repair uniforms, gather firewood, help with preparing rations and generally serve as maids of all work. For a brief introduction, see Esdaile, *Women in the Peninsular War*, pp. 64–93. In consequence, several hundred women accompanied the British troops who were sent to Portugal, but Moore was one of those officers who both regarded the presence of camp-followers as an impediment to the army's operations and was genuinely concerned at the hardships to which they were likely to be exposed, and was therefore anxious in so far as he could to put an end to the practice.

October 15th

Spent the whole of this day in laying in things for our ensuing campaign and long marches: got some flannel, etc. Orders for the men to be supplied well with gaiters and shoes.[47] Mess to parade tomorrow for divine service.

October 16th

Sunday. Had divine service in the morning. Wrote to England and took a walk to an adjoining hut: found myself not being well from a flux. Three Portuguese dined at the mess. Orders for me to mount picket tomorrow evening at the Right's convent.[48]

October 17th

Stayed on picket at the Right's convent all night and day; messes, etc., all regular.[49]

October 18th

Came off picket this day. Orders at Estremoz. Our division under Major-General Paget is likely to move at the shortest notice. Commanding officers of corps are to pay the strictest attention to the following points which are found in the general orders of the 9th and 11th inst., and the returns called for are to be sent in with the least possible delay. The regimental surgeons have the same returns of the sick with the regiments and also those who are left in other quarters, and care must be taken in the march of the regiments of such convalescent men as are not perfectly fit to undertake a long march and not permitted to attend the regiments but to remain

---

47. The stress that is laid on the need for decent gaiters is interesting: although breeches and gaiters were still required for full dress, in the field the infantry increasingly favoured grey trousers.

48. 'The Right' refers to the right wing of the battalion (for the purposes of bivouacking and billeting and, occasionally, the requirements of combat, infantry battalions could be split into two sub-units each one composed of five companies, the manner in which the individual companies were assigned depending on the position which they occupied when the full battalion was arrayed in line.

49. In a letter dated 17 October, Ormsby mentions a development that further blackened the image which most British observers had of the Portuguese: 'The native troops begin to make their appearance and do garrison duty. My taste may probably have been rendered fastidious by looking at our own and the French armies, but, if this be not the case, such soldiers, I am persuaded, have seldom been exhibited since the days of Falstaff. Their appointments are, without exception, ridiculously bad. There is such variety in the shape and colour that it seems as if no uniform has yet been decided on, but that they had all been ordered to procure fancy patterns for approbation, and that no two of them had . . . fixed upon the same.' Ormsby, *Operations of the British Army*, I, p. 156.

in a place which will hereafter be pointed out for the hospital of the division, while a report will also be formed for the baggage which regiments may find it necessary to leave behind. Returns of the horses and mules actually in possession of officers are also to be sent in, and immediate steps are to be taken to provide any deficiency in the number stated in the general orders of the 11th inst. Returns of the names of women and children who are to remain with the heavy baggage for the purpose of being transmitted to the Adjutant General's office in Lisbon, and commanding officers are particularly recommended to impress in the minds of married soldiers that the divisions in this part of Portugal are particularly liable to pass through places where the women will be exposed to the greatest hardships at this advanced season of the year. Regimental Orders: Mr Hutchinson is to send in as soon as possible the returns called for in the divisional orders of this day. Commanding officer called the attention of the married men to that part of the Divisional Orders of this day relative to the hardships which their wives are likely to be exposed to on the march, and as it is utterly impossible to have a man with them, or render them any assistance in the event of them falling sick, he strongly recommends them leaving those who are unable to bear the greatest fatigue behind. Powder horns to be given in with a report of the number. Got myself preparatory to marching made a flannel waistcoat and long flannel drawers.

October 19th

Procured soap, snuff and all necessities for our ensuing campaign. The weather continues here remarkably fine. Got very thick with my landlord and lady. The former informed me we march to Burgos, the distance of 400 miles from this part of Portugal and that the French army were at Pamplona. A lady [is] still in my billet and has been, and still is, excessively kind to me. Her intrigues were very vicious, I believe: she begged to write to me after, and gave me her address, viz. Donha Ana Gertrudis Placida. She was a middle-aged lass and up to romps as much as our English belles.[50] General Paget sent his *aide-de-camp* to invite me to dinner. Dined with him at six o'clock [and] sat till ten drinking fine old port and claret. Had a most excellent dinner.[51]

---

50. There is, of course, no way of knowing exactly what went on in respect of this 'middle-aged lass', but many Spanish and Portuguese women were eager to forge relationships with foreign soldiers as this offered them both a degree of security and a means of escaping lives that were frequently extremely oppressive.

51. As generals are not in the habit of inviting humble subalterns to dinner, from this remark we may assume that Paget was a relative of the two generals of that name.

October 20ᵗʰ

Took a sketch of a neighbouring convent and wrote to Old England; weather remarkably fine. Colonel López of the Spanish army arrived: he gives a very favourable account of matters in that country and likewise of the people intending to rid the country of the French by Christmas.[52]

October 21ˢᵗ

Very long orders given out again concerning the women and the hardships they will be exposed to during the ensuing march; a subaltern officer left behind to take charge of them. Some reports of Sir David Baird having landed. All my sketches lost by Mrs Walker.[53]

October 22ⁿᵈ

Bought a stock of oilskin and some grog preparatory to our next campaign. Saw also an English newspaper: not any news of consequence.

October 23ʳᵈ

Had a very gay party of ladies in my house this night, our Donha Mariana Rita Valente the prettiest of the set and many others. Took a walk with Dobbs to bathe and eat figs.[54]

---

52. An ominous remark that exactly foreshadows the famous 'all over by Christmas' of 1914: in fact it was to be almost six years before the French military presence in Spain was finally extinguished. Yet there is no doubt that expectations were running high amongst Moore's men. By the time that he reached the last town in Portugal, for example, Porter was in a positive fever of excitement: 'We now approach that country whose patriotism has aroused the admiration of England and led our armies with the ardour of a crusade to Spanish shores. I must confess that my heart beats high at the prospect of so soon being introduced to those brave sons of liberty on whose countenances I expect to see the blaze of enthusiasm and from whose energetic examples will shoot that chivalric fire so much needed to inflame the obstinate coolness of some of our too straight-forward heroes. I do not mean too direct in the field but too wedded to common-place modes. They understand not the glorious impulse which arms the undisciplined peasant and makes him, though not a soldier, a dauntless champion of his country's rights. Spain is one in heart and soul, and, while she makes herself the forlorn hope of Europe, it is the policy, as well as the honour, of every independent sovereignty, to support her in so sublime a struggle. We go, and may Heaven's propitious star crown our united efforts!' Porter, *Letters from Portugal and Spain*, pp. 93–4.
53. The identity of this lady is unclear, but it is probable that she was a soldier's wife who was 'doing' for the author and some of his fellow officers.
54. Given the informal context, this is the John Dobbs of *Recollections of an Old Fifty-Second Man* (Waterford, 1863).

October 24ᵗʰ

Sent off my luggage to the store by the _____ and a letter to England by Mrs Walker.[55] Also went out a-shooting but did not see anything except larks and other birds.

October 25ᵗʰ

The German rifle corps arrived here this morning, and most of the army [was] in motion except ourselves.[56] Went out skirmishing this morning: saw a hare and other game. My servant taken ill and not able to do anything. Orders that no officer is on any account to have a soldier for a batman, but a native of the country for whom rations will be drawn and a dollar for work. I spent this day in firing with my pistols: hit three times out of twenty at six paces distant. The following are some orders issued out by Major-General Paget to the soldiers under his command at Estremoz on the 26ᵗʰ.

October 26ᵗʰ

Advanced orders:
Major-General Paget is happy to inform the advanced corps of the army that the moment is arrived at which their efforts are to commence. Between them and the enemy is a very considerable extent of country, in many parts mountainous, rugged and very thinly populated. Under such circumstances considerable difficulties are likely to occur in the movement of a column, but he is well persuaded that it is only necessary to know these must be overcome before the enemy can be conquered to inspire a degree of exertion which must set all difficulties and hardships at defiance. Every arrangement that can be made for the supply of troops on the march and for the conveyance of any men who may fall sick shall be made, but they must be prepared to accept serious deprivations from the nature of the service in which we are engaged and which may prevent the possibility of leaving any of the regimental surgeons behind, and it will become necessary to have any men who from sickness are unable to proceed on the march with their battalions in the charge of the magistrates and such medical gentlemen as the country may afford. Upon this head, however, commanding officers of corps have been furnished with the following instructions:

---

55. The inference here is clearly that Mrs Walker was returning to England: apparently, then, at least some wives took advantage of the arrangements Moore made for the army's camp-followers to return to England.
56. The 'German rifle corps' mentioned in this entry is a reference to the brigade of the Hanoverian officer, Karl Alten. As we have seen, this consisted of the First and Second Light Battalions of the King's German Legion, both of which were clad in dark green and armed with Baker rifles.

No. 1: as no doubts can be entertained that nine cases out of ten of sickness are the result of the immoderate use of the bad wine of this country, the soldiers are exhorted, as they value their health; as they value their honour; as they must feel an ambition to be present with their regiments in the approaching conflict with the enemy; as they must feel reluctance to be left in the care of strangers, to abstain from the use of this most pernicious liquor.

No. 2: the advanced corps will be prepared to march by battalions according to routes which will be sent to them.

No. 3: in order to have one day's provisions always in advance, the corps will advance with one day's biscuit and salt pork cooked for the first day; at the end of the first day's march, the provisions for the second day will be issued and cooked, the men eating the soup but preserving the bread and meat for the following day and so successively, and commanding officers are desired most particularly to see this arrangement systematically established.

No. 4: commanding officers to be very careful to procure good guides; they may be paid 400 *reis* per day.

No. 5: the corps are to march regularly at daybreak, and, when the moon permits, even before daybreak as it is an object of the first importance to the comfort and convenience of the troops to get the march over early in the day; it is [also] recommended to halt for a few minutes every one or two hours.

No. 6: an officer from each battalion is always to be one day forward with the returns of his corps to make every exertion to have the supply in readiness for his battalion.

No. 9: the sick of the several battalions are to be removed to Elvas according to routes which will sent for them; they will be accompanied by an Assistant Surgeon of each corps with a requisite number of nurses selected from men least able to bear the fatigues of a long march; a month's subsistence is to be sent with the men; the Assistant Surgeon having delivered over the sick to the care of the medical officer appointed to receive them, will return to Estremoz and report their arrival to the Assistant Adjutant General.[57]

---

57. It will be observed that there is an apparent error in the numeration here: whether this was because the author of the journal decided to omit the seventh and eighth clauses or because he simply made a slip is unclear.

No. 10: an officer from each battalion of Brigadier-General Alten's brigade with the pioneers and their tools with the mules and the entrenching tools and a good sergeant, two corporal and ten privates, good labourers, of each battalion will repair to Estremoz and report their arrival to the Assistant Adjutant-General; they are to march so as to arrive at Estremoz by the 29th inst; the mules and entrenching tools of the Fifty-Second, Ninety-Fifth and Twentieth Regiments with similar parties are to be held ready to move when called upon.[58]

No. 11: Paymasters to assemble at Estremoz to pay officers 166 days *bât* and forage money and pay to the 24th of November.[59] Officers not in want of immediate cash are requested to take bills.

Regimental order: Major-General Paget has so fully expressed himself in the foregoing orders the commanding officer has only to call the attention of officers and men to them.

Heard of Sir David Baird having landed and, with him the Twenty-Sixth Regiment. Wrote to my old friend Lambrecht.[60] Saw an English paper of

---

58. This clause of Paget's instructions is particularly interesting as it suggests a desire on his part to give his division a battalion of engineers. As the order implies, hitherto each battalion possessed a small number of pioneers – men equipped with axes, picks and spades whose task it was to remove any obstacles that were encountered on the march – while their labour could at need be supplemented by labour drawn from the ranks, but the result of this was that such expertise as existed in this area was badly diluted. What Paget was trying to do, then, was to concentrate his resources in this respect and thereby improve capacity, whilst at the same time ensuring that the rank and file deployed on engineering duties were at the very least men who were both responsible and physically suited to the role (one presumes, too, that the expectation was that, where possible, they would be chosen from men who had some useful skill: carpenters, perhaps, or, still better, miners). Less is said about the officers who were to be involved in this venture than the men, but it is presumed that the intention was to procure an officer of the Royal Engineers – then no more than a corps of highly trained specialists with no rank and file of its own – to command the whole, and that Paget hoped that the officers seconded to the new units would be men with some interest in engineering of the sort who came forward as 'assistant engineers' in each of Wellington's subsequent sieges.
59. The '*bât* and forage money' referred to here was an allowance paid to officers on campaign to cover the transport costs (normally the hire and maintenance of one or more mules.
60. This officer may have been John Lambrecht, an ensign of the Sixty-Sixth Foot who came out to Spain with his battalion in July 1809 and survived to receive the 1847 General Service medal with no fewer than ten bars.

26th September and heard of Sir J. Saumarez's action in the Baltic.[61] The army to Spain to compose 30,000 men. Intelligence from the Spaniards of the French receiving reinforcements of artillery and cavalry.

October 27th

Nothing material.

October 28th

My birthday. An English soldier stabbed by a Portuguese: Boothe of Captain Dobbs' company.[62]

General Order of Sir John Moore

The commander of the forces trusts that the troops on their entry in Spain will see with him how much it is for their honour and their advantage to maintain the high opinion and cherish the good will which that brave and high-spirited people entertain towards the British nation. The troops upon this march will generally be quartered on the inhabitants. The Spaniards are a brave and orderly people, extremely sober, but generous and warm in their temper and easily offended by any assault or disrespect that is offered to them. They are grateful to the English and will receive the troops with kindness and cordiality: this the general hopes will be met with an equal kindness on the part of the soldiers and that they will endeavour to accommodate themselves to their manners, be orderly in their quarters and not

---

61. The naval action referred to here formed a part of Russo–Swedish War of 1808–9. As we have seen, on 21 February 1808 Alexander I had invaded Finland (then a province of Sweden). Sweden being a vital British ally (it was the source of a large part of the timber from which the Royal Navy was constructed), help was immediately provided in the form of a division of troops commanded by Sir John Moore and a naval squadron commanded by Admiral Saumarez. Quarrels with King Gustav Adolf IV over what should be done with the British troops led Moore to abandon the campaign in disgust (an episode which was to have considerable bearing on events in the Peninsula), but Saumarez remained on station, and in late July became involved in a major series of operations in which a Russian battle fleet sallied out in an attempt to drive the Swedish navy from the Gulf of Bothnia. Incompetently commanded, however, the Russian offensive quickly stalled, thereby affording Saumarez time to rush his ships to the aid of the Swedes. On 25 August the British and Swedes launched a joint attack on the Russian squadron off Hango (today Hanko), only for the latter to turn and flee, in the course of which action Saumarez was able to disable and capture a Russian ship-of-the-line.

62. This was not John Dobbs, who was only an ensign in 1808, but rather his elder brother, Joseph Dobbs, who had been a captain in the Fifty-Second since 1804 and was killed in the storm of Ciudad Rodrigo on 19 January 1812.

thank by acts of intemperance a people worthy of their attachments and whose efforts they have come to support in the most glorious of causes, to free them from French bondage, and to establish in their nation liberty and independence. Upon entering Spain as a compliment to the Spanish nation, the army will wear red cockades in addition to their own. Cockades are ordered for this purpose for the privates and non-commissioned officers and will be sent from Madrid, but in the meantime officers are requested to provide themselves [with cockades] and to put them on when they pass the frontiers.

Signed: Henry Clinton, Adjutant-General of the Troops in Spain.
Dined at the mess and found part of my ration [?] stolen. Reports of our marching on Sunday. Did not keep the 28th [i.e. celebrate my birthday].

October 29th

Passed through Estremoz this day the public procession of Santa Isabella, a very paltry thing, all the rest alike. Orders by Lieutenant-General Hope to the troops: the pioneers with parties and entrenching tools of the Fifty-Second [and] First and Second [Light] Battalions, K.G.L., will march tomorrow morning at eight o'clock under the charge of the senior subaltern officer to Monforte and there report themselves to Lieutenant-Colonel Beckwith of the Ninety-Fifth.[63] These two parties are to march with two days provisions for the 30th and 31st and forage for the mules for the same period; the Fifty-Second _____ will be in readiness to march on Monday morning with two days provisions. Much punishment this day, several corporals and privates having been tried.

October 30th

Sunday. Mounted picket this day. Prepared myself for the march tomorrow. The following is a copy from a Portuguese officer of our proposed route.[64]

---

63. The reference to Lieutenant General Hope, i.e. Sir John Hope, is almost certainly an error: presumably the author rather means his divisional commander, Sir Edward Paget. Beckwith, meanwhile, was Thomas Beckwith, a founding member of the famous 'Ninety-Fifth Rifles' and by 1808 the commanding officer of that unit's first battalion. A favourite of Sir John Moore, in 1809 he was given command of a brigade in the Light Division by the then Sir Arthur Wellesley.

64. There seems little point in reproducing this document in full consisting, as it does, of a long list of daily halting places, many of them no more than tiny villages, together with the number of leagues that would have to be covered each day (usually four, five or six). That said, it is not without interest in that it is suggested that Moore's army would be able to march all the way from the Portuguese frontier to Bayonne via Salamanca, Valladolid, Burgos, Vitoria and Irun in an unbroken march of thirty-five days, the fact

October 31ˢᵗ

Monday. Did not march this day according to the orders, the route having not yet arrived. I therefore spent it procuring rum, etc., for the campaign. Orders to march tomorrow at six o'clock, warning bugles to sound at half-past five.

November 1ˢᵗ

At length, the long wished-for day is come: marched from old Estremoz at six o'clock through amazing numbers of boggy lanes and _____ places, four and one half leagues.[65] Light rains during the beginning of the day. Arrived at Monforte and all got most shocking billets, all but two officers. This is a nasty town. Spent my time here in hearing the nuns sing and buying from them sweetmeats. In the convent there [are] fifty-seven, fourteen of which had taken the veil, several of them elegant and pretty girls seemingly _____ heartbroken to get out. Their forehead dress is most curious.[66]

---

that there was a large French army in the way that might have something to say about a hostile force heading straight for the Pyrenees being ignored as something that was seemingly of no consequence whatsoever.

65. Paget does not mention it, but there was much discontent in the army at the delay in taking the field. Thus: 'Why this expedition has been so long delayed, we are, of course, unable to pronounce positively. It is conjectured that the time has been employed in arranging with the Spanish government the place of our destination . . . for it would have been evidently absurd to move till it was ascertained at what point our services were required. But a valuable interval has elapsed and the army has suffered from inaction.' Ormsby, *Operations of the British Army*, I, p. 168.

66. 'Forehead dress' is presumably a reference to wimples. Fantasies with regard to nuns are a common feature of British memoirs of the Peninsular War, it being universally supposed that such women (all of them beautiful, of course) were incarcerated in convents by cruel fathers, stepfathers or other relations and condemned to a life of misery. That some nuns may indeed have been unhappy cannot be denied, but life in most convents was actually one of great ease and comfort, whilst the nuns also enjoyed a wide range of opportunities and life chances that were denied most other women. Also noteworthy here is the fact that when the French attempted to empty the convents by means of offering pensions in exchange for secularisation, the scheme appears to have attracted few takers. In consequence, Porter's story of not just visiting a convent at Salamanca with a group of his friends, but finding 'as free ingress into [the nuns'] cells as if we had been a regiment of confessors' and, not just that, but proceeding to experience 'adventures truly romantic' may be dismissed as, in every possible sense, artistic licence. Indeed, Neale describes precisely the same group of nuns as 'ten or twelve decrepit old women wrapped up in woollen dresses with little of anything like feeling in the lines of their wrinkled countenances'. Neale, *Letters from Portugal and Spain*, p. 229. For all this, see Esdaile, *Women in the Peninsular War*, pp. 164–88.

November 2nd

Halted this day at Monforte which I spent admiring the fine blue distance and the surrounding mountains. Found the quartermaster of the band had deserted. Took up two men of the Sixtieth.[67]

November 3rd

Marched at six o'clock two leagues for Arronches over a delightful country. Met with bad swamps and stoppages on the road. I was greatly amused the whole of this day's march in admiring the distant and magnificent blue mountains which divide Spain from Portugal, each topping the clouds, and the wonderful extent and distance of Spain far exceeded anything I ever in my life beheld.[68] I attempted to sketch it but found my pencil disgrace itself. Arronches is an excessive neat town and is very prettily situated; it is eight leagues from Estremoz. It has two good bridges on each side and is a fortified town. I got an excellent billet, but being on the main road deprived me of walking and making those observations I would have wished.

November 4th

Marched from Arronches at six in the morning, a march of five leagues to Alburquerque. We passed the frontier this day which is divided from Spain by a small rivulet. The fine distant blue mountains surpassed anything I ever before beheld. Three leagues out of the five [were] entirely passes under and over mountains, amazing valleys and descents. We arrived in Spain about twelve o'clock and difference experienced was much: the language totally different in some degree like the German and Dutch; the people in all our opinions excessively uncivil and disobliging (perhaps this is an erroneous opinion). We saw Alburquerque after much rain and wet about two o'clock situated on an amazing high rock

---

67. The regiment mentioned here is the Fifth Battalion of the Sixtieth Foot. Otherwise known as the Royal American Regiment, this was one of the odder formations of the British army, and the only infantry regiment to have five battalions (the norm was two or, at the most, three). Recruited from inhabitants of Canada, its first four battalions were standard redcoat units armed with muskets and spent the whole of the Napoleonic Wars on garrison duty in Canada or the West Indies, but the fifth battalion was dressed in green in a style very similar to the 95th Regiment and, like them, equipped with rifles while it had been raised in England in 1797 from foreign deserters (mostly German). As is suggested by this incident, such men were not entirely to be relied upon, and it may well be this that decided Moore to send the unit back to Lisbon as part of the latter's garrison when he marched for Spain.

68. The author's pen may have slipped here as Arronches lies some miles inside Spain. The mountains referred to are the Serra de San Mamed.

commanding a view not to be expressed, mountains turning upon mountains and exceeding large valleys, rocky and craggy. After, marched into Alburquerque and went to the Officers' Guard which was a stable for mules and asses. Relieved guard at half-past five o'clock, and did not get into my billet till eight or nine o'clock, the people shutting their doors in our faces. Such was our reception in our first Spanish town: I sincerely hope 'twill not be repeated. At last, after going to the *juiz de fora* and summoning a gentleman called an *alguacil*, I made my landlord the Spaniard open the door; [he] gave me a tolerable feed, full of bacon and garlic; his name is Don Manuel. Met Love in the street who asked me to a *baile*; danced till twelve o'clock and for the first time saw the Spanish ladies dance a fandango to the castanets, this having appeared to me excessive rude, the ladies taking the man and hugging them round the waist; the ladies are excessive fine women, and wear their hair (which is amazing long) over their left eye.[69] The bread is very good and white here, eggs hard to be got at two and one half [pence?], goat's milk equally dear. I did not observe much difference in the Portuguese and the Spaniards. The latter seem to have a more worthy idea of themselves, not touching their hats to English officers though civil and cool, yet not appearing so generous as I have heard. Easily offended I am sure they are and, [I] can conceive, jealous. I must say their unanimity is great, for they are determined and make sure of conquest. However, I can assert the English did not meet with that cordiality from the Spanish nation as they expected. However, true it is: a John Bull will never find himself at home abroad, he being some centuries more enlightened than other nations. This is a filthy town but the people [are] somewhat cleaner than the Portuguese; they live chiefly on pork, garlic and vegetables, things to us utterly impossible to swallow. Reports of a battle in which the French lost 18,000 men and the Spaniards 10,000.

November 5th

Rested here this day and took a sketch of the castle adjoining and most beautiful country. Likewise got rum to keep me up during tomorrow as we had orders to march then six leagues or thirty miles. The weather still continues wet and dreary, likewise somewhat cold.

November 6th

Halted this day at Alburquerque and took a sketch of the country and the adjoining castle which is situated on an amazing high rock surrounded by an almost endless valley the skirts of which are bordered by black distant mountains over which boars and wolves are constantly hunted as a friend of my *patrona* brought in one.

---

69. The officer referred to here is Ensign George Love who was lost at sea in 1829.

There was no rain this day. I tried to purchase some worsted stockings, but found nothing but *aguardiente* in the town. Was alarmed at night from a Spaniard coming into my room about some of the soldiers. Orders that the men were to keep in the ensuing day's march to Aliseda close to their battalions as most parts were a total wilderness and roads not to be found and that there would be halts made for them to answer the calls of nature.[70]

November 7th

Marched at six o'clock this morning seven leagues to Aliseda over a dreadful mountainous country covered with heath in most parts and other lavender and myrtle, although the _____ of the country did not make amends for the bad roads which were one sheet of rock: in most parts up to our knees in yellow water resembling *terra firma* for about two leagues. We had not marched an hour from the latter town when in poured a deluge of rain and thunder: we were all wet as if walking through rivers. I supped constantly of rum but the cold and the chill still persisted. We reached Aliseda about six in the evening where, without dinner or anything else, I turned into a tolerable bed after having been dripping the whole of the day. Myself and Calvert slept together; in the morning we were beastly dirty and not a clean thing or even coat to change.[71] My shoes, too, in a bad state.

November 8th

Marched from Aliseda at six this morning four leagues to Brosas. Alas! As usual raining deluges of water and wet to the skin, not a change of anything, and my rum all given to my servant the previous night. Our march was mostly over deserted and dreary mountains having before us a most delightful extent of country which before I never saw equalled. Reached Brosas at two o'clock and dried myself by a few embers at the house of Antonio Roma, a monk. I had to thank God for the blessings of health, a thing which many of my brother officers were destitute of. Our landlord (the _____) told us there had been a great battle between the French and the Spaniards and that the event [i.e. result] was not known (this does not appear possible) and that couriers were arriving every day to quicken our marches.[72]

---

70. The entry for 6 November is somewhat problematic as it appears simply to repeat that for the previous day. Why this should be the case is unclear.
71. Paget's bedfellow at Aliseda was Lieutenant Felix Calvert, an officer of the Fifty-Second who in 1811 secured a captaincy in the Ninety-Eighth Foot as well as appointment as Sir Thomas Graham's principal *aide de camp*.
72. The battle referred to here was probably an action that took place at Zornoza (today Amorebieta) on 31 October in which troops led by Marshal Lefebvre drove back forces of the Spanish Army of the Left that had been garrisoning Bilbao.

Expected to halt three days at Alcántara and to see the Twentieth Regiment. The regiment now marched half one way and half another. Yesterday two companies were lost by their guide and fell in with the other eight again during the hard rain. Much thunder this night and rain.

November 9th

Marched from Brosas to Alcántara nine leagues, which is a tolerable town, very well fortified; the back part is surrounded by mountains, and [it] has some convents in it. Much rain on the march and wet through again as we all waded a river up to our knees and more, the branch of the Tagus. I had nothing to change [into] and, all dirty, dried myself by the fire and got a tolerable billet at the house of Antonio Cavaleria. The people were very civil and the townsmen glad to see us.[73] Instead of staying here three days, stayed one, and another long march to have without a single halting day till our arrival at Salamanca. Also heard here of a battle being fought: event not known, but [we were told] of the Spaniards having 300,000 men and the French 50,000 only, but the former mostly rabble. The country was this day also covered with lavender. Had no breakfast till nine o'clock, and then got some chocolate. After having got a few things to rights and intending the next day [to do what?], I went, thank God, to a good bed, not without wishing myself in that incomparable country, old England.

November 10th

I intended to walk and sketch the Tagus which runs through this place (Alcántara), but from the bad state of my clothes was obliged to get a tailor to mend them and

---

73. Robert Porter, alas, was far less complimentary: 'The governor proved a beast – a vulgar, uncivil animal with little power to serve us and less inclination. He was asleep when we called on him. Indeed, all seemed asleep to the feelings we brought along with us. They received us . . . with an inhospitality they durst not have ventured had they not believed us to be friends. We were wretchedly quartered and the governor's excuse was that he had no authority to force the people to receive us into more respectable houses. The interior of the city [i.e. Alcántara] is nasty, filled with crumbling walls and churches in a desolate state. Dirt reigns here with equal sway as in Portugal. And my expectations of receiving a comforter under these ills from the civility of the people and their blazing enthusiasm evaporating in the general coldness of the place, I could only ruminate within myself on the romantic fables we had heard . . . If these indolent, arrogant Alcantarans be specimens of the army we are to join, I cannot augur a very brilliant campaign.' Porter, *Letters from Portugal and Spain*, pp. 100–5. Porter was not alone in his criticism of the reception given to the British forces in Alcántara. According to one story that later went the rounds, 'a soldier of the Twentieth was poignarded . . . for no other offence, it is alleged, than looking earnestly at a Don'. Ormsby, *Operations of the British Army*, II, p. 6.

my cap. Some row last night with our men and the Spaniards. Alcántara is an excessive old place, strongly fortified, and a fine bridge near it, also an excessive high hill at the back. Orders to march tomorrow. Was bit in the most striking manner by the mosquitoes and my face covered with bad pimples. Was reduced to the necessity of leaving some of my luggage behind not being able to carry it, viz. a smart little box.

November 11th

Marched at six o'clock this morning to Zarza Mayor three leagues. The bridge of Alcántara is excessively beautiful and would have made a fine drawing, but, being obliged to buy worsted stockings, gloves and neck cloth hindered me from taking it. The road is here excessively rocky and hilly, covered mostly the commons with lavender and myrtle. You have on this country a vast extent of country to view before you, mountains peeping above the horizon and tipping their heads on clouds; indeed, every day seems to _____ the beauties of nature. The Spaniards begin to get more kind every day. Arrived at half-past eleven at Zarza Mayor and got tolerable billets. I took a sketch of it and the adjoining country. Found my feet began to blister much. Saw several men who wore badges for thrashing us at Ferrol, also several Spaniards who spoke about the shameful capitulation [i.e. the convention of Sintra]. My landlord's name is Antonio Gazabo; indeed, here all are Antonios.

November 12th

Marched at six o'clock through a deserted country covered with corks and olives; we saw several eagles on the way. Crossed the [Gata] and waded up to our knees. At twelve arrived at Moraleja four leagues from our last place. The country this march is beautiful (I mean the distance as our way was all desert). Got a tolerable good billet at the house of Luando de Torre: there is a pretty girl with fine hair. Given me by a Spanish officer a gazette of 8th November: no news. Lost myself this night and was conducted home by a monk. Rose to march at seven. Moraleja is a pretty little *villa*: the [Gata] runs through it and there is fishing and a good bridge.

November 13th

Marched at seven this day. Roads at the beginning tolerably fair, and country flattish – corks, olives and orange trees. The latter end the roads craggy and mountainous. Arrived at nine o'clock at Perales two leagues from the last. It is a dirty, beastly hole, very small, though a good market of chestnuts, turnips, potatoes and such like. The Spaniards as well as the Portuguese live chiefly on vegetables. Orders for the right wing to march tomorrow, and the left to remain here. Saw Colonel Offeney who told me our next place was far worse than this and the roads dreadful.[74] Got some cheese here from my dame and wet through getting some soldiers a lodging: thirteen of them and the town excessive small and a very few decent pigsties and the people full as bad.

November 14th

Half the regiment marched this morning and the other half remained behind. It rained much in the morning. We marched at six: the road consists of mountains and woods, the beginning for a league tolerably fair, the remaining three entirely cliff and rock so that no artillery or cavalry could pass. The sight was beautiful and for two or three leagues we saw the clouds floating under our feet in the most extensive and beautiful valleys. We passed two large woods entirely of oak and waded a river which I believe is the Tagus, not being able to get information. At twelve arrived at Peñaparda, a very filthy, brutal hole. Quartered on a peasant and he and self slept in the same room (call it pigsty, 'tis more applicable). Heard of the murder of the *corregidor* of Ciudad Rodrigo for being in favour of the French, supposed, at least, to be so.[75] Much rain all this day. The Spaniards are now tolerably kind to us though for my part I do not see their generosity. The more I see of them, the more I adore and praise that country, England, which no other in the world has equalled.

November 15th

Marched at seven o'clock this morning to [Fuente]guinaldo. The road is tolerably good running through a forest the whole way: it consists entirely of oaks and extends an immense way on both sides. We waded a river up to our loins and now found ourselves in the province of Old Castile which is reckoned the most rich part of Spain.[76] Got a good billet here which Colonel Ross of the Twentieth had quitted on the 13th. Reported our being nine days behind the rest of the army through a mistake of General Hope's. [Fuente]guinaldo is a very decent little place. It stands on a hill, has a good church and commands a view of the most never ending forest. Heard of Sir J. Moore having been at Ciudad Rodrigo. Orders to halt here tomorrow for refitting.[77]

---

74. Paget gets the rank wrong here, the individual referred to being Lieutenant Colonel Wilhelm Offeney, an officer in the Second Light Battalion of the King's German Legion who was serving on Moore's staff as Assistant Quarter Master General.
75. Although this passage reads as if the murder of the *corregidor* (i.e. chief magistrate) of Ciudad Rodrigo had just occurred, it had actually taken place at the very onset of the Spanish uprising in the last week of May 1808.
76. Fuenteguinaldo is in León rather than Old Castile.
77. In the period 1811–12 Fuenteguinaldo was on three occasions to figure as Wellington's headquarters.

November 16th

Got the tailor to make me a pair of trousers and a cover of oil-skin for my cap. Intended to get my jacket turned up but had not time. Went out shooting with a Spanish peasant: saw some birds but could not get near them [and] was chased by a great dog home. Had a running match in the evening on the beautiful green on the right of the village where there is a chapel surrounded on all sides by crosses. Orders to march tomorrow.

November 17th

Marched at seven o'clock to Ciudad Rodrigo, the capital city of Old Castile, four leagues excellent road from Fuenteguinaldo.[78] At twelve arrived at Ciudad Rodrigo and found the Twentieth Regiment there who had orders to march the next day. Looked out for Champion [?], but did not find him. Hear of the French army being reinforced by 60,000 men and their being at Burgos. Ciudad Rodrigo is a large town situated on the banks of a very pretty river over which there is a good bridge. It has a very neat fortification and plenty of tolerable shops: in fact I admire [it] more [than] anything I have yet seen.[79] Had a deal of trouble getting my billets, six out of which [I] was disappointed [in].[80] Foster of our company died in the convent

---

78. The diarist is under a misapprehension here: as already remarked, Ciudad Rodrigo is not in Old Castile, but rather León, while the capital of that province is, logically enough, the city of the same name.

79. Paget was not the only officer who was impressed by Ciudad Rodrigo. Let us here quote Adam Neale: 'After passing several small villages, we reached the brow of a gently rising hill, whence we had a view of a fine fertile plain bounded by a range of lofty mountains in part covered with snow. At the further extremity of the plain rose the white towers of Ciudad Rodrigo. To which we approached by a very handsome bridge of ten arches thrown over the River Agueda on whose banks the town is proudly situated on a sandstone rock. Overlooking the bridge is a large square tower with battlements and loopholes connected with a lofty stone wall round which the road winds for a short distance and then enters the town by a strong turreted gate. The streets are remarkably clean, which strikes one the more forcibly from the filthy state of those in Portugal . . . There are two handsome squares, one of which is close to the cathedral and surrounded by several good-looking houses belonging to the clergy; the other, still larger, contains a market house and several shops adjoining . . . The masonry of the houses is very good. They are all composed of a fine, rich ochre-coloured free stone which looks very well. The cathedral is a handsome building, at least the exterior, for I have not been able to procure admission into it.' Neale, *Letters from Portugal and Spain*, pp. 205–8.

80. The reference to difficulty getting billets appears to reflect much more unfavourable comments that appear in other sources. For example: 'D. had rode on before me, but had not been enabled to procure our billets in the same house as had always been

here where the men were billeted. Hear Sir J.M. [i.e. John Moore] has just left this.[81]

November 18th

Halted this day at Ciudad Rodrigo. The tailors all employed and could not get them. Foster buried at three o'clock. Got a knife, cockade and some lead for bullets, also a basin of goat's milk for breakfast. A little rain this day. Some of the Ninety-Fifth Rifles arrived this day, a very fine set of men. Orders to march tomorrow and to perform our march to Salamanca in three days instead of four as was intended: from this something appears odd. Intended to sketch this town, but the weather and my duty prevented me as it always does in a soldier's life. My billet at last a damned bad one, stinking shockingly and my hostess weeping all day because her *patrona* [*sic*: this should read *patrón*, i.e. the man of the house] was gone to Salamanca to move food for the troops.[82]

---

the case in Portugal. He complained much of the incivility of his landlord, an old, overgrown priest, who on his arrival immediately retired, and ordered his housekeeper to show the Englishman upstairs to a dreary attic room in which there was a miserable *bracero* . . . What annoys me most is the *sang froid* and stupid wonder with which these people seem to regard us in passing along their streets. I can hardly help thinking that I read in their physiognomy sentiments that do not exactly correspond with what we were inclined to expect from them. By the way, I must not omit to inform you that something like a commotion has almost taken place in this town in consequence of our soldiers having requested a little salt from the people on which they were billeted. I dare say you will have some difficulty in giving credit to this fact which is, however a real one.' *Ibid.*, pp. 206–13 *passim*. Still more damning was Captain John Patterson of the Fiftieth Regiment of Foot: 'We now passed the frontier of Portugal into Spain, and halted for the night at Ciudad Rodrigo. On approaching the city, we were horrified by the sight of lofty gibbets, four of which were planted on the entrances, having appended to each the quarters of some unfortunate malefactor whose limbs were blackening in the sun. These sickening emblems of their cruelty impressed us with no very good opinion of the people with whom we were about to hold friendly intercourse, and their conduct on this night was quite in character with their gibbets. A more atrocious set of men we never had the honour of being acquainted with, and so much did they appear in favour of our enemies that we were convinced they would gladly have delivered us into their hands if it had been in their power to do so. An officer of the Seventy-Ninth unfortunately got involved in a dispute, and, while passing through one of their dark and narrow streets, was barbarously assassinated by an unknown hand.' Patterson, *Adventures of Captain John Patterson*, p. 73.

81. Foster appears to have been a member of the rank and file: certainly, the Fifty-Second had no officers of this name.

82. We see a glimpse here of the impact of war on the civilian population: many thousands of Spanish women found themselves separated from their husbands and in

November 19ᵗʰ

Was on the baggage guard this day and was obliged to wait an hour behind the regiment for the hospital cars. At last started though with bad bullocks. The road at first is good, but for a league upwards afterwards 'tis very bad, and from the incessant rain the whole of the day 'twas the greatest hardship to keep up and together, but, wandering on a march of thirty miles this day to a place called San Múñoz with a mist before our eyes, not able to see a bit and having no guide, was puzzled to death to find the road. Towards three or four o'clock endeavoured to find bullocks at a village we passed though, but none [were] to be met with. I therefore got Mr Maling [?] to go forward. I was in a dreadful pickle here, having given away all my rum to keep the wet from a soldier's wife. I had, however, the good fortune to get a little ham and bread here for a *pisette*: though half done, 'twas good. General Paget passed the cars at this village, the entrance of which was a perfect bowling green. We started in half an hour with bullocks procured by Dr [*sic*] Maling, but [as it was] growing dark and seven o'clock at night, [we] could not find our road and acted entirely by chance and the tracks of the commissaries' cars. We saw a light and believed it to be the wished for town, but on approaching it found it to be peasants amusing themselves. I was in the rear now, my corporal acting guide, when I hear a dreadful crash which was a car tumbled down a precipice with a woman and sick man on it, neither of them, thank God, badly hurt. I was here put to the greatest task to put it to rights, all with me except two rank and file being sick and ill, in an unknown road, no guide, raining and chilly cold, surrounded on all sides by an almost endless wood of corks. At last through much exertion got it upright, but shortly our bullocks knocked up and here again a pretty test, but, encouraged by a light in the wood and shooing the bullocks on, [we] supposed we had reached the long-sought-for town. But, travelling a league, we found it to be nothing but men burning charcoal to ash, and here again I determined to persevere and see the town if possible. About half a league further on [we] beheld another light, and, thank God, this proved to be the asylum of my regiment. I now carried

---

consequence left in a situation that was extremely vulnerable, if not wholly destitute. Meanwhile, Ormsby has some interesting comments on the garrison, a force known as the Voluntarios de Ciudad Rodrigo which had enlisted in exchange for a promise that it would never have to serve beyond the walls. Thus: 'There is a great deal of bustle here among the native troops or rather the recruits of the insurrection. They are not numerous, nor of a very encouraging disposition: the sons of some, and the grandsons of more, ought to supply their places, not that I would speak irreverently of the patriotism of old age, inefficient though it may be, for the example cannot fail to stimulate and rouse the younger into action.' Ormsby, *Operations of the British Army*, II, p. 7.

all the ophthalmic men and lame on the cars and, just going into the town, found before our feet a river to cross and no bridge. Here again a wading match and after this another. However, at ten o'clock arrived, thank heavens, safe and sound. After marching from six in the morning, I was, God knows, fatigued _____ _____ and in bad billet after eating a dish of steaks [?] and onions slept most soundly.[83]

November 20th

Woke at six and roused with my bones full of pains and aches. Marched over a charming country and good roads to Don Diego, four or five leagues, and got a most miserable hole indeed; however, slept well in it after drinking plenty of milk and carrying the colour.[84]

November 21st

Marched at seven this day over the most extraordinary country I have seen yet, perfectly flat and cultivated, roads excellent indeed, and day lovely. A vast deal of cultivation indeed in this part. We were to reach Old Salamanca this day, and about twelve o'clock had a view of that most renowned and famous city so extolled in the books of G. Blas and Don Quixote.[85] It appeared about a league off, something like

---

83. The road travelled over by the author and his convoy was one that was fated to be the scene of much suffering on the part of Wellington's army. Thus, exactly four years later, it was to witness the culmination of the terrible retreat from Burgos: according to some of those who took part in both operations, the suffering that the army endured between Salamanca and Ciudad Rodrigo surpassed anything which had been experienced on the road to Corunna.

84. As each battalion would have had two colours and a minimum of ten ensigns, Paget would not have had to carry a colour more than once every five days. Meanwhile, it was about this time that the first news began to reach the troops of the fighting that had now been raging for almost a month between the French and the Spaniards though it was still far from clear what was going on. Charles Kinloch, for example, was still with the 2/52nd: 'There is a report today of a courier having arrived late last night from the Spanish army with accounts of their having gained a complete victory, but there is no relying on the truth of anything that is said here there are so many contrary accounts. Indeed, it is ridiculous in me attempting to give any except what one actually sees: the first correct account we get is generally from the English gazette.' *Cit.* Glover (ed.), *'Hellish Business'*, p. 30.

85. 'G. Blas' is a reference to *Gil Blas*, a picaresque novel by the French writer Alain Lesage and set in sixteenth-century Spain, which was well known in Britain, and provided many officers who fought in the armies of Sir John Moore and the Duke of Wellington with their first introduction to Spanish society, albeit one that was highly stereotypical. So rooted were images generated by Lesage's romance and others like it that the belief took hold that Spaniards continued to dress in the costume of the sixteenth century: hence the insistence of cartoonists on portraying Spaniards in this

Canterbury only much finer; poorer when I entered it. We billeted the men in a convent where they got good beds and rugs. Sir J.M. was here, we found, and our second battalion, the Twenty-Eighth, [the] Queen's and, in fact, most of General Beresford's division and General Paget's. Breakfasted with the second [i.e. General Paget] who I was very glad to see.[86] They all had good billets. Salamanca I like as it very much is a pretty, clean and large town. There is an opera and coffee houses, a very famous and gaudy college which holds about thirteen of our Irishmen who came here to study. There are also a vast number of convents, good houses and buildings, the people mad for their cause and glad to see us as I firmly believe.[87]

---

fashion, not to mention the astonishment voiced by a number of officers when they discovered that, in fact, in the towns and cities the inhabitants dressed in much the same fashion as people anywhere else.

86. Again, note the inference that Charles Paget was in some way connected to Henry and Edward Paget, and impression that is strengthened by his evident friendship with Forbes Champagné (see below).

87. This is not the impression conveyed by other memoirs and journals. Here, for example, is the German commissary, Auguste Schaumann: 'The Spaniards rely entirely upon us, and, after leading us into a most dreadful mess through their deceitful and mendacious promises, they run away and say, "Now try to get out of it as best you can!" This is the general feeling, and it is shared even by cultivated and enlightened Spaniards. The people . . . have the effrontery to look upon the English troops as exotic animals who have come . . . to engage in a private fight with the French, and now that they are here all the fine Spanish gentlemen have to do is to look on with their hands in their pockets. They do not regard us in the least as allies . . . they simply regard us as heretics . . . Poor General Moore is . . . in a parlous plight, and the more one sees of the Spaniards, the more discouraged one gets. Everything that has been so blatantly trumpeted in the papers about their enthusiasm, their great armies and the stampede to join them is simply lies. It often looks as if Spain [is] not even willing to defend herself. In all the hamlets, villages and towns, the inhabitants . . . lounge about in their hundreds, completely apathetic, indifferent and gloomy, and sunk in their idleness. Is this the daring, patriotic and impetuous race about which the press have raved so bombastically?' Ludovici, *On the Road with Wellington*, pp. 79–80. Someone who was equally scandalised, meanwhile, was the surgeon, Adam Neale: 'I have hitherto been . . . amongst the most sanguine in the Spanish cause, but since my arrival here I have witnessed so much apparent apathy and indifference that . . . I cannot help at times asking myself if I am in the midst of Spain. The beings I see muffled up in long cloaks, sauntering . . . in listless indifference under the piazzas, are so very different from that bold impassioned race which my heated imagination has been contemplating that I wish rather to believe myself in the midst of a Spanish city in Paraguay or Peru . . . We have all mounted the patriotic cockade which is composed of red cloth which is composed of red cloth stamped with the initials of "Viva Fernando Septimo" ... Every Spaniard, down to the poorest muleteer, bears this badge, and indeed this seems nearly to be the extent of their patriotism in Salamanca at least as far as we have been able to

There is an amazing good square in Salamanca of excellent houses similar to
Lisbon, though, for my part, [from] what of I have it seen, I like it much better and
think it far superior on every point.[88] It is at present full of troops. Divers reports
of the enemy: some say they are at Valladolid and others retreating to Burgos, and
some (which is most credible) [have] Blake firmly licked and routed.[89] Sir D. Baird
is daily expected with the artillery: they are to halt one day at Madrid.[90]

---

discover. In other respects you would imagine the country was in a state of profound
peace: no energy, no bustle, no alacrity, "everything flat, stale and unprofitable".',
Neale, *Letters from Portugal and Spain*, pp. 219–23. In fairness, however, it should be
noted that Patterson was far more complimentary about the inhabitants of Salamanca
than he had been about the inhabitants of Ciudad Rodrigo. Thus: 'The officers of our
regiments were no less highly gratified than we were by the affability and kindness of
the people, who exerted themselves to make our residence among them as happy as we
could possibly desire.' Patterson, *Adventures of Captain John Patterson*, p. 73.

88. In general, Salamanca was much admired. Though Neale described it as 'an intricate
maze of dirty narrow streets', he also admitted that the city's 'lofty bell-towers and
cupolas … grand gothic cathedral … and beautiful bridge beneath which glides the
waving Tormes form a landscape of the first order.' Neale, *Letters from Portugal and
Spain*, pp. 224–5. In the words of James Ormsby, meanwhile, 'The different colleges
are noble and spacious buildings, and, bringing to the recollection our Oxford and
Cambridge, a comparison naturally ensues. For splendour of edifice, the preference
must be given to Salamanca, for … there is not a single building here which does not
warrant admiration, not one which is inelegant or obscure.' Ormsby, *Operations of the
British Army*, II, p. 27. Sadly, a great many of the university buildings were levelled by
the French so as to provide clear fields of fire for the network of forts which they built
on the south-west edge of the city after they took possession of it in December 1808

89. 'Blake' is a reference to the commander of the Spanish Army of the Left, Joaquín Blake
y Joyes. One of a considerable number of Spanish officers descended from the so-called
'Wild Geese' of the late seventeenth and early eighteenth centuries, he had in fact been
heavily defeated at Espinosa de los Monteros in a two-day battle on 10–11 November. As
we shall see again, Paget is extremely restrained in his remarks on this development. To
take just one example, Porter was exceedingly worried: 'Little hope can now be entertained
of forming the intended junction with Sir David Baird. Under the circumstances we are
in, we cannot advance against the enemy until General Hope arrives with the infantry
and cavalry. The country in our front is one continued plain extending nearly to Burgos
so that should the French come up with us here in any force, we must . . . fall back on the
strongholds of Portugal. But in such a case what will become of our right column? I do not
like to think of it.' Porter, *Letters from Portugal and Spain*, p. 144. Meanwhile, still more
unsettling, were growing rumours of treason in the Spanish camp. To quote Ormsby, 'We
were . . . informed by an Irish student of Salamanca who is employed in the commissariat
that . . . Burgos was in the hands of 20,000 French, and that the governor, the bishop and
three generals were discovered to be in the interest of the enemy and . . . sent to Madrid
in irons.' Ormsby, *Operations of the British Army*, II, pp. 154–6.

90. Another slip: Paget means not Sir David Baird but Sir John Hope.

November 22ⁿᵈ

Spent this day chiefly in getting a map, shoes, etc., etc., and looking about the place. The large square affords a deal of commerce.[91] In it there are several good shops of jewellery and linen commerce, also some remarkable good houses. A proclamation made to save the milk for the British troops by the *corregidor*, and our regiment to be inspected by Sir J.M. on Thursday. Reports of our being the Reserve.

November 23ʳᵈ

Bought some pencils, knife, castanets, etc. Asked Champagné to dinner.[92] Ordered a sketch and journal book. Also gave my *patrona* cash to purchase me a vocabulary. Weather very fine. Report of General Blake having licked the enemy and divers other things. Saw Major Pack of the Forty-Third Regiment by the university which I intended this day to see, but many things hindered me.[93] A man of the Sixth Regiment [was] hung a few days back for theft.[94] Sergeant-Major Winterbottom [is] made Adjutant.

---

91. Neale provides an amusing picture of the scene in the square: 'The windows of my lodging command a view of this place [i.e. square] and, as I contemplate the busy scene of petty traffic, it gives me some idea of the habits and character of the inhabitants. I observe that the women of the lower classes are irascible to a degree. There is generally a pitched battle amongst them eight or ten times a day: their tongues are the grand weapons of attack, and, as far as I can judge from the excessive rapidity of their vituperation, the language they use is not much inferior to that of the fair inhabitants of Billingsgate.' Neale, *Letters from Portugal and Spain*, p. 226.
92. The officer referred to here is Lieutenant Forbes Champagné. An extremely well-connected young man – the son of another Forbes Champagné who had commanded the Twentieth Foot in 1795 and was currently Commander-in-Chief, India, he was also a first cousin of an uncle of Generals Henry and Edward Paget – Champagné was wounded at Roncesvalles on 25 July 1813, but survived the battle to be rewarded with a post on Wellington's staff. His mother being Henry and Edward Paget's sister, Jane, it is conceivable that he was Charles Paget's cousin.
93. Who the Major Pack referred to here was is unclear: there was no officer of this name serving in either the Forty-Third or any of the other infantry regiments present in Salamanca at this time.
94. This incident is mentioned by none other than Sir John Moore himself in a diary entry dated 14 November: 'On the 8th I reached Almeida where I found Brigadier-General Anstruther who had been sent to take possession of it with the Sixth Regiment [of Foot] . . . Their conduct has been bad and their officers have been shamefully negligent. I spoke to them with great severity and told them that I should not take them into Spain: their conduct was unworthy of it. One man had been sentenced to death by a general court martial and I ordered him to be executed.' J.F. Maurice (ed.), *The Diary of Sir John Moore* (London, 1904), II, p. 278. Drunkenness, in particular, was a serious issue in the army well before the unfortunate episodes

November 24ᵗʰ

_____ this morning at a quarter before eight. Weather very cold indeed.[95] Spent this day in writing letters to England and drawing. Two hundred carts of ammunition arrived today and several artillery [batteries]. No courier arrived yet.

November 25ᵗʰ

Wrote letters to England all this day from twelve to three. Drilled and marched in line before Major-General Paget. The Fiftieth Regiment arrived. Weather very cold.[96]

---

witnessed during the later retreat, Schaumann, for example, recording an incident at Villa Velha when a large part of the Thirty-Second Foot drank itself into insensibility when it chanced upon a large store of brandy. Ludovici, *On the Road with Wellington*, pp. 60–1.

95. The bitter weather was remarked on by many veterans of the campaign. Joseph Sinclair, for example, was currently heading toward Salamanca with the column of Sir John Hope: 'It was one of the severest nights of cold I ever endured in my life. At the time we wore long hair formed into a club at the back of our heads. Mine was frozen to the ground in the morning, and, when I attempted to rise, my limbs refused to support me for some time [while] I felt the most excruciating pains all over my body before the blood began to circulate.' Anon., *Journal of a Soldier of the Seventy-First*, p. 63. Meanwhile, the cold came as one more shock to an army that had been expecting something entirely different. To quote Porter, 'Not any of us being apprised that we should encounter such severity, I fear that all the officers are in a similar predicament to myself . . . I have not brought a single item of warm clothing with me . . . Indeed (ignoramuses that we were, not better to inform ourselves), we did not harbour a thought that, in a country so famous for glowing suns, we could ever experience such hyperborean blasts.' Porter, *Letters from Portugal and Spain*, p. 181.

96. Arriving in Salamanca, this day, Ormsby describes a number of events of which Paget says nothing whatsoever. Thus: 'The first information we obtained on our arrival was of an unpleasant nature, no less than the probability of an immediate retreat and everything was yesterday arranged for carrying it into effect. An alarm was spread on the previous night of the approach of the enemy, and [the army] being without ammunition, it was determined we should fall back upon our stores . . . This false alarm originated in one of our regiments coming in at a late and unexpected hour, and was strengthened by the green colour of their uniform, being a rifle corps and the first of that description seen by the Spaniards. But it is known that the French have pushed some strong patrols of cavalry in front of Burgos and they are even stated to have entered Valladolid. They cannot be in force, and the consternation of the people at the rumour of their advance is a proof of the defenceless state in which they are at present.' Ormsby, *Operations of the British Army*, II, pp. 17–19.

November 26th

Wrote to Mrs Young and Mrs Miller this day. Drilled in the morning. Dined with Captain King yesterday and today.[97] No news in particular.

November 27th

Orderly officer this day all night. Wrote to Colonels Robinson and Stapleton. Was asked to dine with Seward of the Ninth Regiment tomorrow.[98] Heard from a staff officer the enemy had 170,000 men and Napoleon was actually in Spain.[99] Saw a convent this day, the top of which was crammed with nuns looking through wooden blinds. Poor girls: they waved their handkerchiefs and hands to me. Long orders given out by Sir John Moore concerning the loss of the ammunition.[100]

November 28th

Dined with Seward this day and had an excellent dinner at the Colegio de Santa María Magdalena. Gave my coat to be turned.

---

97. It has not been possible to establish who this officer was.
98. 'Seward' was Ensign William Seward. Though wounded at Barrosa in March 1811, he survived the war and was still alive to claim his Military General Service Medal in 1847.
99. This remark is highly suggestive: Napoleon had actually crossed the frontier into Spain on 5 November.
100. The orders referred to here were essentially a lengthy condemnation of the practice engaged in by many soldiers of selling a few rounds of ammunition so as to procure money for drink. Thus: 'When the army began its march from Portugal, the regiments were complete in all their equipment, and every soldier was furnished with his full allowance of ammunition. From the general character of this army the commander of the forces felt confident that every soldier in it would take pains to keep all of his appointments in the best state for meeting the enemy and, above all, that his ammunition would be the first object of his care. The general is therefore disappointed to find that, besides the great deal of unserviceable ammunition which has been damaged by the rain, there is in many regiments a considerable deficiency in the number of cartridges. This the general has ordered to be made good, but, as these deficiencies can only have arisen from the men having sold their ammunition, or through a degree of negligence almost as culpable which can only take place in regiments which are ill-regulated and whose officers do not do their duty, the commander of the forces directs that, in addition to any measures which commanding officers may feel necessary to adopt to check a practice so disgraceful and injurious to the character of the regiment, each soldier shall pay, now and in future, three pence for every cartridge made away with.' General Order of Sir John Moore, 26 November 1808, *cit.* Ormsby, *Operations of the British Army*, II, pp. 244–5.

November 29th

Took a long walk in the country, which affords a large number of beautiful rides, and attempted to take a sketch of the town, but the fog prevented me. Went out to drill this morning before breakfast: my head ached abominably from drinking too much Málaga wine the previous night. Orders for the sick to march all to Almeida. The Ninety-First and Twenty-Eighth to form part of the Reserve with ourselves. Various reports concerning the enemy. Mail from England arrived and went: no letters for me. Asked to dine tomorrow with Champagné of the Twentieth Regiment. Took a long walk over Salamanca this evening: saw some beautiful and superb architecture and one of the cathedrals.[101]

November 30th

The Rifle Corps [i.e. the Ninety-Fifth Regiment] had orders to march at twelve this day, which they did. Heard of the enemy being at Toro and an officer the other day having fallen in with their outlying pickets. The Twentieth had orders to march tomorrow also at twelve o'clock. An express came from General Hope's army, contents to me unknown. Dined this day myself and Dick with the Twentieth Regiment; was made a present of a snuff-box.[102] Looked out to get some stockings changed, but could not find the house. Took a pleasant walk with Harcourt into the country. Various reports of the enemy being at Burgos, Toro, Pamplona and in fact all over the country: Toro lies north from this town twelve leagues.[103] Certain it is, however, we had orders this day to hold ourselves in readiness to turn out and not to be without sound of the brigade. An alarm last night at the magazine and [the] drums beat to arms: no mischief whatsoever.

---

101. Although they are constructed side by side and in effect form one building, Salamanca has two cathedrals, a Romanesque one dating from the twelfth century and a Gothic one commenced in 1532.

102. The Dick referred to here is a Lieutenant James Dick. A lieutenant in the Fifty-Second since July 1805, he transferred into the Commissariat the following month and reached England safely, only to leave the service altogether in August 1809 and die of natural causes a few months later.

103. As the author was writing these lines, a large column of French troops headed by Napoleon himself was forcing the Somosierra pass in the Sierra de Guadarrama. In Salamanca, meanwhile, there was little or no understanding of the situation. As James Ormsby wrote on 30 November, 'Some Spanish soldiers are to be seen arriving daily, but they are fugitives from Blake's defeated army, which from the accounts they give is completely routed and dispersed. The inhabitants are not dejected by this misfortune and are confident of ultimate success. Their reliance is placed upon Castaños who is said to have a force of 80,000 men.' Ormsby, *Operations of the British Army*, II, p. 36.

December 1ˢᵗ

Parade this morning at half-past six o'clock for punishment: two men flogged for making away with their necessaries.[104] Skirmished this morning and formed hollow squares against cavalry. The Twentieth Regiment marched so that we were now in the brigade left by ourselves. A change [has] taken place in the brigades and divisions. Report of a very decisive engagement having taken place between Sir D. Baird and the enemy in which Sir D. lost his left arm and took fifteen pieces of cannon, together with many killed and wounded.[105] Several deserters arrived from the Spanish army, also two French prisoners who told us that the Spaniards said that, as soon as we could eat [*sic*] all up that we could get, we should take to our shipping and be off. The Junta has, I heard, been petitioned by several noblemen to yield to the French yoke. Hear of Lord Holland having been in Spain and returned not well satisfied with the Spanish Patriots.[106] Settled my accounts with Butler and gave him a draft for £40 on Morland at ten days after sight. Found £12-10 shillings of my *bât* and forage money was coming to me. Got my short stockings changed. Walked a deal this day in the square. Got my razor ground and at last my coat to be turned. Resolved to get some cigars, etc.[107]

---

104. It is sometimes implied that flogging was completely abolished in the Fifty-Second and other light-infantry regiments: though resort to that punishment was certainly much reduced, as this entry shows the lash continued to be used in serious cases. One soldier of the Ninety-Fifth who was certainly flogged at Salamanca was a man named Robert Liston who was sentenced to 700 lashes by a general court martial for supposedly throwing a stone at his battalion commander. Hibbert (ed.), *Recollections of Rifleman Harris*, p. 67.

105. No such action had taken place: at this stage, indeed, the French were almost completely unaware of the presence of Moore's troops, let alone those of Baird.

106. The Lord Holland mentioned here is Henry Vassall-Fox, third Baron Holland. An ardent hispanophile who had visited Spain during the Peace of Amiens, Holland was a leading figure in Whig society and politics and served as Lord Privy Seal in the disastrous 'Ministry of All the Talents' of 1806–7. Much excited by the news of the Spanish uprising, which he believed to be an exemplar of a people rising in revolt to reclaim its historic liberties in the face of centuries of absolutism, he and his wife travelled to Spain in the autumn of 1808 and spent a few days in Corunna before travelling on to Seville (in the wake of the fall of Madrid to Napoleon on 4 December the provisional capital) via Oporto and Badajoz. Clearly, then, the author's report of his doings is more than somewhat garbled: Holland certainly did not return to England at this time, while, notwithstanding the growing evidence that the tale of the uprising against Napoleon had been much exaggerated, he never ceased to proclaim his belief that the Spanish people were the key to victory. For an interesting account of his party's many adventures, see Ilchester, *Spanish Journal of Elizabeth, Lady Holland*.

107. It was the Peninsular War that first popularised cigar smoking in Britain.

December 2nd

Did not march today as expected. Heard of the Spaniards having licked the French very much near Zaragoza, the report not quite confirmed; that with a very entertaining *señora*. General Hope is expected tomorrow for certain. Lent Old Dobbs ten dollars and Young Dobbs one dollar, the former for the mess and the latter for cigars.[108] Order to march is expected every day. Turned off my washing woman, Mrs Gurwood, and got Mother Sutcliffe. Tailor sent in his bill: a damned rascal. Weather much finer than usual and more mild.

December 3rd

Report this day of the Spaniards having been completely routed and beaten: they all seem much displeased though I hear several petitions have been sent in from the first families to yield to the common enemy.[109] I went with Dundas to see the cathedral which is a high and handsome building with a vast number of smaller

---

108. Here we see the two Dobbs' brothers united in a single sentence. 'Old Dobbs' was the captain, Joseph, and 'Young Dobbs', the ensign, John.
109. The battle referred to here is that of Tudela and had taken place on 23 November. In brief, commanded by the victor of Bailén, Francisco-Javier Castaños, the 26,000 men of the Spanish Army of the Centre were drawn up on a 10-mile front from Tarazona to Tudela blocking the road to Zaragoza. Far too weak to hold so extensive a position on their own, they were supposed to be reinforced by the garrison of Zaragoza, but the commander of this force, José Palafox, hated Castaños and did not release any troops to him till the last minute, the result being that when the French attacked they were able to break through almost immediately. Left alone by the French, most of whose attention was concentrated on the troops who had come from Zaragoza, the bulk of Castaños' men got away, but even so the Army of the Centre was unable to resume offensive operations until the middle of January 1809. As for Paget's reaction to the news, he was either remarkably phlegmatic or just as remarkably insouciant. Thus, other observers were in a state of consternation and rightly so. Here, for example, is Robert Porter: 'Did we live in the days of witchcraft, surely Napoleon would lose all his titles in that of sorcerer! It seems as if we are spell-bound and shut up by the magic seal of this Gallic Mahommed within the walls of Salamanca to do [nothing], but to wonder at our fate. Victorious in Portugal, waved on by enthusiasm herself to lock the outward gates of Spain against the flying enemy, where now are our triumphs, where the promised patriots in arms? All we expected to meet have made themselves air! The voice that summoned us is silent; the country is filled with a conquering foe; the Spanish armies are dispersed, and we find ourselves in a snare! Whithersoever we turn, rumour brandishes the scythe that is to mow down our withering laurels and perhaps our ranks into the bargain . . . A terrible report is in circulation that Castaños, who commands the only force of any strength, has been defeated! If this be true, our destiny must soon be decided, and, I fear, retreat will be inevitable.' Porter, *Letters from Portugal and Spain*, pp. 162–3.

steeples, somewhat resembling Westminster Abbey.[110] The outside is famed for the amazing [and] beautiful architecture which, cut in the most minute manner, [represents] Our Saviour's birth and the Wise Men, the flight into Egypt and other familiar things. The inside is also excessively beautiful, having amazing high pillars of stone and beautiful painted glass. The _____ are made chiefly of different saints carved in marble and relics of saints. There is an excessive handsome room on the right side of nearly twenty large looking glasses and an immense table of marble in the centre. Out of this there is a small closet which has in it Our Saviour on the cross carved in the most elegant and tasteful manner. There are also in it several glass cases filled with the relics of saints, Saint John and various others. I also saw yesterday a beautiful library of various books in the convent on the right of the nunnery which also I visited the day before. Got my coat turned, etc. Gave John Jack two dollars for shoes and mending. Mr Brawdy dined with us who had been to Madrid through Segovia and the Kingdom of Murcia. He gave a very flattering account of the people in Madrid: they were all boasting of the number of Frenchmen they had killed, and the theatres represented the siege of Saragossa with the various stratagems they practised [for] destroying the French in that place. They [i.e. Mr Brawdy and his companions] were nearly attacked on their march several times, and lay one night out in a thick wood to avoid the enemy's cavalry, formed at the same time in a hollow square, the baggage, etc., being placed at the centre.[111] A courier arrived which brought certain information of the defeat of the Spanish army. The Ninth, Second Battalion/Fifty-Second Regiment and the Forty-Third had orders to march tomorrow to Ledesma, a town to the north-west of Salamanca. Bought some cigars and saw Major Hull of the Forty-Third.[112]

December 4th

Walked out with Lieutenant James Hay to see a brigade of artillery arrive.[113] Sir John Moore also rode out of the town to see General Hope. Intended to have

---

110. Paget's companion was the Ensign Thomas Dundas previously encountered in Lisbon.

111. Who this Mr Brawdy was is unclear, though he was certainly not one of the liaison officers that had been dispatched to Spain by the British government following the outbreak of the Peninsular War. Whoever he was, though, he was clearly something of a fantasist.

112. This officer was Edward Hull; on 8 September 1808 he had in fact been promoted to the rank of lieutenant colonel, but either Paget was unaware of this fact or he forgot the change when he came to write up his diary.

113. The James Hay mentioned here is not to be confused with the Lord James Hay who was killed at Waterloo, not to mention several other officers of the same name. A lieutenant in the Fifty-Second Foot since August 1807, he eventually transferred into

finished my sketch of Salamanca in my new book, but had not time sufficient to finish more than the bridge, which has hung over the gate [?] the head of a traitor. Various reports concerning the Spaniards and of our facilitating a retreat. Appearances give such a report very good credit at this time.

December 5th

Slept at the convent last night on picket, myself, _____ and Ferguson; came off this evening.[114] Went out in the morning for a field day: marched about two leagues and advanced in line nearly two miles and got to Salamanca about two o'clock where I made a second breakfast. Our second battalion advanced to Ledesma this day at five o'clock. Reports of the Spaniards having been more thrashed; some general arrived to consult Sir J. on the subject. The Sixtieth countermanded marching.

December 6th

A courier arrived this day which brought the intelligence of the French having entered Madrid on the 1st of December at the gate of Saint Barbara and that the Spaniards blew up a mine which put to death 12,000 men and finally ended in their defeat, and added that the people from their balconies flung down iron gratings which fouled the feet of the cavalry and thereby threw their riders. Indeed, the enemy were repulsed with great slaughter, but Joseph Bonaparte assured his army that he would be crowned king the 24th of the month at the same time. But the inhabitants of Madrid assert they would sooner be buried in the ruins.[115] The Twentieth and Ninety-Fifth Regiments arrived and we hear that the retreat of the artillery is countermanded and that a courier has been sent to Sir D. Baird to countermand his ordered retreat. Some say we shall march to Madrid immediately and [there are] various opinions on the subject. The inhabitants here did not seem much pleased about it; indeed, this province is remarked to send less men for soldiers than any other, so much so that a proclamation was this day stuck up concerning it. I see daily at least a thousand idle fellows, young men doing nothing.[116] Mustered this

---

the First Regiment of Footguards and served as an *aide de camp* to several generals including Sir John Sherbooke and Sir Stapleton Cotton.

114. The Ferguson referred to is a Lieutenant Dugald Ferguson; having transferred to the Ninety-Fifth in 1809, he died of sickness at Salamanca in 1812.

115. The intelligence reported here was completely fictitious: although Napoleon arrived before Madrid on 1 December, it was not attacked until 3 December, and then made only the most trifling of resistance. As Porter wryly noted, 'The most absurd reports are in circulation which bewilder the brains of the inhabitants and sometimes are very likely to mislead us.' Porter, *Letters from Portugal and Spain*, p. 147.

116. This assertion is repeated by other observers. Thus: 'To judge from the inertness of the people here, it might be inferred that they were in a state of profound tranquillity

evening at three o'clock as the paymaster had arrived. Bought some cigars this day and also some cloth for gaiters; also paid my tailor, washerwoman and shoemaker. A mail from England arrived and papers up the 15th *ultimo*. The retreat the army was about to perform is now put a stop to by this circumstance.[117]

December 7th

Took a sketch this day of the cathedral and Salamanca which I was ill able to equal. Punishment this morning at half-past seven. Heard for certain we are now going to advance: there was a meeting of general officers this day, viz. a council of war, and it is believed they determined on the advancement of the army. Two or more

---

and at peace with all the world. They lounge, or rather strut, around the square from morning till night . . . and content themselves with talking of Napoleon . . . when they ought to be rushing to the field for his destruction . . . Not one military movement on their part is here discernible, [though] the town could contribute to the common cause 10,000 troops with very slight exertion.' Ormsby, *Operations of the British Army*, II, pp. 35–6. Finding this situation hard to conciliate with the stories of patriotism that had dominated the news from Spain ever since the outbreak of the uprising against Napoleon, the same author took refuge in a combination of Spanish national character and the want of organisation and firm leadership in the insurgent camp: 'I do not mean to insinuate that the inactivity which pervades the people here proceeds from an indifference to the cause of freedom, being satisfied that they are enthusiastic and sincere in their abhorrence of the French. This quiescent apathy is rather the result of their national characteristic, pride; of their contempt for the enemy; of their confidence in their own armies; and, above all . . . the want of an established government to give a direction to their spirit and an impulse to their energy.' *Ibid.*, p. 37. As explained elsewhere, such factors were, perhaps, a part of the story, but they certainly cannot be regarded as sufficient explanation.

117. This last remark reads oddly. The author seems to imply that the mail from England carried orders forbidding Moore to withdraw to Portugal, but, if such was his belief, he was sorely mistaken: rather, as we have seen, Moore cancelled the retreat because he was under the impression that Madrid was attempting to defend itself. Meanwhile, widely reported, the apparent apathy of the populace after everything they had heard prior to coming to Spain was something which bewildered Moore's troops and left them struggling to find an explanation. 'The Spanish people', wrote Private Anthony Hamilton of the Forty-Third Regiment of Foot, 'though still influenced by fierce and unmitigated hatred of their invaders, were no longer animated by that uncalculating and convulsive energy which in the commencement of the struggle had goaded them like madness into furious resistance. The fierceness of the paroxysm had passed, and, though in the cause of their country every Spanish hand was prepared to grip the sword, the blows it dealt were directed by an erring aim and a feeble arm. Their detestation of a foreign yoke was undiminished, but it had become a fixed and inert sentiment rather than a fierce, uncontrollable and all-prevailing impulse.' Hamilton, *Hamilton's Campaign with Moore and Wellington*, p. 22.

couriers arrived from the Spanish army: various reports in circulation. Napoleon undoubtedly is in Spain. The Ninety-Fifth arrived.

December 8ᵗʰ

Had a field day and came home about eleven o'clock. Nothing particular happened except various reports concerning the enemy. Went to the cathedral with Love, and afterwards to my lodgings: expected to march shortly.

December 9ᵗʰ

Orders to march tomorrow in the morning at length arrived after staying at Salamanca three weeks, but towards evening the order was countermanded and we were not to march till the day after with the Twentieth, Ninety-Fifth and Ninety-First Regiments [it is] supposed towards Toro where report says there are 6,000 French. Had a field day under General Paget. Saw Sir John who looked very well and in good spirits. Took brandy into our mess. Orders given out for a mail to England to be closed tomorrow: wrote to William this night. Bought a bottle of rum [and] some worsted gloves, and sent my manservant out to look for a Toledo blade having broken my own. Weather excessively cold indeed. Report of the Junta having written to Sir John to say he [should] either advance or quit the kingdom; heard they had returned to Badajoz: no good sign. Also heard of Lord Holland having returned to England describing the Patriots.[118]

December 10ᵗʰ

Rested at Salamanca and got some little necessaries, a blanket mat, etc.

December 11ᵗʰ

Marched at last to Villa del Rey [actually Villares de la Reina] where I got a tolerable billet alone: six leagues this day. Heard of an action with the Fifteenth [Light] Dragoons in which there were twenty-five French and fifteen English: fifteen of the former were taken and five killed and the rest escaped by the swiftness of their horses.[119]

December 12ᵗʰ

Arrived at Toro.

---

118. See footnote 181. Paget is again quite wrong here. At this moment Holland was en route for Seville where he remained until July 1809. At the same time, the last sentence seems to be either incomplete or miswritten: in the context, though utterly mistaken, 'decrying the Patriots' would make more sense.

119. Probably written up at a later date, this entry is erroneous: the clash with the French cavalry took place on 12 December.

Part 2: 10 December 1808–17 January 1809[120]

December 10th

Halted at Salamanca.

December 11th

Stopped at Salamanca and got some things washed.[121]

December 12th

Marched to Fuentesauco, five leagues. An action took place between some of our dragoons who behaved in a most glorious fashion, the Tenth, I believe.[122]

---

120. Entitled 'Journal from Salamanca', the second part of the journal is, as already noted, much less accessible than the first, and, as witness the very brief nature of many of the entries, was clearly written in haste and, at least in some instances, in arrears: in its very form, then, it bears the scars of a campaign notorious for the misery, fatigue and suffering which it involved. What is less easy to explain, however, is the duplication of the entries for 10, 11 and 12 December, and, still more so, the discrepancies between them.

121. This statement is incorrect. As various other accounts make clear (and the author himself claims in his first version of events), General Paget's brigade marched from Salamanca on 11 December rather than the next day.

122. Paget remains characteristically reticent on the subject of the advance of Moore's army deeper into Spain. However, in the circumstances, it could not but give rise to much discussion among officers and men alike. As Porter wrote, for example, 'We are not to retreat, but to advance, an order we should gladly have obeyed weeks ago, but better late than never, and, as so great a change from the obvious movement, has taken place, the general sentiment is that some advantage not dreamt of by those out of the secret is now perceived by the dictators of this onward march . . . Such is the conversation with us, but in my own private opinion I cannot perceive whence any advantage is now to arise. I know there are none to spring from Spain as it lies beaten and humiliated, and to expect that the enemy will give us any is a fancy more wild than Don Quijote's encounter with the windmills . . . I therefore bask not my military ardour in such extravagant imaginations, but in sober probability suppose that our brave commander-in-chief has received urgent wishes from home that he would not retreat.' Porter, *Letters from Portugal and Spain*, pp. 193–4. As for the idea that the capital might somehow stage a second Zaragoza, the same author was openly scornful: 'After the advantages gained by the French troops over the army of Castaños and Palafox . . . the victors advanced to Madrid. They attacked the place but received some checks as the inhabitants, aware of their danger, had fortified the most vulnerable points. This resolution is certainly in the spirit we expected to have found pervading the whole country, but, as it is without able direction and hopeless of support, I fear their efforts will prove abortive and that the loss of the capital

December 13ᵗʰ

Marched to Toro, six leagues from the latter place. It is a large town situated on an immense cliff on the Duero. Got a billet in a tobacco shop.[123]

December 14ᵗʰ

Walked with _____ Wallace to an adjoining village.[124] Another action equally gallant took place with our dragoons. [Joseph] Bonaparte in this town three days before the British entered had been proclaimed king.[125]

---

must speedily follow the defeat of their generals . . . Unhappy nation! As a free man and an ally I bemoan your fate and . . . execrate from my soul the wretches in power who barter your liberties and their own for victory in a debate, a little temporary influence, or, finally, the gold of their enemies.' *Ibid.*, pp. 190–1.

123. Toro was found by many observers to be a more imposing place than this brief note suggests. As Porter wrote, 'We halted a day at Toro which gave me an opportunity of viewing the buildings . . . Every step in this town presents some object highly interesting, and nothing can be more picturesque than several points both within and without is walls. It is celebrated . . . particularly for a great battle that was fought between Ferdinand of Castile and Alfonso, King of Portugal . . . in 1576.' *Ibid.*, p. 207. Though Paget has little to say on the march, desperate to catch the French unawares, Moore pushed his men extremely hard. John Harris, for example, was with a parallel column that crossed the River Duero further west at the town of Zamora. 'I remember on the march from Salamanca seeing many men fail: our marches were long and the weakly ones were found out . . . As for myself, I was nearly floored by this march, and, on reaching . . . Zamora, I fell at the entrance of the first street we came to: the sight left my eyes, my brain reeled, and I came down like a dead man. When I recovered my senses, I remember that I crawled into a door I found open, and, being too ill to rise, lay for some time in the passage, unregarded by the inhabitants.' Hibbert (ed.), *Recollections of Rifleman Harris*, p. 48. Pushing the troops so hard had its disadvantages, however. According to William Gavin, then a sergeant in the Seventy-First Foot though later promoted to the rank of ensign: 'Marched to Toro: the weather was dreadful [and] the whole face of the country covered with snow. In this town the troops committed dreadful depredations.' G. Glover (ed.), *The Diary of William Gavin: Ensign and Quarter-Master of the Seventy-First Highland Regiment, 1806–1815* (Godmanchester, 2013), p. 53.

124. Assuming that the Wallace referred to was an officer, this must have been Major William Wallace of the Twentieth Foot: although Wallace is a name that figured frequently in the officer corps, no other officer named Wallace was serving with Moore's army.

125. As Joseph Bonaparte had been proclaimed in June and had never renounced his claim to the throne, this reference reads a little oddly. It is, then, probably, a reference to the so-called 'degrees of Chamartín', a series of ordinances issued by Napoleon shortly after his entrance into Madrid.

December 15ᵗʰ

Marched to Pedroso del Rey, five leagues. Country as yet from Salamanca particularly flat. Every day the Spaniards appear to wear off in civility to the English.[126]

December 16ᵗʰ

Marched this morning towards Tordesillas when suddenly we changed our route to Tiedra, reason unknown to me; marched two leagues.[127]

December 17ᵗʰ

Halted here and spent the day with Wallace in shooting pigeons. I had a large pistol and he a Frenchmen's gun, short and excellent.

December 18ᵗʰ

Marched six or seven leagues to Bau [almost certainly Barcial de la Loma], a dirty little hole where every incivility was shown us. Our left wing rested at an adjoining *villa*. Got in about eight o'clock at night.

---

126. Given the fact that Madrid had fallen without the British army firing a shot, this sentiment is scarcely to be wondered at. As Neale had written of public opinion at Salamanca in a letter dated 11 December: 'I am happy, I must confess, that we are at length likely to do something as the people here have lately become very anxious to see us out of town. For the last week they have been unceasing in their enquiries to know when we meant to march and have lately begun to make some very extraordinary remarks upon our apparent inactivity . . . As the great mass of people here are excessively ignorant, indeed infinitely beyond what I had conceived possible, they have thought that the delay has been somehow or other occasioned by an unwillingness on the part of some of our generals to meet the French.' Neale, *Letters from Portugal and Spain*, p. 244.

127. This march was accompanied by the onset of fresh cold, whilst it traversed an area that was remembered as being especially bleak. Thus: 'On the 16th we recommenced our march and took the road towards Castronuevo. The country . . . seemed particularly dreary. Not a tree, nor even a shrub, was seen to enhance the barren prospect . . . This was an apt scene in which to change our climate: it appeared as if by some invisible agency we had been transported to the naked tracts and killing blasts of Siberia. The weather became piercingly cold, and the saturated air hung a corroding damp upon us that portended even another alteration for the worse.' Porter, *Letters from Portugal and Spain*, p. 209. Meanwhile, the sudden change in the direction of the march was occasioned by the fact that a dispatch from Napoleon's chief-of-staff, Marshal Berthier, to the commander of the troops guarding Napoleon, Marshal Soult, whose bearer had been set upon and killed by the inhabitants of a small village near Segovia, had suddenly turned up at Moore's headquarters, the result being that it had become clear that Soult was much further north than had initially been anticipated.

December 19th

Marched back a league to Villalpando.

December 20th

Marched to Valderas, six leagues. It is a tolerable town: got coffee and sweets. Myself and Dundas billeted together: got a good straw mattress. Another action took place with our dragoons who with much inferior numbers conquered.[128]

December 21st

Marched about three leagues to Santa Marta and got a most vile hole, a little smoky closet for nine of us. Our mule and horse as yet kept up well.

December 22nd

Marched to Grajal de Campos, two or three leagues. Heard of the French being in a strong position under Marshal Soult and [that they] waited our attack.

December 23rd

Halted at Grajal de Campos and shot pigeons but, the Queen's being near, our sport was stopped by order of General Paget. A deal of _____ on the enemy [?]. Got some pistols and a letter from my brother, John, from a Mr Ady, and _____. He [i.e. Mr Ady] breakfasted with me today and set off to join the Second Battalion, but could not walk, the ground being so very slippy. Orders to get away at six o'clock, which was done, when we marched off intending to attack the enemy at break of day. The whole army was in motion when at twelve o'clock at night, we faced to the right-about and took up our old quarters. The reason I know not: some

---

128. The action referred to is the battle of Sahagún. In reality, this took place in the early morning of the following day, but the cavalry brigade involved set off to attack the enemy the night before so the diarist's mistake in this respect is of little consequence. The classic eyewitness account of Sahagín is that offered by Captain Alexander Gordon of the Fifteenth Light Dragoons: 'On our arrival at Sahagún we . . . discovered the enemy formed in a close column of squadrons near the road to Carrión de los Condes . . . The interval between us was perhaps 400 yards, but it was so quickly passed that they had only time to fire a few shots upon us before we came upon them . . . The shock was terrible: horses and men were overthrown, and a shriek of terror, intermixed with oaths, groans and prayers for mercy, issued from the whole extent of their front. Our men pressed forward until they had cut their way quite through the column. . . . The French were well posted, having a ditch in their front which they expected to check the impetus of our charge; in this, however, they were deceived.' Wylly (ed.), *Cavalry Officer in the Corunna Campaign*, pp. 101–2.

say he was reinforced, others that he quitted his position. The night was very cold. Two or three false alarms a few days ago had been given to us.

December 24th

Came off picket from sickness this night, being very chilly and ill. But better towards morning. Shot off my pistols. Orders to march tomorrow and now begins our dreadful retreat from Sahagún.[129]

December 25th

The day was damp and raining and the road ankle-deep in mud from the snow. Marched to Mayorga six leagues from this place, three leagues in deep mud and ploughed fields, and for the last two leagues it rained incessantly. Got a fiend of a billet and supped with Captain P. Campbell's company. Also a _____ and a little native wine. I had _____ except a blanket and therefore my clothes dried on me.[130]

---

129. So riven with hindsight is the last sentence of this entry that it all but constitutes proof positive that the section of the diary dealing with the retreat was written up at a later date. Meanwhile, the author is remarkably understated in what was generally perceived as an appalling turn of events. Here, once again, is Joseph Sinclair: 'On the 24th of December our headquarters were at Sahagún. Every heart beat with joy. We were all under arms and formed to attack the enemy. Every mouth breathed hope. "We will beat them to pieces and have our ease and enjoy ourselves", said my comrades. I even preferred any short struggle, however severe, to the dreadful way of life we were pursuing. With heavy hearts we received orders to retire to our quarters. "And won't we be allowed to fight? Sure we'd beat them", said an Irish lad near me. "By Saint Patrick! We'd beat them so easy. The general means to march us to death and then fight them after."' Anon., *Journal of a Soldier of the Seventy-First*, pp. 64–5. Particularly serious from the point of view of the Anglo-Spanish alliance was the development recorded by Ensign Robert Blakeney of the Twenty-Eighth Foot: 'Subsequently we were informed that the Marquis of Romana either mistook or wilfully failed in his engagements to co-operate and that the attack must consequently be postponed. Thenceforward a hatred and contempt of the Spaniards in arms filled the breast of every British soldier.' Sturgis (ed.), *Boy in the Peninsular War*, p. 35. It was a bleak Christmas. Like Paget and Blakeney, John Harris was in Edward Paget's Reserve Division: 'Some of the men near me suddenly recollected as they saw the snow lying thickly in their path. The recollection soon spread among the men, and many talked of home and scenes upon that night in other days in Old England, shedding tears as they spoke of the friends and relatives never to be seen by them again.' Hibbert (ed.), *Recollections of Rifleman Harris*, p. 72.

130. Some more details of the events of 25 December and the days immediately thereafter, and with it the state of almost total ignorance of the gravity of the situation that prevailed among the rank and file, are provided by John Harris: 'There was a sort of

December 26ᵗʰ

Baggage guard this day. Marched by Valderas to Fuentes de Rupel, seven good leagues. Valderas scarcely was _____ as myself and Dundas went in; lent him three dollars to buy sugar with. It rained all this day, very chilly and _____. Redden on picket. Dobbs and me slept in a bed, several soldiers in the house. No change.[131]

---

thaw on this day and the rain fell fast. As I passed . . . I observed General Craufurd as he sat upon his horse . . . and remarked the peculiar sternness of his features: he did not like to see us going rearwards at all, and many of us judged there must be something wrong by his severe look and scowling eye, "Keep your ranks there, men!" he said, spurring his horse towards some riflemen who were avoiding a small rivulet. "Keep your ranks and move on: no straggling from the main body!" We pushed on all that day without halting, and I recollect the first thing that stuck us as somewhat odd was our passing one of the commissariat wagons overturned and stuck fast in the mud and . . . abandoned without any attempt to save any of its contents. A sergeant of the Ninety-Second Highlanders just about this time fell dead of fatigue, and no-one stopped, as we passed, to offer him any assistance. Night came down without our having tasted food or halted . . . and all night long we continued this dreadful march. Men began to look into each other's faces and to ask the question, "Are we ever to be halted again?" Many of the weaker sort were now seen to stagger, make a few ineffectual efforts, and then fall, perhaps to rise no more. Most of us had devoured all we carried in our haversacks and endeavoured to catch up anything we could snatch from hut or cottage in our route. Many even at this period would have straggled from the ranks and perished had not Craufurd held them together with a firm rein . . . Thus we struggled on night and day for about four days before we discovered the reason for this continued forced march. The discovery was made to our company by a good-tempered jolly fellow named Patrick McLachlan. He enquired of an officer, marching directly in his front, the destination intended. "By Jesus, Mister Hills", I heard him say. "Where the devil is this you're taking us to?" "To England, McLachlan", returned the officer with a melancholy smile upon his face as he gave the answer. "If we can get there.'" Hibbert (ed.), *Recollections of Rifleman Harris*, pp. 71–2.

131. Paget is here complaining of the fact that he had no change of clothes available. As usual, he is rather laconic, but the want is more than made up for by Porter: 'At Valderas the conveniences we had hitherto enjoyed might be sought, but could not be found. The number of our troops occasioned not only the men, but the officers to be billeted in crowds together, and, for want of sufficient stabling, many of our horses were left in the open air. Here, then, I bade adieu to the cleanliness and regularity we had hitherto been able to obtain. We were now entering seriously into the privations of war, and this privation, I must own, I do find difficult to bear with the indifference becoming a soldier!' Porter, *Letters from Portugal and Spain*, p. 212.

December 27ᵗʰ

Marched at six. Orders to keep close together as we expected to be attacked hourly by cavalry. Road more muddy and unpleasant. At six o'clock took possession of the pass at Benevente with some of the Germans and three pieces of cannon. Stood to our arms all day, and [were] relieved at five o'clock at night by our second battalion and the Forty-Third Regiment: a gallant action had taken place between Lord Paget and the enemy, we as usual victorious. Slept at Benevente this night; dined with Abney.[132]

December 28ᵗʰ

Halted at Benevente. A false alarm given, [we] got under arms and the whole army took up their position; rained dreadfully and returned wet to the skin. The bridge was blown up here though not effectually. Billetted with Colonel _____.[133]

---

132.   The Abney referred to here is one Edward Abney, a lieutenant in the Second Battalion of the Fifty-Second. The cavalry action, meanwhile, was probably the one that took place at Mayorga in which the Tenth Hussars routed a regiment of enemy light cavalry that had temporarily cut them off from the main body of the army though in fact the British horse was in action in various places most of the day.

133.   The bridge referred to here was not at Benevente itself but rather a mile or two to the east near Castrogonzalo, a small settlement just the other side of the River Esla. As Paget implies, Anstruther's brigade saw no action here, but Crawfurd's men took part in a rearguard action against several squadrons of French cavalry that launched an attack on the bridge the evening before, fighting going all night and into the next day as well: 'The enemy's cavalry were on our skirts that night and as we rushed out of a small village, the name of which I cannot now recollect, we turned at bay. Behind broken-down carts and tumbrils . . . and everything we could scrape together, [we] lay and blazed away at the advancing cavalry, whilst the inhabitants, suddenly roused from their beds to behold their village almost on fire with our continued discharges, and nearly distracted with the sound, ran from their houses, crying "Vivan los ingleses!" and "Viva Francia!" in a breath, men, women and children [all] flying to the open country in their alarm. We passed the night thus engaged, holding our own as well as we could . . . Towards morning we moved down towards a small bridge, still followed by the enemy, whom, however, we had sharply galled and obliged to be more wary in their efforts. The rain was pouring down in torrents on this morning, I recollect, and we remained many hours with our arms ported, standing in this manner and staring the enemy in the face, the water actually running out of the muzzles of our rifles . . . Meanwhile, the Staff Corps had been hard at work mining the very centre of the structure, which was filled with gunpowder, a narrow plank being all the aid we had by which to pass over. For my own part, I was now so utterly helpless that I felt as if all was nearly up with me, and, that, if I could steady myself so as to reach the further end of the plank, it would be all I should be able to accomplish. However, we managed all of us to reach the other side in safety, when, almost immediately

December 29ᵗʰ

Marched to La Baneza eight leagues. Roads covered with ammunition, dead horses and cars [i.e. wagons].[134] Got the opthalmia. General Lefebvre taken in the action of the day and the Imperial Guards quite defeated. He forded the river and behaved well, but _____. Very wet today indeed and knee-deep in mud: gaiters broke and all destroyed; arrived excessively fatigued indeed.[135]

---

afterwards, the bridge blew up with a tremendous report and a house at its extremity burst into flames. What with the explosion and the tremulous state of my limbs, I was thrown to the ground, and lay flat upon the ground for some time almost in a state of insensibility. After a while, I somewhat recovered, but it was not without extreme difficulty, and many times falling again, that I succeeded in regaining the column.' Hibbert (ed.), *Recollections of Rifleman Harris*, pp. 77–9.

134. Even at this early stage of the retreat, Moore's army was suffering great distress. Having been part of the rearguard at Benevente, John Harris was at the rear of the column: 'The sight was by no means cheering. On the road behind me I saw men, women, mules and horses lying at intervals, both dead and dying, whilst far away in front I could just discern the enfeebled army crawling out of sight, the women huddled together in its rear, trying their best to get forward amongst . . . the sick soldiery who were now unable to keep up with the main body. Some of these poor wretches cut a ludicrous figure, having the men's greatcoats buttoned over their heads, whilst, their clothing being extremely ragged and scanty, they looked like a tribe of travelling beggars . . . It was still raining, I remember on this morning, and the very dead looked comfortless in their last sleep as I passed them occasionally lying on the line of march.' *Ibid.*, pp. 98–101.

135. Gavin is equally succinct in his description of the march to La Baneza: 'No food, nearly naked, the worst of roads. Dreadful weather.' Glover (ed.), *Diary of William Gavin*, p. 56. One suspects that the brevity of this account was not just the result of fatigue in that Benevente witnessed the first of a series of episodes of mass drunkenness in which hundreds of men broke into the town's wine cellars and drank themselves into oblivion. Meanwhile, the action described here took place on the banks of the River Esla as Moore's army withdrew from the town, a leading role in the action being taken by Sir Charles Stewart, later Marquess of Londonderry: 'A body of five or six hundred horse were observed about nine o'clock to try a ford not far from the ruins of the bridge, and . . . a few moments afterwards they crossed and began to form on our side of the river. Instantly the pickets which had been appointed to do the duty of a rearguard made ready to oppose them. Though they mustered little more than 200 men, they boldly advanced . . . against the mass, repeatedly charging its leading squadrons and keeping it fairly in check till Lord Paget and the writer of these pages arrived when the former made haste to bring up the Tenth Hussars whilst the latter put himself at the head of the detachments already in the field. Many charges were now made on both sides and the squadrons were repeatedly intermingled, whilst the pickets were ordered to give ground as it was intended that they should. But the Tenth were now ready . . . and they needed no entreaty to dash against the enemy.

December 30th

Arrived at Astorga and also La Romana's army from León, all peasants and mob, though fine pieces of cannon. In three days the whole army deserted and the cannon were by chance dragged on to Lugo and there fell into the enemy's hands.[136] Knee-deep in mud this march. Several men fell out from fatigue and _____ dead by

---

One cheer was given, and, the horses being pressed to their speed, the enemy's line was broken in an instant. They fled in great disorder to the river . . . leaving behind in our hands their colonel, General Lefebvre[-Desnouettes] with upwards of seventy other officers and men.' Londonderry, *Narrative of the Peninsular War*, I, pp. 207–8. An eyewitness to the fight was John Harris: 'The shock of that encounter was tremendous to look upon and we stood for some time enranked, watching the combatants. The horsemen had it all to themselves: our dragoons fought like tigers, and, although greatly over-matched, drove the enemy back like a torrent and forced them again into the river. A private of the Tenth Hussars – his name, I think, was Franklin – dashed into the stream after their general ... assailed him, sword in hand in the water, and brought him a prisoner on shore again.' Hibbert (ed.), *Recollections of Rifleman Harris*, p. 80.

136. Astorga was remembered by other veterans as the very acme of chaos. Here, for example, is William Gavin: 'The confusion in the town beggars description. The motley groups of half-naked, half armed Spaniards with the way-worn dispirited English, bullock-wagons, artillery, etc., rendered it quite impassable. The writer of this [journal] went to a convent and saw in the course of a few minutes no less than forty dead bodies carried out for interment.' Glover (ed.), *Diary of William Gavin*, p. 57. Moore's army was universally shocked by the terrible condition of La Romana's forces. To quote Alexander Gordon, 'This Spanish force amounted to about 6,000 men in the most deplorable condition. They were all ill-clothed; many were without shoes and even without arms; a pestilential fever raged amongst them; they had been without bread for several days and were quite destitute of money . . . I spoke to some of the men who were evidently suffering from famine and disease: they declared they had eaten nothing for three days, and, when we gave them the remains of our dinner and money to buy wine, their expressions of gratitude were unbounded.' Wylly (ed.), *Cavalry Officer in the Corunna Campaign*, pp. 145–7. Other observers were even harsher in their judgement. 'Here we found the army of La Romana', wrote Joseph Sinclair. 'I can convey no description of it in words. It had more the appearance of a large body of peasants driven from their homes, famished and in want of everything, than a regular army. Sickness was making dreadful havoc among them.' Anon., *Journal of a Soldier of the Seventy-First*, p. 70. Some British writers have been inclined to make use of such quotes as weapons to lambast the quality of the Spanish army in general, but, whilst this force had many problems, it would be unfair to judge its capacities from the troops on show at Astorga: badly beaten in a fiercely contested battle at Espinosa de los Monteros on 10–11 November, they had since then been retreating almost continually through the wilds of the Cantabrian mountains and had just sustained a further defeat in the face of impossible odds at Mansilla de los Mulos.

the enemy, also all our sick.[137] Billetted in a convent knee-deep in bullocks' blood
_____. Got a pair of good English shoes.

December 31st–January 1st

Marched five miles to a small village, most dreadfully _____, and mountainous,
which is the gateway of Galicia, till now being perfectly flat. Got some straw and
broke open the door of a convent to sleep in. La Romana's army flying everywhere.
Marched at ten o'clock at night through a most mountainous country; indeed, we
went eight leagues, up hill mainly. It was most bitter cold and [there were] falls
of snow in the night. The road was covered with clothing, cartridges, dead horses
and men of all sorts. Arrived at Bembibre at eleven o'clock on the first of January.
Orders to march at five, but [these were] contradicted. Got some straw in an old
house with the men.[138]

January 2nd

Marched from Bembibre to Cacabelos, four leagues. Excessively muddy _____
and cold. Got some ham here at two o'clock, also some good wine, but no bread
could be got with. We had an excellent billet.

January 3rd

Three men were sentenced to be hung but reprieved by General Paget. The French
being at hand, was under arms all this day. In the evening engaged the enemy, who
had two large columns but no artillery. Poor Captain Bennett of the Ninety-Fifth
was killed and two others wounded. Marched through Villafranca at eight o'clock

---

137. This sentence is difficult to read in the original and the sense even of what can be read
    clearly is hard to follow. If the suggestion is that the French massacred the army's
    sick, the author is very much in error: though the unfortunate men concerned were
    indeed taken by the enemy, they were well cared for.
138. The author is here being excessively reticent. Thus, as Astorga had done the day
    before, Bembibre witnessed yet another episode of mass intoxication. Much more
    forthcoming is an ensign of the Twenty-Eighth Foot named Robert Blakeney:
    'Bembibre exhibited all the appearance of a place lately stormed and pillaged.
    Every door and window was broken, every lock and fastening forced. Rivers of
    wine ran through the houses and into the streets, where lay fantastic groups of
    soldiers . . . women, children, runaway Spaniards and muleteers, all apparently
    inanimate . . . while the wine oozing from their lips and nostrils seemed the
    effect of gunshot wounds . . . The music was perfectly in character: savage roars
    announcing present hilarity were mingled with groans issuing from fevered lips
    disgorging the wine of yesterday; obscenity was public sport.' Sturgis (ed.), *Boy
    in the Peninsular War*, pp. 49–50.

at night; raining much; bridge was effectually blown up. Excessively muddy; men fell down asleep; rocky and a river by the road.[139]

January 4th

Arrived at a village: slept here a little.

January 5th

Marched to a village, six leagues over a most mountainous country. Got a billet with the men and some salt pork.

January 6th

Marched six leagues to a small villa; billeted with the men.[140]

---

139. The story of General Paget reprieving the deserters is widely attested to. In the action at Cacabelos a brigade of French light cavalry commanded by Auguste Colbert successfully drove in the pickets protecting the utmost rear of Moore's army, but then made the mistake of trying to rush the rearguard-proper even though the only access was across a narrow bridge. The result of such folly being all but inevitable, the French cavalry were routed with heavy losses and Colbert himself shot down by a rifleman named Tom Plunkett. One participant in the action was Alexander Gordon of the Fifteenth Hussars: 'The French continued to threaten us by various manoeuvres until near two o'clock when orders were received for the regiment to fall back and join the main body of the army at Villafranca. We retired very slowly to allow the Reserve time to break up their encampment and the enemy followed at the same pace along the highroad . . . Our rearguard kept them at bay until, on approaching Cacabelos, the leading squadron gained a rise in the road which enabled them to discover the mere handful of troops opposed to them upon which they immediately charged and drove us a few hundred yards, but at the entrance of the town we fronted them and fought hand-to-hand, disputing every inch of ground. For some minutes we were so jammed together in a narrow street that it was impossible for either part to advance or retire . . . The Ninety-Fifth should have lined a wood on the right of the road . . . but they were not posted when the enemy came up and the *chasseurs* dashed in upon them and threw them into confusion.' Wylly (ed.), *Cavalry Officer in the Corunna Campaign*, pp. 163–4. For a more detailed account of this action, see Appendix 4. The Captain Bennett mentioned was not in fact killed, but rather merely severely wounded; that said, he died of his wounds at Corunna on 14 January.

140. The journal does little or nothing to convey the horrors of the retreat here. Joseph Sinclair once again makes an excellent eye-witness: 'There was nothing to sustain our famished bodies or shelter them from the rain or snow . . . Fuel we could find none . . . The road was one line of bloody foot-marks from the sore feet of the men, and on its sides lay the dead and dying. Human nature could do no more . . . We felt there was no hope . . . There was nothing but groans, mingled with execrations, to be heard between the pauses of the wind. I attempted to pray and recommend myself to God, but my mind was so confused I could not arrange my ideas. I almost think

January 7ᵗʰ

Marched and [were] attacked by the French. Took our position for the night. Dollars 90,000 lost.[141]

I was deranged . . . How I was sustained I am unable to comprehend. My life was misery. Hunger, cold and fatigue had deprived death of all its horrors . . . Words fail me to express what we suffered.' Anon., *Journal of a Soldier of the Seventy-First*, p. 70. Another soldier struggling on through the chaos was one Stephen Morley: 'We had neither an adequate supply of food or clothing, and our feet were dreadfully hurt from want of shoes; many were actually barefooted . . . The poor women were deeply to be pitied. One of them . . . with no covering but her tattered clothes . . . gave birth to a son . . . The road all the way was strewed with men unable to proceed . . . Discipline was forgotten, none commanded, none obeyed.' S. Morley, *Memoirs of a Sergeant of the Fifth Regiment of Foot containing an Account of his Service in Hanover, South America and the Peninsula* (Ashford, 1842), pp. 61–2.

141. The loss of the money referred to in the journal was one of the more embarrassing episodes of the retreat, the chests in which it was being carried being emptied into a ravine beside the road rather than risk them falling into the hands of the enemy when the horses pulling the wagon concerned foundered under the strain. Infinitely worse, however, was the fact that in many regiments discipline had now broken down under the strain, the ever more desperate soldiery in many instances literally running amok across the Galician countryside. As Anthony Hamilton of the Forty-Third Foot wrote: 'It is melancholy to contemplate the condition to which we had . . . been reduced . . . The rain came down in torrents; men and horses, sinking with fatigue, covered the roads; and the soldiers whose strength still enabled them to proceed, maddened by the continued suffering of cold and hunger, were no longer under subordination. In such circumstances, pillage could not be prevented. Wherever we came, the inhabitants fled from their villages and sought shelter among the mountains. Enormities of all kinds were committed: houses and even villages were burning in all directions. The ravages of the most ferocious enemy could not have exceeded in atrocity those perpetrated by a British army on their allies.' Hamilton, *Hamilton's Campaign with Moore and Wellington*, p. 43. Needless to say, in many sources these scenes were invariably blamed on the Spaniards and often minimised to boot. For example: 'Reciprocal ignorance of language . . . diversity of religious customs and local prejudices were perpetually interposing to frustrate the endeavours of the officers to preserve amity between the soldiers and the Spaniards. Besides, as in Galicia . . . there is more specie than real property, our soldiers were frequently incensed at finding that the offer of a dollar would not induce a peasant to part with a morsel of rusty bacon, a few garlic sausages or a bit of bread, [items] which, often, in fact, were not worth one third of the sum. On [our men] arriving of an evening at their villages after a most fatiguing march ... these unfeeling mortals often refused ... to run to the adjoining fountain for a pitcher of water or to procure a few heath roots to make a fire. Hence frequent bickerings ensued and often a few blows which the Spaniards generally deserved. That the British soldier is incapable of wanton cruelty, I could convince you by a few anecdotes.' Neale, *Letters from*

January 8ᵗʰ

Marched all night after lighting our fires ten leagues, and arrived at twelve o'clock a league beyond Lugo: billeted in a pigsty. Three young men joined. Heard from John [i.e. his brother, the naval officer encountered at the beginning of the journal] and the joyful news of the *Ville de Paris* at Vigo.[142]

January 9ᵗʰ

Very rainy. My servant lost me a pistol, a map, a sock and a pair of shoes, and I was now destitute of everything except a dirty shirt, a knapsack and a white waistcoat which I picked up from the spoils on the road. An alarm given, all turned out while it rained a deluge, and [I was] obliged to leave some apple dumplings in the camp kettle. Wet march to Lugo and our staying till dark in the rain [*sic*]. The Guards were slightly engaged. Quartered in a convent this night: wet to the skin and no change whatsoever as our baggage was sent on to Corunna. Laid me down in my wet things, but could not sleep much. Orders for the men each to have seventy rounds of ammunition.[143]

Portugal and Spain, pp. 337–8. Indeed, there are even those who sought to put the boot on the other foot: 'The apathy with which the inhabitants of this mountain country . . . have witnessed our misery is revolting. They were to be seen in large armed hordes far away from us in the mountains . . . when . . . they might have been very useful to us and covered our retreat. But not only did these puffed-up patriots . . . give us no assistance, but they also took good care to remove all cattle and all foodstuffs out of our way . . . and in addition murdered and plundered our own men who fell out left and right along the road.' Ludovici, *On the Road with Wellington*, pp. 127–8.

142. HMS *Ville de Paris* was a first-rate ship-of-the-line built and launched at Chatham in 1795. Her strange name is accounted for by the fact that she was named after a French ship taken at the battle of the Saints in 1782 but lost immediately afterwards in a storm.

143. In the units of Paget's rearguard division, the constant presence of the enemy helped keep the men together. However, in much of the rest of the army, the situation was now quite desperate. Herewith William Gavin's account of the situation on 9 January: 'We reached Betanzos. On the way bags of biscuit, casks of port and barrels of rum were placed on the road: [they had been] sent from Corunna and the wagons returned for a further supply. The rum caused the death of hundreds: the heads of the casks were knocked in and the men drank to such excess that they many of them lay down to rise no more . . . Of our brigade which at the commencement of the retreat consisted of 2,500 men, not more than 150 marched in with the colours, and they barefoot, covered with old blankets and many without arms.' Glover (ed.), *Diary of William Gavin*, p. 60.

January 10th

Marched off at 5 a.m. to offer the French battle; took our position opposite the enemy in a furzy plain. _____ got a few turnips and a _____ made me a dish of soup: each cooked now and kept himself from starving. My shirt was worse than all being visited by vermin, but many others were ate up with them. Marched at eight o'clock, a mere (shameful to say) three hours since we reached Lugo.

January 11th

Kept marching and halted at two o'clock to cook. Myself and _____ fell asleep in a hovel and [were] nearly taken by the enemy.

January 12th

Kept marching on. [On the] report of a French picket being seen, took our position. In the event saw them fire [at] and prick [?] the fatigued stragglers which troubled us not a little. Marched on and took up our position this side of Betanzos and slept amongst the straw under a hedge; got a blanket. Some rum given to the troops.

January 13th

Marched to Corunna. I went on before as I now had walked my shoes and stockings off my feet and was badly blistered. Got there at two o'clock [and] got a bed at a tailor's shop for half a dollar, but, alas, no shipping.[144]

---

144. The brevity of this comment is again either testimony either to the author's exhaustion or evidence that he was writing from memory after the event. Thus, it was on this day that the approach of the French led to the destruction of Moore's reserves of powder – some 4,000 barrels – in an explosion that is claimed to be one of the biggest ever recorded prior to the First World War. Herewith the account of Captain Gordon of the Fifteenth Hussars: 'The whole town was thrown into considerable alarm at about nine o'clock this morning by a tremendous explosion, which shook the buildings like an earthquake. A number of windows were broken by the concussion, and the inhabitants . . . rushed into the streets – many of them half-dressed and with terror in their countenances – and, falling upon their knees, began to repeat their 'Aves' with an energy proportioned to their fright . . . The account I heard of the cause of this explosion . . . was that Sir John Moore had ordered a magazine to be destroyed . . . as there was not time to remove the powder it contained, amounting to 1,500 barrels. It was said, however, that there was another depot of nearly 5,000 barrels in an adjoining building, but that this circumstance was concealed . . . by the Spanish officer in charge of the magazine. The consequence was . . . an explosion infinitely more violent in its effects than had been calculated. Some of the men who were employed on this occasion were blown up. The inhabitants of the village in which the magazines were situated had been sufficiently warned of their danger . . . but they paid little attention to the cautions they received, and

January 14ᵗʰ

Got some shoes and some stockings. Heard the regiment was near the bridge.[145]

January 15ᵗʰ

Joined my regiment and sent on fatigue with a sergeant and a corporal _____ of the rifle corps to receive my orders from the Adjutant General. I did so and 'twas to pick up all the stragglers: found none. Asked to dinner by an officer of the Twenty-Third Fusiliers [i.e. the Twenty-Third Regiment of Foot, the name of this unit being the Royal Welsh Fusiliers].[146]

January 16ᵗʰ

Reported myself to the Adjutant General and to the colonel about some stragglers of the Second Battalion. Ordered me to repair to the convent of San Francisco and collect the convalescent men and see them embarked. Towards three or four o'clock I heard there was skirmishing and at last [it] turned to a general action. I wished to join myself but the order I [had] received prevented me. Slept aboard the *Ville de Paris*.[147]

January 17ᵗʰ

Went ashore and embarked several sick and straggling men. Found my regiment had embarked last night and was but slightly engaged. Embarked on board the *Ville de Paris* for good, but without leave, it being a perfect scramble and my brother on board her. Got a cot _____ for me [and] some cold meat, English wine and butter, also a clean shirt and stockings from John. The French batteries opened on us, but, the transports getting under way, [they] did not do us much injury. We had twelve

---

it is probable that many of them perished owing to their obstinacy as the place was reduced to a heap of ruins'. Wylly (ed.), *Cavalry Officer in the Corunna Campaign*, pp. 197–9.

145. The bridge referred to here is the one that spanned the estuary of the River Mero at El Burgo.

146. Paget's failure to discover any stragglers belonging to the regiments of his brigade is not entirely surprising: although some regiments were hit very badly by straggling, those belonging to the Reserve held up much better than much of the rest of the army, not least because they were in constant danger from the French cavalry and therefore had the stimulus of action to sustain them.

147. Whilst it is not extraordinary that Paget missed the battle that marked the culmination of the campaign, the same cannot be said about his failure to mention the death of Sir John Moore, and all the more so given the general's close connection with the Fifty-Second.

sail of the line here under Sir Thomas Hood and Admiral de Courcey. I was now, thank God, rid of Spain. Three transports [that] ran foul of each other got ashore and were burned by the boats of the fleet.[148]

---

148. Paget had some distinguished company on his journey back to England: among the other passengers on the *Ville de Paris* were Sir David Baird; the brother of the Earl of Aberdeen, Colonel Alexander Gordon; and Sir John Colborne. The 'perfect scramble' noted by Paget is confirmed by other sources. Not the least of the problems was the desire of the masters of the transports to get away with as little delay as possible. Here, for example, is how William Gavin described the night of 16 January: 'The captains of the transports were ordered to hoist a lantern in the rigging of their mainmast to announce their admission of the poor soldiers and, when complete, to lower it, but they lowered the light before they had half their complement . . . The people were [therefore] bundled into whatever ships they could get alongside of so that scarcely standing room was in some of them, while others were half empty. I got on board a transport where parts of fourteen regiments were huddled together . . . As soon as daylight appeared, the French discovered our retreat . . . and brought their guns to bear on the shipping from the heights of Santa Lucia. The masters of the transports immediately cut their cables and in the confusion four transports ran aground and were abandoned.' Glover (ed.), *Diary of William Gavin*, pp. 63–4. That the evacuation was chaotic and marked by scenes of near panic is confirmed by Schaumann: 'We marched along the quay and then down some steps . . . to the water's edge. The sloops from the men-of-war were already waiting and we were just on the point of boarding them when on the height of Santa Lucia there was a sudden terrific outburst of fire, and it seemed as if the Day of Judgement had come. Shot and shell whistled about our heads and striking first the water, then the sloops and anon the ships themselves made hearing and seeing almost impossible . . . Then followed a scene which I shall remember to my dying day . . . The minute the bombardment started . . . there arose an extraordinary tumult and outcry . . . All the transports immediately cut their anchors and began to get under way. They ran into one another, and damaged and smashed each other's bowsprits, rigging and yards. Five ships which attempted to escape between the island of San Antonio and the citadel got into such terrible confusion that one of them ran up on a bank in the direction of the French and was stranded and had to be abandoned by its crew and blown up . . . Only the men-of-war remained, and they had to take many thousands of troops on board. At last one of the shots ricocheted over the water and struck the wall quite close to us whereupon . . . one of the naval officers called to us from the boats and told us to turn back and march through the town to the lighthouse where we would be more protected and they would await us . . . We therefore marched out . . . to the opposite shore, which was very rocky and over which the breakers were beating furiously. The sloops from the men-of-war could not come up close, but were kept at a safe distance by means of their oars while we had to go to the edge of the rocks . . . and, then, with the water splashing over our heads, take hold of one of the oars. Then we were grasped by the mighty fists of the sailors . . . and dragged in like sheep.' Ludovici, *On the Road with Wellington*, pp. 143–5.

January 18th

Wednesday. Sailed from Corunna with a fine breeze aft . . . with the *Resolution* (76), *Tonnant* (80; Admiral de Courcey), *Barfleur* (98; Sir John Hood); *Ville de Paris* (100), *Victory* (100), *Elizabeth* (74), *Plantagenet* (74), *Zealous* (74), *Norge* (74), *Implacable* (74), *Audacious* (74), *Endymion*, *Semiramis* and _____ frigates, some cutters, brigs and schooners.

January 19th

Wind fair. Had 900 troops on board and seventy officers, also the officer sent home with the dispatches from Sir John Hope.[149]

---

149. As so many of the transports had sailed for home half-empty, for many of the returning troops conditions were wretched in the extreme. Schaumann, for example, had embarked on a transport called *Nimrod*: 'Twenty-two officers and 220 men were on board, in addition to the crew and the servants. There was not enough water or provisions on board to supply half of them for a fortnight . . . At bedtime there was the utmost confusion in the cabin . . . Colonel Alten and Major Hay of the Eighteenth Hussars . . . had taken possession of the bunks, while the rest of us had to lie packed together like sardine on the floor. As there was very little room, we had to assume the following order: three rows were formed, the first row [spreading] out their legs and [allowing] the second to lay their heads between them, and the third row [lying] with their heads between the legs of the second. We were . . . not allowed to use drinking water to wash with, but it was impossible to use sea-water because soap will not dissolve in it and it does not remove any dirt. In the morning we received a pailful of porridge with a large lump of butter floating in the top of it . . . At midday we had peas and salt meat with a portion of rum that looked quite black and at night we had a little hard cheese and some ship's biscuit.' Ludovici, *On the Road with Wellington*, pp. 146–7. Just as graphic is the account of Adam Neale, though this is that much more interesting on account of the reference that it makes to symptoms of post-traumatic-stress disorder, a phenomenon that is certain to have occurred with some frequency, but is but little mentioned in the memoir literature: 'I am a good deal indisposed and not much the better for being shut up in a little noisome, damp cabin with six other officers. Four of them are extremely ill and generally raving all night long. Their complaints are the fruit of over-exertion, and their distempered and horror-struck imaginations are perpetually pursuing some dreadful hallucination connected with the casualties of war, famine and shipwreck. It was only last night that one of them, in a temporary fit of insanity, hurried me and one or two more on deck in our shirts in the rain by screaming out that the ship had sprung a leak and was going down. On ascertaining the cause of the alarm, we went below and found the poor fellow . . . crawling in the utmost distress of mind to effect his escape from the phantoms of his own bewildered brain. God knows whether we may not experience the reality before long, for one half of the crew are so ill that they cannot get upon deck while it is blowing such a gale . . . that I can write no longer.' Neale, *Letters from Portugal and Spain*, pp. 327–8.

January 20ᵗʰ

Fine weather, but calm during the night. Some men flogged on board. Found ourselves by observation to be at 47-12 north. Heavy weather: fleet much scattered.

January 21ˢᵗ

Received permission from by telegraph from *Tonnant* to proceed to Portsmouth for the benefit of the general [i.e. Baird].[150] Heavy weather, light winds: all possible sails set.

January 22ⁿᵈ

Strong gale from the eastward. Saw land (Lizard Point).[151]

January 23ʳᵈ

In the morning quite calm. Came on a brisk breeze from the southward. Made all sail in the Channel. At noon Portland lighthouse north-east-by-east two or three leagues distant.

January 24ᵗʰ

Blowing hard from the westward; thick, heavy weather. Beating off and on the back of the Isle of Wight. Weather too thick to allow our visiting Saint Helen's. Saw an Indiaman homeward bound, signal of distress flying, having lost her main top mast. Blew too hard to send a boat on board.

January 25ᵗʰ

Fresh breezes and clear. Made sail in for the land. Saw the Isle of Wight and Saint Helen's. Three line-of-battle ships and a frigate coming out of Spithead. Anchored at three o'clock at Spithead: a number of officers went ashore. Found a great number of men-of-war at Spithead.

January 26ᵗʰ

Heard of General Brownrigg being at Portsmouth. Orders to land sick and wounded. Strong gales from the westward with rain.

---

150. Baird had lost his left arm at Corunna.

151. The gale referred to here inflicted one last disaster on Moore's army. In brief, 2 transports – the *Dispatch* and the *Smallbridge* – were wrecked on the Cornish coast with the loss of 296 officers and men, most of them members of the King's German Legion. Oman, *Peninsular War*, I, p. 596.

January 27th

Went ashore. Bought boots, pantaloons, etc. Play in the evening. Met my old friend, Cole. Dined at The Blue Posts. Eighty-Second disembarked.

Appendix 1

The Account of Captain John Dobbs, Fifty-Second Foot[1]

[p. 4] Having arrived off the coast of Portugal on the 21st August 1808, on which day our second battalion took an active part in the battle of Vimeiro, we got orders to land the following morning and had to abandon any sea-stock which we could not carry in our haversacks and canteens, and, having a quantity of spruce beer

---

1. Occasionally mentioned in Paget's text, like so many officers in the British army, John Dobbs was a Protestant from Ireland. Originally hailing from Dublin, in 1806 he had acquired a commission as a lieutenant in the Armagh militia at the age of just 15, and the following year transferred into the First Battalion of the Fifty-Second Foot. In all this, also typically enough, family connections mattered a great deal. Dobbs' father, Francis Dobbs, was a barrister who had served as a member of the Irish parliament whilst he also happened to have been a school fellow of none other than Sir John Moore. Meanwhile, such patronage was also evidently of great help not just to John Dobbs but to his family as a whole, for one brother (Joseph) had proceeded him into the ranks of the Fifty-Second, in which he had enlisted as a gentleman-volunteer, whilst a second (Alexander) became a captain in the Royal Navy and two others (William and Francis) officers in the Armagh militia (Francis Dobbs senior had died in 1801, leaving his wife and children in a state of reduced means, the result being that there was no option for his sons but to pursue a career in the army). As for John Dobbs, like the rest of his unit, following his return to England in January 1809 he was sent to take part in the abortive Walcheren expedition, and then returned to the Peninsula, where, still with the Fifty-Second, he fought in the battles of Sabugal, Fuentes de Oñoro, Salamanca, Vitoria and the Pyrenees, not to mention the assaults on Ciudad Rodrigo and Badajoz. Offered a captaincy in the Fifth Regiment of Caçadores, on 1 September 1813 he transferred into the Portuguese service, and in this capacity took part in the crossing of the Bidassoa, the battles of the Rivers Nivelle and Nive, and the siege of Bayonne. Having come through the whole war without a scratch, he was badly wounded in the sally the French launched from Bayonne on 14 April 1814, and is generally accepted as the last British casualty of the campaigns in the Peninsula and the south of France. Originally published in Waterford in 1859 as *Recollections of an Old Fifty-Second Man*, his memoirs re-appeared in a new edition in 1863 and it is from this latter work that the extract is taken.

which was beginning to fly, our amusement the evening before was fixing a mark in the ceiling and letting the corks fly at it. We attempted to land in the flat bottomed boats, but one or two of the first that attempted it were swamped by the surf and the men drowned. It was therefore necessary to use the men-at-war boats and we were changed into them, in which operation I had a [p. 5] narrow escape of losing my leg between the two boats: I, however, escaped with a severe bruise which did not prevent me marching with the regiment. Immediately after landing on the 22nd, we had to cross over several extensive vineyards to the great delight of the troops who helped themselves to the grapes, the roots of which are at a short distance from one another. Having been bared of the old branches for firing, the new branches are covered with clusters of them: the appearance at a little distance is like that of field peas. When ripe, they are carried into houses having large shallow reservoirs which they are spread over, having sufficient slope to let the juice run to a spout prepared for emptying it into casks ready for its reception. When the grapes are spread, a number of persons (with not very clean feet) are sent into the reservoir who tramp them till the juice runs off. After this, the skins are collected and put into the press which is a coil of rope several feet high, a heavy beam moving on a pivot, being a powerful lever, [then pressing] the coil of rope till all the remaining juice is pressed out of them; the juice thus obtained is allowed to ferment in large vessels. In Spain it is conveyed from place to place in pigskins turned inside out and coated with tar [which] are slung on the backs of mules whose pack saddles are well adapted for the service; when exposed to the heat of the sun and the skins not very new, the tar and hair becomes blended with the wine which becomes anything but agreeable. Wine was frequently issued in place of the ration (rum) and, until accustomed to it, it was considered a grand thing by the men to be drinking wine.

To the great joy of the men, they were relieved from hair-tying which was a burden grievous to be borne. And our huts being close to those occupied by the men, we could hear them joking one another on the subject: one of the principal ones was calling on their comrade to tie them, which was impossible as their hair was gone.[2]

Our first day's march was a short one, but the weight each man had to carry was tremendous: in addition to heavy knapsacks, there were their muskets and

---

2.   Described elsewhere as cone-shaped constructions built by leaning substantial branches against one another with their foliage uppermost so as to function as rudimentary thatching, the huts mentioned here had been constructed some days earlier by the French troops sent to check the British at Roliça. As for the relaxation in respect of the soldiers' hair, this was indeed a great blessing: up until this point, British soldiers had had to wear their hair pulled back tightly from the scalp and tied in a pig-tail, the whole being coated with a mixture of flour and grease that stiffened

ammunition, a blanket, a mess kettle and a wooden canteen; they and their officers [also] had three day's provisions. The weather was very hot [and] our [p. 6] caps and leather stocks gave us great annoyance, the former by day and the latter both day and night. As we slept in our clothes, we remedied the former by boring two small holes in the sides, and the officers the latter by clasping them over the knee and the men by slipping them over the ramrod.[3] We each of us had a small tin tot which we carried with a knife and fork made to shut up like a common clasp knife. The tot was in constant requisition: on getting up, it was paraded with water to wash my mouth; at breakfast it answered for a tea-cup; on the march for drinking out of; at dinner for soup; after dinner for rum, punch or wine. After some time I supplied its place with a small silver cup for the same uses [and] also [acquired] a silver fork, both of which, being easily cleaned, were great luxuries.

As we had no change of clothes till our arrival in Lisbon, we had to take advantage of some running stream and wash our shirts as well as we could, sitting by till they dried. We were billeted in Lisbon for some days and took the opportunity of visiting remarkable places about it, amongst others a gambling house greatly frequented, and were surprised to find the most active persons to be the priests and monks, some of them partners in the concern. As I passed through the streets, every corner had a woman frying and selling sardines, which appeared very plenty and gave occupation to a great many fishermen. An image of their patron saint [was] in the bow of each boat with a small begging-box under it, having a slit in the top and [a] lock attached. As their prayers were addressed to the saint for success in their fishing, when they are disappointed they fly into a rage with the saint and duck his image, giving him all sorts of abuse. The key of the money box is kept by a priest who relieves it of its contents from time to time.[4]

Another thing which strikes the strangers is the constant assassinations, a number of bodies being found every morning – some stabbed by enemies, others

---

the whole assembly and allowed the display of elaborate curls at each side. Horribly uncomfortable in itself, wearing the hair in this fashion meant that many soldiers were woken up at night by rats chewing at their heads.
3.   Though rendered exactly as per the text, this last remark is, to say the least, very obscure. However, the suggestion seems to be that the leather of the stocks was somehow softened a little.
4.   It is, perhaps, worth pointing out here that fishermen of the sort depicted here were frequent recruits to the anarchism that became so vibrant a force in Spain a century later. Meanwhile, contained in Dobbs' words is a hint of an attitude to religion which has little in common with the blind devotion of legend. Far from the Church having the massive influence generally attributed to it, it was often regarded with considerable loathing by the populace. Here, for example, is Adam Neale on the mendicant orders that were so significant a feature of the Church in both Spain and Portugal: 'Collected

by bravos hired for the purpose. What applies to Lisbon is equally applicable to all the larger towns and cities in Spain and Portugal . . . At the end of the war the native merchant on whom I was billeted [in Oporto] told me the following anecdote which was told himself by a [p. 7] friend . . . Having in a fit of anger hired a bravo to murder a friend, on becoming calm [the individual concerned] went to the bravo's house to prevent his doing the deed. The man not being at home, he asked where he was to be found. The answer [being] at church . . . he followed him and observed him earnestly engaged in his devotions. As soon as they were over, he asked him how he could engage in prayer when about to commit such an act [and] the bravo replied that he was asking for success in the job. The weapon used for assassinations is a stiletto. It has a straight handle and blade, the latter tapering to a point. It is carried in the sleeve, and, when about to use it, the handle is turned with the blade backwards along the arm which hides it from observation. The bravo passes the person on the left side, giving him a back stroke which strikes into the heart, he still moving on as if nothing had happened. They are very dextrous in throwing it: this is done by laying the handle in the palm with the blade outward,

---

in a body of five or six persons, [the friars] arm themselves with a crucifix or a wooden image or a picture, and, bearing a few lighted tapers, they sally forth after sunset through the streets of the towns roaring forth the most discordant tunes in praise of Saint Francis or the Madonna, while a few imps, whom they keep in pay and are well instructed for the purpose, run before the procession, and with a large stone or huge cudgel thunder on the door of each house till the owner, trembling for his locks and hinges, starts from his bed, curses the disturbers of his repose and, chucking a testoon [an archaic term for a shilling] or a couple of *vimtems* out of his window, creeps back to his miserable straw pallet and wishes from the bottom of his soul that the whole crew of Franciscans, Benedictines and bare-footed Carmelites were in the very lowest depths of purgatory.' Neale, *Letters from Portugal and Spain*, pp. 143–4. According to some observers, indeed, the whole edifice of monasticism was increasingly regarded with scepticism by the populace on whose shoulders it rested. As Porter reflected after having visited a convent in Salamanca, 'The brotherhoods and sisterhoods of these tombs of the living already lose the reverence with the people which they once possessed, and, from what I can observe, I do not believe that the country at large would regret if they were abolished at once.' Porter, *Letters from Portugal and Spain*, p. 155. Attendance at church was still very heavy, indeed, almost universal, but many observers claimed that there was an air of routine about the practice, and, further, that much of the congregation seemed but little interested in the service. To quote Porter in respect of a funeral on which he looked in, 'I could not help remarking the little feeling, either of regret or of decency, which was exhibited in almost all present, as smiles and conversation amused them during what ought to have been considered the most awful of ceremonies.' *Ibid.*, p. 157.

and, with a jerk, discharging it up, down or straight forward with so certain an aim as to strike a mark of one penny piece at twelve paces distance.[5]

The building occupied by the Inquisition was not to be seen [i.e. not open to visitors], but the Inquisition itself had been suppressed by the French, not only in Lisbon, but in the whole of the Peninsula. In Madrid the whole system was exposed by them, all the subterranean apartments having been discovered by one of their engineers who suspected them to be under the chapel [and] poured a quantity of water on the flags which found its way through the joining on the flag that covered the staircases leading to them. It is a slur upon the English that the French have done more to suppress this dreadful institution than the English authorities who call themselves Protestants.[6]

The Fifty-Second, having crossed the Tagus a little above Lisbon, marched through the Alemtejo. Our first day's march was distressing from want of water,

---

5. Fact blends with fantasy in this passage. That violent death was frequent in the towns and cities of eighteenth-century Iberia cannot be doubted: famously enough, Charles III of Spain prohibited the voluminous woollen cloaks affected by many Spanish men on the grounds that they made it too easy to carry knives undetected. However, the number of deaths was almost certainly far smaller than Paget implies, Ormsby going so far as to state, 'I have not heard any instance of assassination by the charge of which the natives are, I believe, of late years unjustly calumniated.' Ormsby, *Operations of the British* Army, p. 148. At the same time, to the extent that it was reality at all, the situation was the result not of the personal quarrels and family vendettas suggested here, and, indeed, envisaged by many other foreigners, but rather clashes between rival gangs, simple tavern brawls and the street crime produced by the endemic poverty. At the same time, whilst it cannot be proved that stilletos did not make an appearance from time to time, the weapon that was most typical of the lower classes was in fact the *navaja*, this being an over-sized general-purpose clasp knife. Note, however, the way in which the issue is used to confirm the idea that Spaniards were cowards, men who hired others to do their dirty work for them or struck down their victims without warning.

6. Dobbs displays the most absurd prejudice here: whilst the record of the Inquisition is scarcely edifying, for the British government to have sought to impose so controversial a measure on Spain would have been politically disastrous even if there had been any means of effecting it. At the same time, too, in neither Spain nor Portugal was the Inquisition anything like the force which it had been in past centuries. Torture and burnings at the stake were things of the past (the numbers of burnings were in steady decline throughout the eighteenth century, the last such cases in Spain and Portugal taking place in 1746 and 1794 respectively), while the institution had in effect become little more than a board of censorship, and, what is more, one that concentrated on political texts only (scientific works, by contrast, were largely ignored). Even the numbers executed – perhaps 5,000 in Spain and another 1,500 in Portugal, and that over a period of roughly 300 years – were not especially great.

not a drop being to be had from the time we started till we got into quarters for the night. The consequence was that the men fell out by the hundreds, but even this had some advantage as [p. 8] they marked the road for those in the rear. While on the advance to Estremoz, we met the French garrison of Elvas on its way to Lisbon for evacuation. Having halted in this neighbourhood, an Irishman of the name of Patrick Donovan deserted to us. It appeared he had been implicated in the Irish rebellion and banished to the continent. He said he had been made a present of to the King of Prussia and entered his services. When that country had become subject to Bonaparte, he had been transferred to the French army and shared in most of Napoleon's victories. He had now made his escape with a hope of getting home to his own country. He was a noble soldier: he joined my brother's company and served throughout the Peninsular campaign. His experience of French tactics and his fear of being recaptured kept him always on the alert, and when he found us careless, he would caution us to be on our guard, and [he] always kept a sharp look-out himself.

We waited till the beginning of November at Estremoz and enjoyed the fruits of that country in all their perfection, melons, water melons, oranges, figs, grapes, and what I observed at Lisbon, as it regards sardines, might be observed here and elsewhere of chestnuts, every corner having stoves for roasting of them. We were greatly annoyed by the constant ringing of the church bells: they never ceased. We were also surprised to find a list of sins and prohibited articles hung at each church door with a price attached for which they might be indulged in . . . We never paraded for Protestant worship, but were paraded for a Roman-Catholic ceremony and presented arms to the host which did not give us any concern at that time. At this place I witnessed the interment of a beautiful young female at one of the churches. She was in full dress and carried on a bier. A flag had been taken up and a grave dug in which she was laid, and when a few inches of clay had been laid over her, they began to pound it with a piece of wood made like a paving mallet until nearly all the earth taken out was forced back.

In the beginning of November 1808, we entered [p. 9] Spain. In the first village we had a sample of Spanish welcome: we were told that we were not welcome, that they could fight their own battles without our help, etc.

A number of houses were told off for the company's quarters, but we had great difficulty getting in the doors being closed against us. One of the houses appeared to be untenanted, and we were going to break the door open when an old woman put her head out of a window over it and then held out an old matchlock gun in order to frighten us away, her hand shaking with age and fright. When we got to Salamanca, we found a change for the better. At least, I did: the old lady on whom I was billeted used to send me a cup of chocolate and a thin slice of toast every morning before I was up and paid every attention to my comfort while I remained with her, which was till the 11th of December 1808.

On the 23rd we were quartered at Sahagún after Lord Paget and his hussars had driven the French dragons out of it. At this time Napoleon with 60,000 men was marching out of Madrid to intercept us while Soult had 30,000 in our front and we were only 22,000. Sir John Moore's object was to give the Spaniards an opportunity to rally by drawing off the French force, but it was of no use.

On the 23rd of December 1808, we had a night march to attack Soult. The snow lay on the ground several inches deep and we were forbidden to speak. Unexpectedly, about midnight the word was passed from the rear to counter-march, and we returned to our quarters. On the 25th we were in full retreat, the reserve in which the Fifty-Second were being the rearguard with the exception of the Hussar Brigade, who remained behind till we entered the mountains and then passed us.

At Benevente, Bonaparte overtook but failed in intercepting us. When he made his appearance on the heights over the bridge, the Reserve got under arms and drew up in front of the town, the Hussar Brigade being on the plain between us and the river with their pickets at the bridges and fords. On this occasion for the first and last time I saw Napoleon I: he had a numerous staff in attendance, but, my brother's glass being a good one, I was able to distinguish him as he reconnoitred us. [p. 10] Finding that we had slipped through his fingers, he took his departure after seeing his Imperial Guard very roughly handled by the Hussar Brigade who were left behind while we continued our retreat. On this occasion the French lost a general and seventy prisoners with a number of men killed and wounded.

Just before the enemy's advance to Cacabelos, the Reserve were halted on the heights above it for the purpose of hanging three marauders. Everything was ready and a square formed round the gallows when a hussar rode in from the rear, reporting to General Paget that the enemy were close at hand. He coolly received the report and proceeded to address the troops, stating the disgrace attached to the crime, but [saying] that he would pardon them if they would refrain from such excess, but that, if this promise was not made, they should die [even] if the enemy were firing into the square. There was a general exclamation of 'We will! We will!' He made a sign to the Provost Marshal who immediately liberated the prisoners. The troops were at once moved off, some to cover the retreat on this side of the river, while others crossed and took up a position to cover their retreat over the bridges. After repulsing the enemy, the retreat was continued.[7] It may be well to state that Sir John Moore superintended the various operations necessary to retard

---

7.   For a fuller account of the events at Cacabelos, please see Appendix 4.

the advancing enemy, taking advantage of every height and defile, placing a gun where it could tell on their advance and throwing a shrapnel shell so as to discharge itself into a column of infantry or cavalry as required. This was our occupation by day which delay had to be made up for at night. The want of rest made us subject to optical illusions, [and] one remarkable one I think worthy of mention. The head of a column came to a small stream running across the road which became magnified in their sight to a broad river of unknown depth. The front rank halted and, of course, all in their rear did the same, and all sat down in mud nearly knee deep and at once fell fast asleep. Some staff officer discovered the mistake or it is likely we should have remained till morning.

There was a great deal of suffering from dysentery and there were prisoners taken by the enemy in consequence of men being obliged to fall out. In this the Highlanders [p. 11] had a great advantage over the Reserve who wore trousers.

As there is a prejudice against low-sized men, the fact that the lowest man in my brother's company (I don't think he was five feet three inches, men being scarce in those days), in addition to his own knapsack, carried that of our right-hand man, who was fully six feet high, for the latter part of the retreat is worth noting, this being a case of breadth making up for length.[8] The retreat of the Reserve occupied eighteen days, the distance [being] about 230 miles. The French army under Soult, after Napoleon left him, was 60,000 men and ninety guns, while Sir John Moore's army only consisted of 19,000, 3,000 having been sent to Vigo.[9] During the greater part of the retreat, we had to march all night and halt by day to allow the baggage stores and stragglers to get off, [and] when we moved on the rear files of the rifle corps and the advance files of the enemy were constantly engaged. No new hand could stand the night work: some officers who joined us on the retreat having come out with Sir David Baird . . . were so ill after the first night's exposure that they had to go back to Corunna. The roads were nearly knee-deep in mud and

---

8.   The original of this sentence being almost completely unintelligible here, the editor has therefore taken the liberty of both adding a few words and making a single change in the order of the various clauses. Meanwhile, the implication of the reference to men being scarce is that the soldier mentioned here was accepted for service despite the fact that he was below the normal minimum height.

9.   Dobbs' figures are wildly out here: in fact, the effective strength of the army on 19 December 1808 was 29,357 men, of whom 26,199 were eventually disembarked in England. As for Craufurd's brigade, this numbered just 1,900 men rather than 3,000. For all this, see Oman, *Peninsular War*, I, pp. 646–7. As for the French forces, while there were plenty of reserves on the way, including, most notably, the corps of Marshal Ney, Soult had only 20,000 men and 40 guns on the field at Corunna. As Moore had 15,000 men in line even after getting many men on board ship, the discrepancy was by no means overwhelming.

part of the mountains with snow. When we got to Lugo, we were relieved for the night and occupied a convent. All the officers of the Fifty-Second were crowded into one small room having closed the window shutters and door, and, having a charcoal-pan lighting, our adjutant, who was the first to lie down, was seized with convulsions. [However,] being carried out, he immediately recovered which showed us the danger we had escaped and its cause.

Having offered battle to the enemy at Lugo, our baggage was sent to the rear: unfortunately, our rations, cloaks and blankets were on the mules and we never saw them again. One of the men having thrown away half his blanket to lighten his load, I picked it up and, turning down a foot of the end over a string which I tied around my neck, it answered all the purposes of a cloak. Having got a bullock's heart from one of the butchers, we had it hot and cold for breakfast, dinner and supper till our rations became due. It may be imagined what we suffered during the rest of our retreat, again being the [p. 12] rearguard. Our shoes being worn out, we got some of those sent out, I believe, for the Spanish troops, and these, being supplied by contract, were so bad that a few hours' marching left them without soles. In this state we arrived at Corunna and were allowed to go into some houses in the neighbourhood.

During the retreat, we were in such need of rest that we often fell asleep whilst marching, and, as I had to carry one of the colours, the unfortunate man in my front often suffered from the pole, whilst I, in return, frequently knocked my head against the butt end of his musket. None but staff officers were allowed to have horses. On our coming in sight of Corunna, no fleet was there to convey us off, but it arrived shortly afterwards . . .

On the morning of the 16th of January 1809, the day of the battle of Corunna, while preparing our breakfast of flour and milk, a tremendous explosion took place and a quantity of matter from the roof fell into the vessels, completely spoiling the contents. This was done by the destruction of the powder magazine which was done to prevent it falling into the hands of the enemy.[10] On [our] inspecting the quarters, the men lay as if dead over the floors, but the enemy had hardly fired his first gun before every man was up and ready for [the] action in which they [were] immediately engaged . . . [p. 13] The village we occupied was about half a mile in the rear of General Hope's division. About three o'clock, [the enemy] opened fire from a battery of eleven guns which had been masked with straw. Under the cover of this fire, [they] advanced to the attack in four columns, two of which attacked the right and centre: that on the right was met by the rifle corps, while that on the centre was received by Lord William Bentinck. Brigadier-General Paget was

---

10. Dobbs' memory evidently failed him here, the destruction of the powder magazine rather occurring on 13 January.

ordered up with the reserve in support, and [p. 14] the Fifty-Second [was] ordered to relieve the rifle corps, their ammunition being expended and most of their swords out of order, which we did in extended order sending the colours to the rear.[11] Sir Sidney Beckwith [*sic*] met us calling out, 'Come here with your bayonet! Come here with your bayonets!'[12] Reynett's company, in which I was[, was] one of the first engaged, and the first man hit was close by me: he fell apparently dead by the ball, it having entered the forehead and passed out at the back of the head so that I said nothing could be done for him . . .[13] What was my surprise afterwards to discover to find he was not killed, the ball having passed round the head under the skin. On [his] recovering his senses, he was taken by some passers-by to the rear and re-embarked; he was recovering from the wound when he was attacked by fever and carried off. We continued to drive the enemy before us till, getting on [their] left flank, they had to withdraw the other column attacking our centre at Elvina and return to the strong position which they had left for the attack . . .[14]

As soon as it was dark, we lighted our fires as if we were going to remain for the night, but afterwards began to move off. On getting to the beach, we found

---

11. 'Swords' here means 'sword bayonets', all troops equipped with the Baker rifle carried by the Ninety-Fifth being issued with such weapons rather than the much shorter blades used in conjunction with the muskets carried by the rest of the army.
12. Dobbs' pen slips here, Beckwith's Christian name rather being Thomas. For further details, see note 63 (p. 91).
13. The Reynett referred to here was Captain James Reynett. However, he was not serving with the battalion, having rather secured a position on Moore's staff as Deputy Assistant Quartermaster General.
14. This account of the Fifty-Second's participation in the battle of Corunna is interesting as it provides clear evidence of the unique ability of British light-infantry regiments to deploy in their entirety as skirmishers. Though somewhat cursory, the account given by Dobbs of the participation of Anstruther's brigade in the fighting is fair enough. In brief, whilst the main body of Soult's infantry launched a frontal attack on the British forces holding the ridge surmounted by the village of Elvina, a brigade belonging to Mermet's division attempted to outflank the defenders by circling round the western end of the high ground, it being this force that was attacked by Paget. Supporting the French was a substantial force of cavalry, but this was precluded from taking an effective part in the action by the fact that the ground was extremely broken, a veritable maze, indeed, of patches of scrub, rocky outcrops and stone walls. Meanwhile, the advance was very successful. With the Fifty-Second in the lead, Paget's infantry pushed deep into the French positions and in fact got so far forward that they came within striking distance of the French artillery positioned on the heights from which Soult had launched his attack. For a somewhat highly coloured account, we can turn to Robert Blakeney of the First Battalion of the Twenty-Eighth Foot: 'Shortly after our arrival . . . [Sir John Moore] ordered the Ninety-Fifth to be detached . . . to keep the heavy dragoons of Lorge and Franceschi's light cavalry in play. Between the rifles

the boats waiting for us and immediately pushed off, but lost one another in the darkness, and, some of us not knowing where to find our ships[, we] got on board the first we came to, sending back the boats for others who were waiting for them . . . As soon as the enemy found that we had embarked, they brought a battery of guns to play on us, and, as the consequences of a raking fire in our crowded ship would [have been] very bad, we made our captain cut his cable.[15]

and the right of Baird's division the Fifty-Second formed a loose chain across the valley . . . In the meantime the battle kindled along the whole line . . . The enemy's column [which had] passed by Baird's right . . . moved sternly forward, certain, as they thought, to come in rear of our troops. But as they advanced they met the Reserve . . . coming on with aspect as severe and determined as their own . . . A thousand passions boiled in every breast. Our opponents, madly jealous at having their . . . fame tarnished by the many defeats which they sustained during the march, [were] determined to regain those laurels to them for ever lost. We, on the other hand, of the reserve had many causes to rouse our hatred and revenge. We painfully recollected the wanton carnage omitted on the defenceless stragglers of all ages and sexes at Bembibre . . . The haughty and taunting insults, too, of our gasconading pursuers were fresh in our memory . . . Thus urged forward by mutual hate . . . we joined in fight . . . Our foes stood firm. But the time occupied in firing was but short: we soon came to the charge and shortly the opposing column was dissipated. Their cavalry now thought it prudent to retire behind their great battery; the Ninety-Fifth, freed from their presence, joined us; and the Fifty-Second, who had slowly retired as the enemy's column first advanced through the valley also united with [the] division . . . We now pushed on all together and turned the French left and were preparing to charge and carry the great French battery. Had Fraser's division, [which] had not fired a shot, come up now and joined the reserve . . . if Napoleon the Great himself had been there, his escape would have been impossible.' Sturgis (ed.), *Boy in the Peninsular War*, pp. 115–18. Despite the protracted nature of the fighting, the Fifty-Second's casualties were not heavy, its total losses coming to five rank and file killed and another thirty-eight wounded. Oman, *Peninsular War*, p. 593.

15. Obviously enough, this last remark is extremely damning, what makes it still worse being the fact that it was not just common soldiers who were implicated in the mutiny. Such, however, was the state of disarray into which a large part of the army had fallen.

Appendix 2

The Account of Captain Charles Steevens, Twentieth Foot[1]

[p. 52] On the 20th of August 1808 we disembarked at Maceira near Peniche and lay on the beach that night, and the following morning we took part in the battle of Vimeiro: we were in Major-General Ackland's brigade and the army was commanded by Sir Arthur Wellesley.

The old Fiftieth were much engaged in this action and behaved very gallantly. Only part of the Twentieth were present at the battle of Vimeiro under the command of Lieutenant-Colonel Campbell as headquarters could not land for want of boats: all on board were dreadfully annoyed, when they heard the firing, that they could not join the remainder of their comrades, but such is the fate of war.

I was detached during the action and was with two companies of the Ninety-Fifth (Rifles): we were engaged in driving some French riflemen [*sic*] out of a wood that was in front of the centre of our army. My company behaved nobly on this occasion: I had only one man wounded [while] [p. 53] we knocked over several of the enemy and took many prisoners. The French hid themselves behind the trees and kept up a very heavy fire, but we advanced on them very rapidly and drove them away in all directions, pouring in volley after volley of musketry. Several pieces of cannon were taken that day and we lost an immense number of men. We had one officer killed (Lieutenant Brooke) and one officer wounded (Lieutenant Hogge).[2] I was excessively ill during the action and suffered a great deal of pain, but, having command of the Light Company, I could not bear the idea of being left on board ship, so I landed with my men, and got through the fatigue of the day better than I expected.

---

1. Born in Essex on 15 January 1777, Charles Steevens secured a commission as an ensign in the Twentieth Foot in December 1795 while still a pupil at a school run by a Dr Barrow in Soho Square in London. Having survived the war unscathed, he rose to the rank of lieutenant colonel and died at Cheltenham on 9 March 1861. His account is extracted from Steevens, *Reminiscences of my Military Life*, pp. 52–77.
2. These two officers were Lieutenant George Brooke and Lieutenant John Hogge; the latter survived the war and ended it as a captain.

The French at Vimeiro were commanded by Junot and they were beaten at all points.

We camped afterwards at Becarinha near Sintra, not far from Lisbon. We were hutted when we could get wood; otherwise we were exposed to all weathers, never taking off our clothes.

The army in and about Lisbon was under the command of Sir Hugh Dalrymple as, after the action, Sir Arthur was superseded in his command, two generals, Sir Harry Burrard and Sir Hugh Dalrymple, having been sent out from England. Both, I believe, were senior to Sir Arthur Wellesley, and then that unfortunate Convention of Sintra was entered into. I call it 'unfortunate' because the very garrison of Lisbon under Junot [p. 54], who were allowed to embark for their own country although prisoners of war, opposed our army again in Spain soon after. It was a great pity that convention was ever concluded, as, no doubt, if Sir Arthur Wellesley had not been superseded in his command, the result would have been very different. The army was very much dissatisfied, and indeed so were the people in England, at the French garrison being allowed to escape, consisting, as it did, of many thousand men: if our army had advanced and attacked Lisbon, not a man of them would have escaped, but they must all have been taken prisoner.

After this treaty was concluded we moved from our encampment at Becarinha on our way to Elvas, my regiment having been ordered there, and we were the first English regiment ever quartered in that place. On our march we crossed the river to . . . Montemor Novo . . . Arraiolas, Estremoz . . . Villa Viçosa and from thence to Elvas, the frontier town of Portugal. At Estremoz the inhabitants were particularly kind and civil to the regiment: they made us a present of a couple of fine bullocks, and gave fruit, wine, bread, etc., to the men as well as to the officers. The bullocks' horns were decorated with ribbons and they were driven out of the town at the head of the regiment.

We remained at Villa Viçosa a few days and during our stay we received a handsome present from the Lady Abbess and nuns and were invited [p. 55] to go into the convent there. The present consisted of two large dishes of sweetmeats and cakes ornamented with coloured cut paper, flowers, etc.; they were beautifully arranged and, of course, very sweet, and were a delightful treat to us. We were very politely received by the Lady Abbess on our entering the convent, and we thought it a high honour to be admitted within the walls. We sat chatting to the Lady Abbess and the young nuns, for many of them spoke French as also Italian. I managed to get on pretty well with the French language for foreigners will always help you out when you are at fault. Many of the nuns were both young and handsome, and we thought it was a great pity to see so many fine young women excluded from society, but they appeared cheerful and happy, and were particularly pleasant and agreeable, and we were very sorry when the time came for our departure: we used now and then, afterwards, to go and talk to them through the iron grating, but, if I recollect well, the Lady Abbess was always present.

While at Villa Viçosa, I amused myself fishing in a pond close to the palace where I was quartered. I fished out of one of the windows, and my tackle was not much suited to the angler, for it consisted of a piece of stick for a rod and a string with a crooked pin tied to it. One of my subalterns, Harding (whom I have mentioned before) managed to catch a dish of fish now and then with my assistance, but I am almost ashamed to say what they were – nothing more nor less than gold and silver fish. One [p. 56] day our little mess gave a dish of these fish for a fore-quarter of mutton to another mess, for we could not all meet at one dinner, but generally a company or two of officers dined together as we used frequently to do on service.

Part of the regiment was quartered at Elvas and part at Fort La Lippe.[3] The inhabitants of Elvas were particularly friendly and attentive to us and, never having seen a British regiment before, they made much of the old Twentieth. Our colonel (Ross) speaking the language of the country and also French very fluently was a great advantage. Previous to our occupying Fort La Lippe, the French had a garrison there, but, being included in the Convention of Sintra, they marched out soon after our arrival at Elvas and were escorted to Lisbon to join their own army there, and, I believe, opposed us again some months after in Spain. At Elvas I was billeted at a gentleman's house: the family consisted of himself, wife and daughter. The daughter had a very pretty black horse which I wanted to purchase: her father was not unwilling if she were inclined to part with it, as it was entirely at her own disposal, and I often asked her to let me have the horse. One day I was talking to Colonel Ross about it [and] he said 'Show her twenty guineas and the horse is yours (dollars were not so tempting as guineas: nothing like the head of the old guinea with the head of good King George III upon it – that coin passed everywhere).[4] As I had nothing but dollars, Colonel Ross lent me the twenty guineas [and] I laid them on [p. 57] the table before the young lady: the horse was immediately mine. The little horse afterward met with a sad fate, being one of the number that were shot near Corunna just before that action, more of which affair will be mentioned hereafter. Here, as at Villa Viçosa, we used to chat with the nuns through the iron grating, and one of our officers (Lieutenant W.),

---

3. Fort La Lippe is a detached fort surmounting a conical hill perhaps half a mile from the northern walls of Elvas. Though open to visitors, it is in a sad state of preservation. As Steevens goes on to say, the views it offers are as extensive as they are dramatic.
4. The Colonel Ross mentioned here was actually Lieutenant Colonel Robert Ross. By the end of the war a brigade commander, he was killed in action near Baltimore in August 1814.

a handsome young fellow, fell in love with one of them, a very pretty girl.[5] The affection seemed reciprocal, and I believe they were both equally sorry when the regiment marched away.

We afterwards moved into Fort La Lippe: it was a very strong place, stood high above the town of Elvas, and opposite (at about six or eight miles' distance) was Badajoz, the frontier town of Spain, a fortified place; at this time it was not in possession of the French, but was garrisoned by the Spaniards. Fort La Lippe was a fine, healthy situation from which we had a very extensive view both of Spain and Portugal. While we were here, our horses were taken to water down the hill outside the fort to a cistern of fine spring water: for some days I found my horse bled very much at the mouth, [and] on examination it was ascertained to be caused by leeches, several having been found about his tongue.

After being quartered in this fort some little time we marched thence into Spain. Our first day's march was to Campo Mayor in Extremadura and from thence to Alburquerque, Alceda, Brosas [p. 58], Alcántara, Zarza Mayor, Moraleja, Perales, Peña Pardas . . . and Fuenteguinaldo to Ciudad Rodrigo where we remained some little time . . . From Ciudad Rodrigo we were ordered to Salamanca, and marched to San Martín del Río and Canillas de Abajo and from thence to Salamanca. On our route from Fort La Lippe to Salamanca, we passed through an extensive forest: it was nearly two days' march to get through it . . . There were many wolves about at night, and the people were obliged to shut up their horses, cattle, etc., after dark, for they had been known to eat part of an animal alive.

We remained at Salamanca for some weeks awaiting the arrival of the remainder of our troops, which, from the force being so large, were obliged to march by different routes. When collected we mustered, including cavalry and artillery, 40,000 men. We experienced some fatiguing marches between Lisbon and Salamanca, nearly 400 miles. I marched on foot all the time and I never had better health. Sir John Moore was in command of the army, and we thought ourselves very fortunate in having so fine a fellow at our head.

[p. 59] Salamanca was a large town on the River Tormes, over which there was a handsome bridge to enter the town. It contained a fine cathedral and several colleges, but the streets were very narrow and dirty. In the river was a bird called a diver which afforded some of us a little amusement: he used to be close to the town, and some of the inhabitants related an odd story about this diver which they called by the name of 'Bonaparte': they said it had been there about twenty years, and no-one could shoot it. One morning, three of us, poor Bent, Harding . . . and I

5.　The officer mentioned here was almost certainly an Ensign James White; he was not promoted to the rank of lieutenant until July 1809.

took our fowling pieces, determined, if possible, to shoot this celebrated bird.[6] We found him on the river and so placed ourselves that, whenever he came up after diving, he was always between us. We got several shots at him, but he was always so quick in getting under water after the trigger was pulled that we never could touch him, and, after firing till our patience was quite exhausted, we gave it up. Others besides ourselves were equally unsuccessful at various times, so we left him as we found him, and when we quitted Salamanca, 'Bonaparte' was still alive. If we had had detonating locks, no doubt we should have bagged him in spite of the superstitious notions many had concerning this bird.[7]

At Salamanca I was billeted at the house of a Spanish gentleman who drove six mules in his carriage and seemed a person of good fortune, but whether Tory or radical I know not. [However,] I should rather suppose the latter, for he never paid me a [p. 60] visit nor paid me any attention . . . In the meadows round about Salamanca were immense quantities of mushrooms: we . . . gathered bushels of them [and] used to have them . . . cooked in various ways. I cannot say exactly how long we remained at Salamanca, but it was a few weeks, and it was reported that our retreat was finally decided on before we marched from that place, for the Spaniards gave us no support and their soldiers were sneaking away to their homes in all directions – frequently a dozen or twenty together – leaving us to fight their battles, and, without their assistance, our force was too small to cope with the enemy, for we had not more than 24,000 afterwards at Corunna and the French had about 40,000 – very great odds. . . .[8]

As soon as we moved from Salamanca, it was looked upon then as the commencement of Sir John Moore's retreat as it was called. From Salamanca [p. 61] we went to Castellanos de Moriscos, San Cristobal de la Cuesta, Villa Excusa, Toro, Pedrosa del Rey, Tiedra, Villalpando, Valderas, Santierce, Grajal de Campos,

---

6. The two officers referred to hear are Captain James Bent of the Twentieth Foot and Colonel John Harding of the Royal Artillery. The former was killed at the battle of Orthez in February 1814.

7. 'Detonating locks' are a reference to the percussion caps introduced in place of flints from the 1820s onwards, the advantage that they offered sportsmen being that they ignited the charge instantaneously whereas with the flintlock there was an appreciable delay between pulling the trigger and the ball exiting the barrel.

8. Hatred of the Spaniards was one of the most pernicious effects of the campaign: indeed, it continues to distort the historiography down to the present day. Amongst the many to express his views on the subject was Edwin Griffith of the Fifteenth Light Dragoons: 'There cannot, I think, be a more disagreeable nation: deceitful, passionate [i.e. quarrelsome], bombastic, imposing, inquisitive, vain and satirical.' Cit. G. Glover (ed.), *From Corunna to Waterloo: the Letters and Journals of Two Napoleonic Hussars, 1806–1816* (London, 2007), p. 93.

Mayorga, Fuentes de Carvajal, Benevente, La Baneja, Astorga, Combarros, Bembibre, Cacabelos, Villafranca, Herrerías, Nogales, Constantino [and] Lugo, and thence we marched one league to Milarosa where we took up a position on high ground [in] a commanding situation, and the French were in a position just opposite to us. We remained one whole day there, expecting the enemy would attack us, but we only looked at each other, and not a shot was fired on either side.

As soon as night came on we retired about three leagues and took up another position, and I think it was in this position that we had a little skirmishing, the French having attacked us, but it was very trifling. From thence we went to Cordela and to Monillos which was about a league from Corunna: here our brigade remained a day or two, and the other part of the army was cantoned in and about Corunna as the ships that were expected for us had not arrived. Otherwise it was expected that the army should have embarked immediately on its arrival at Corunna, but, being delayed, the French had plenty of time to bring up their force, [and] we were therefore obliged to take up a position.

We suffered great privations during the retreat, which was seriously commenced on Christmas Day 1808, and from that time till the battle of Corunna, January 16th 1809, the enemy kept pretty close to [p. 62] us and at times harassed us a good deal. We were frequently within musket shot of one another and [we] occasionally had a brush with them.

On the evening of Christmas Day I recollect going through a stream of water, and rather a deep one: we might just as well have gone over a small bridge close at hand, for we got wet to our waists and had no opportunity of drying our clothes, and this on a Christmas evening when our friends at home were enjoying themselves at their firesides was no joke, but General Anstruther, who gave the order, thought it would have caused too great a delay to go over so narrow a bridge. However, I was none the worse, being of an age at this time to go through a great deal.

On this same day we lost one of our men in a melancholy way, and a fine young man he was: he was in the grenadier company [and] was eating a piece of roll or new bread while walking along and talking to his comrades on the march when part of it stuck in his throat and choked him. Our excellent kind Surgeon, Arnott, was called immediately to his assistance, but could not save him and the poor man was soon after buried.[9]

One day, I recollect, there was a little skirmish with the enemy, for, after the excessive fatigue we [p. 63] underwent, we were obliged occasionally to halt to recruit ourselves, and then the French used to attack us. On one occasion they had

9.   The Surgeon Arnott mentioned here was one Archibald Arnott. In 1821, the Twentieth then forming part of the garrison of St Helena, he was one of the doctors who ministered to Napoleon in his last illness.

a party led on by an officer on a grey horse: a man of the Ninety-Fifth, and he was seen to witness it. Colonel Ross and all of us who witnessed it were very sorry as he seemed to be a remarkably gallant fellow, but such, alas, is the fate of war.[10]

The French had much the advantage of us in these petty warfares, for I have frequently seen their light troops mounted behind their dragoons so that, when they came to a favourable place to make an attack, these fellows dismounted quite fresh, and our light troops, who had been always marching, had to oppose them. Still, we managed to beat them off.

At a place called, I think, Cacabelos, a soldier of one of the regiments, who was a straggler and had been taken prisoner, managed to get again into our lines although severely wounded in several places. His wounds being chiefly about his face and arms, he was, poor fellow, able to walk, but the French had cut him about terribly: he was a dreadful object to look at and greatly to be pitied; [p. 164] though perhaps his condition had been brought on by his own irregularities, still we could not help feeling for him. Colonel Ross led him through the ranks of our regiment to point out to the men the way in which the French would serve them if they lagged behind through drunkenness. I believe the poor sufferer, after all, was left behind a day or two after as we had not the means to carry him on, and, in all probability, the surgeon said, he would not survive as he had so many wounds. It was supposed he had been drunk when taken prisoner and, having resisted, no doubt the enemy ill-used him, for many hundreds of stragglers who reached our lines and were not at all mutilated.

It was at this same town (Cacabelos), I think, that I met with a radical priest who treated the French very differently from our troops, but he paid for his folly. We had been quartered in this priest's house, but the men of my company had been indifferently accommodated, having no straw in their rooms, and, when I remonstrated with this priest, he said that he could not procure any straw, so we were obliged to go without, but he appeared very civil and I concluded that it was out of his power to make our rooms more comfortable. We marched out of the town to continue our retreat, but, unexpectedly, we were ordered to return, and the different companies of the regiment were directed to occupy their old quarters. I took my [p. 165] light company back to the priest's house, and, lo and behold, all the rooms were knee-deep in straw as the French were expected in the town that day if we had not returned. Of course, my men were very much exasperated against the priest for his deceitful conduct, so I was determined to punish him in some way. The priest himself was not forthcoming, as you may well suppose, [but]

---

10. This is clearly a reference to the death of General Colbert at Cacabelos: note that Steevens makes no mention of there being anything extraordinary about the circumstances in which he was shot. See note 7 (p. 179).

he happened to have a little store of bacon in the house, so I had a piece served out to each of my men, and, after all, I believe it was no loss to him, for no doubt the French would have helped themselves to it as soon as they arrived as was generally their plan. Except in this instance, we always paid for what we had, and the night before I had paid the priest for a pint of wine and some bacon for each man, [so] after his behaviour, I think he was rightly served.[11]

We suffered a good deal from fatigue wet and cold besides the want of provision. One day I had nothing to eat but a few raw turnips. The chief brunt of the retreat fell upon us, the regiments composing the Reserve under the command of General Paget.

I commanded the light company of the old Twentieth: a fine company it was, and I was not a little proud of them. The regiments took the duty of rearguard alternately. One day I was in the rear of all our troops with my light company and my two [p. 66] subalterns, Lieutenants Lutyms and Harding.[12] We had a large medicine chest in charge which I had orders to destroy if the bullocks that were drawing it knocked up which unfortunately turned out to be the case. This detained us some time, the chest being so well and closely packed, for it was just as it came from Apothecaries' Hall and was very valuable. The chest was taken out of the cart and every bottle, jar, case, etc., thrown out of it and broken to pieces, the men using stones and butt-ends of their firelocks [while] we afterwards destroyed the chest itself by jumping upon it: in short, I do not think we left anything worth having for the enemy when they came up which they did very soon after we retired.

We were often within shot of the enemy's first file of dragoons, but we did not fire at each other, our object being to reach Corunna as expeditiously as possible and to avoid engaging, our army being so inferior in point of numbers, for the strength of the French was about double ours.

At a place called Nogales on our retreat there was a bridge to be blown up and my company were nearly taken prisoners through some mistake with respect to an order. I received orders to post my men on the side of the bridge next to the enemy so as to cover it whilst preparations were being made for [p. 67] blowing it up. However, by some mistake they forgot to recall us. We anxiously listened for [a]

---

11. This story is less far-fetched than it seems in that the Church was divided in the face of the French invasion: rightly fearing for their futures, the Religious Orders were inclined to be very hostile, but the parish clergy had much to gain from Joseph Bonaparte. However, rather than being an out-and-out collaborator, it seems more likely that the priest in question rightly judged the French to be a greater threat than the British and therefore held back such resources as he had for their use.

12. Lutyms was Engelbert Lutyms (sometimes Lutyens), who was wounded in the battle of the Pyrenees, and ended the war as a captain. However, it has not been possible to trace Lieutenant Harding.

bugle signal, [but there was] still no sound. At last one of my subalterns (Harding) said to me [that] he thought we ought to retire or we should be left behind, for I was told, before we took up our position, that we should be there but a short time. I took his advice and immediately made for the bridge, the advanced guard of the French cavalry being but a short distance from us [though] they did not pursue us. We retreated in double-quick time and it was fortunate we did so, for, as soon as we passed the bridge, our engineer (Captain Pasley, I believe) blew it up.[13] If the bridge had been blown up a few minutes earlier, we should have been just in time to be too late, and many of us might have been taken prisoners [though], at any rate, we should have tried the river which would have been the only chance of escaping.

During the retreat Captain Byrom commanded the grenadier company of the Twentieth, and we used often to say, 'Who will knock up first, the grenadiers or the light bobs. He soon gave in and went on board ship on the sick-list; Lieutenant Telford was one of his subalterns.[14]

The French were not much impeded by the bridge at Nogales being blown up, for they discovered a ford not a great way from the bridge, and their cavalry soon overtook us and frequently harassed us a good deal.

[p. 68] We witnessed many painful sights: it was dreadful to see the numbers of dead lying by the roadside, consisting of men and sometimes women and children – once or twice I saw a little infant lying close to its mother, both dead – also horses, asses, mules and oxen, some frozen to death, having been overcome by fatigue, others . . . shot (for the orders were that, whenever any animals were unable to proceed, they were to be made away with).

Several officers of my own regiment were walking without shoes, but fortunately we came to a place where we had some stores under the charge of a commissary, and those who were in want of shoes supplied themselves. I threw away an old pair and got new ones, but the exchange, though necessary, was not a very agreeable one, for I suffered very much from my new shoes being too large and from their being so thick, as they were what we soldiers called ammunition-shoes, being intended for the men. We likewise supplied ourselves with some salt provisions and what we could take with us. We set fire to everything we left behind, and some little time after we had quitted the place – for it was towards night when we moved on – we

---

13. This officer was Captain Charles Pasley of the Royal Engineers; he survived the war and lived till 1861.
14. Captain Byrom was an Edmund Byrom; interestingly, he saw no further action after the Corunna campaign. Lieutenant Telford, by contrast, served throughout the war and reached the rank of captain. Wounded at Orthez, he died in Cheltenham in 1829.

could see the fire raging, most likely in the possession of the French, for they were always pretty close to us and annoyed us whenever an opportunity offered.

We were repeatedly soaked with rain and had no opportunity to change our clothes. I . . . sometimes had my joints pretty stiff with rain and cold, [and, although] my health continued perfectly good . . . I have [p. 69] often thought that of the retreat had lasted many days longer, I should have been perfectly done up, for most of us had gone through almost as much as we were able to contend with: we were nearly all young men, but still our privations were very trying. The regiment used sometimes to march left in front, and one day, as I was walking alongside Colonel Ross at the head of the regiment, I observed that he frequently fell fast asleep and nearly fell off his horse being almost worn out.[15] I was also so over-fatigued that I very often fell asleep as I walked along, waking up to find myself in the rear of the regiment, thus adding considerably to my fatigues by having to work my way up to the front again.

I recollect [that] one day we took up our position to cover the retreat of the stragglers, which at this time, it was supposed, consisted of about 1500 or 2000 men. It was a dreadfully wet day and our limbs were stiff with wet and the extreme cold and severity of the weather. On this day many of the stragglers came in: some . . . had been left behind through fatigue and sickness and many – too many – who had strayed through drunkenness (one man, who was supposed to have been dipping his canteen in a large butt of wine was actually drowned in it). The scenes of drunkenness were truly appalling, [and were] such as I never before nor since witnessed, but it was chiefly among the young soldiers who landed at Corunna and came out to join our army.

Our regiment lost hardly any men, for they were [p. 70] generally between the ages of twenty-five and thirty-five and able to go through a great deal of fatigue; besides our colonel (Ross) gave orders that, whenever we did happen to get into a town, the officers were not to go to their billets, but were to remain with their men. The consequence was that we were always a check upon pour men and prevented them from drinking (for of course they liked a buckhorn of wine as well as any other soldiers) and also, if we had been called upon in the night, we were then always ready to turn out with our different companies.

Our stragglers being so numerous and being, of course, armed, the enemy did not venture to attack them. However, one day the French seemed to be making some demonstration for an attack and a sergeant – I believe one of the Forty-Third Regiment's – formed up the men and made a good fight of it, beating off the

15. To march left-in-front means to proceed with the battalion's companies in inverted order of precedence, this meaning that the light company would occupy the head of the column and the grenadier company the rear rather than the other way about.

enemy. I heard afterwards that he was very properly rewarded by promotion, for he displayed much judgement and coolness with his bravery and was, no doubt, by his skill and valour the cause of many stragglers rejoining their regiments.[16]

One day, inconsequence of the oxen being overcome with fatigue while drawing a cart laden with dollars, we were obliged to throw the money away, amounting to about £25,000. It happened that, at the time we were throwing the money away, we were in a high situation, that part of the road being [p. 71] upon a hill and perfectly visible to the enemy. It was an unpleasant sight for us to see the little casks of dollars thrown down into the valley on the side of the road, some of them breaking when out flew the dollars in all directions. Many of the soldiers' wives went into the valley and loaded themselves with dollars; the French, not allowing any women to be with their army, sent them back into our lines in double-quick, but without the money.[17]

There ought not to have been any women with our army after we commenced our retreat. Our women received a liberal allowance to pay their way back to Lisbon, but, after being absent a few days, they again made their appearance and many of them, poor things, perished. One I recollect perfectly well from being a particularly well-conducted woman: she had been with the Twentieth Regiment about eleven years and was of a delicate constitution so that she was unable to undergo the hardships to which she was subjected. She was missed during the retreat: it appeared that her daughter – quite a young girl – lost her mother in the dark one night and never heard of her again. I have said a good deal about this person, as her mistress at Liverpool – where she lived as a servant – spoke of her in the highest terms, and was sorry she married a soldier. Her end was certainly an unfortunate one, but she was an example of good conduct.[18]

The money which we had thrown away was [p. 72] soon in the possession of the French and fine pickings they had: £25,000 was no bad haul for a morning's work.

Previous to the money being thrown away, it was proposed, I heard, that the officers and men should carry a certain number of dollars, but, whether from being so hard pressed by the enemy, we had not time to distribute the money, or whether

---

16. The sergeant concerned was one William Newman whilst his reward was a commission as ensign in the First West-India Regiment, a colonial unit composed entirely of black troops that, like many others of its type, provided a home for many officers who were promoted from the ranks.

17. Steevens is mistaken here. In fact, the French did allow women to travel with their field armies, but, at least in theory, all of them had to have a licence to operate as *cantinieres*, *vivandieres* or *blanchisseuses*: unlike in the British army, then, they were not just there as soldiers' wives.

18. In view of the evil character given campfollowers in many journals and memoirs, this testimony is worthy of particular note.

the men were unwilling to carry it, I cannot exactly say, but I believe that the latter was the case, for everyone seemed so fatigued that they wanted no additional weight to carry. For my own part I should have been sorry to have carried even twenty or thirty dollars in my pocket such were my feelings at the time, wishing to keep myself as light as I could, and I am sure many were of my opinion . . .

[p. 72] During the retreat a little boy was found whose parents were supposed to have perished. I think he was picked up by Colonel Ross, for I recollect perfectly well seeing him with a child in front of his saddle, but whether or not this little boy was the same I cannot exactly say. This orphan was taken care of by our regiment and brought to England, and one of the soldiers (an armourer as I recollect he was, but I forget his name) adopted him and treated him as his own child. After a few years the poor orphan died, much to the grief of the worthy philanthropic soldier. I . . . often [saw] the boy in the barracks: he was well taken care of and very well behaved, and the man who adopted him was much attached to him.

Among the numerous things that were destroyed in our retreat was one which most of the officers were sorry to part with: it was our big drum and a most excellent one it was, being a very fine mellow-toned instrument. As it was thought very cumbersome to carry, our colonel gave orders to have it destroyed. No sooner said than done: the drum was broken to pieces by jumping upon it. It seemed a pity to destroy it, for we never had a good one afterwards, and we often regretted when our band was playing that we had not our old drum, the sound of which we had heard for many years on many a day's march and on many a parade both abroad and at home.

While we were in the neighbourhood of Corunna, [p. 74] an immense magazine of gunpowder (4,000 barrels) was blown up by order of Sir John Moore that it might not fall into the hands of the enemy, and such an explosion I never witnessed before: the sound was tremendous and the volume of smoke, thick and black, that ascended, was a wonderful sight. Lutyms, Harding and I were sitting in the chimney corner in our cantonment near Corunna when the magazine was blown up: the soot fell all about us and we were ignorant of the cause of this terrible report until we ran out of the house to see what was the matter . . .

A day or two before the battle of Corunna I witnessed a very different sight, and a very painful one too, such as I hope never to see again. There being no ships provided for the embarkation of horses, an order was given out for them to be destroyed and an order was given out for them to be destroyed, and it was a cruel sight to witness the destruction of our fine English horses: many of them were brought to the edge of the rock overhanging the sea, some shot and others stabbed, and then thrown down. Of course, very many of them reached the bottom alive and there lay on the sands, poor things, where there were men placed to dispatch them, frequently with a hammer. Occasionally I saw a poor animal clinging to a rock previous to reaching the bottom. I could bear the scene but a short time: I never witnessed anything more horrible and painful . . .

[p. 75] The day the reserve arrived at their cantonments near Corunna, I was ordered to remain [i.e. stay behind] with my company, [which was] detached from the regiment. Sir John Moore happened to pass through the village where we were as he was riding round the outposts. Seeing us, he rode up to me and asked who I was. I told him I was captain of the Twentieth's light company [whereupon] he immediately said [that] it was a mistake our being left there, and ordered me to join my regiment as he wished that the Reserve should have a little respite, having recently gone through so much during the retreat. I thought that Sir John . . . made [p. 76] his enquiries and gave his orders in such a mild gentlemanly way [that] I was quite struck with his engaging manners, and so were my two subalterns, and I am sure the men of my company seemed, all of them, to be particularly pleased with him. Alas! A few days afterwards he was no more . . .

At Corunna one fine winter afternoon, the 16th of January 1809, when we were all making ourselves as comfortable as circumstances would admit by changing our linen and the men cleaning themselves (I mean the Reserve, for the troops of the other divisions had had opportunities before), a sudden firing was heard, both cannon and musketry, which made a great stir among us, and we all equipped ourselves as speedily as possible, and in less than half an hour we were under arms and marching towards the point attacked, for the French had commenced an action and were marching towards our lines . . . On our way there, Lutyms and I had a narrow escape: a cannonball pitched close in our front, but, the ground being soft, it buried itself and only saluted us by throwing up the dirt around us. . . . Many of our regiments suffered severely, and we unfortunately lost our brave and excellent commander, Sir John Moore, but the French were beaten on all points, and as soon as the action was over, it was [p. 77] decided that the troops should be embarked.[19] The first to embark were the Reserve, an arrangement made a day or two before by Sir John Moore in consequence of the fatigue they underwent during the whole of the retreat . . . Happy enough were we to get on board ship . . . We then turned into our beds, and had the luxury to sleep without our clothes, and once more to get into a bed, [for] the first time for some weeks. In the morning, soon after daylight, we sailed out of the harbour, glad enough to get out of the country.

19. As this extremely cursory account suggests, the Twentieth were not heavily engaged at Corunna, their role being limited simply to supporting the advance of the Fifty-Second and the Ninety-Fifth.

Appendix 3

The Battle of Vimeiro as Recounted by George Landmann[1]

[p. 198] At between seven and eight o'clock, some distant firing of small-arms announced that the advanced pickets were engaged . . . Everything was now in movement [and] the drums were beating to arms . . . A brigade [i.e. battery] of guns being required to pass out of the park to join the left wing, I found it necessary to fill up a hollow road close at hand, for which purpose I employed my very own small number of men and collected a few more from the Irish Commissariat Corps. This work took up half an hour during which time the enemy's light infantry had pressed forward with so much vigour that, although the work on which we were engaged was at least 300 yards in the rear of the line, the musket shot [p. 199] occasionally dropped in amongst us . . . One of them passing through the shovel of one of the commissariat men, he threw it down as if it had suddenly become red-hot and burned his hands, and, with extreme terror painted in his looks, after wildly staring at the shovel a second or two, screeched 'Ah, murder!', and ran off as fast as [his] legs could carry him.

At this moment, I heard, in the valley leading to the sea, a strange uproar and confusion of female voices, and soon discovered running towards me by the side of the Maceira rivulet a great many women, perhaps thirty or forty in number, no doubt the wives of some of our soldiers. As they approached, it was evident that an event greatly irritating to their temper had occurred, and all I could make out, for they all spoke at once, was that they were heaping execrations and most desperate menaces on a party not then mentioned or invisible. At length, when one of them came sufficiently near to me, I enquired into the cause of so much uproar and disturbance. 'Faith, and I think we [p. 200] have had enough to make us cry

---

1. Born in London in 1779, George Landmann was the son of a professor at the Royal Military Academy in Woolwich, and enlisted in the Royal Engineers in 1791. Reaching the rank of captain in 1806, when the Spanish uprising broke out, he was serving in a division that had been sent to Gibraltar under Sir Brent Spencer. Among the troops left by Sir John Moore to hold Lisbon, in 1809 he secured a commission in the Spanish engineers, thereafter continuing to serve with the Spaniards until he was invalided home in 1812. His account is extracted from G. Landsmann, *Recollections of my Military Life* (London, 1854), pp. 198–234.

murder: weren't we all washing, down there in the river, as safe, as we thought, as if we had been on the banks of dear Shannon, when we was all pounced upon by a party of French dragoons. The villains were not satisfied with taking the greatest liberties with us, but had the impudence afterwards to rob us of our shoes, which, please your honour', she continued, 'was a dirty, unmanly, mean, vile, cowardly trick to pass off on us poor harmless creatures, who had never once given them an ugly word.' On my making some remark on the first part of their grievance, she repeated, louder than before, 'Oh, the dirty villains! To take away our shoes was worse than anything!'[2]

By this time, the way across the hollow way had been completed, and, having seen the brigade pass safely over . . . I mounted my horse . . . and rode off towards the two windmills, where I saw the reserve guns had taken up a position . . . [p. 201] which induced me to believe that I should there find Sir Arthur Wellesley.[3]

In order to reach that place, I necessarily passed though the village of Vimeiro. The shutters and doors of all the houses were closed, yet here and there a face expressive of great anxiety was seen peeping through a shutter partly, and as if very cautiously, opened. At one of these I saw a very interesting young woman with an infant in her arms, and, on my stopping my horse and looking at her attentively, she beckoned me to her. On my approaching the window she immediately begged [if] I would advise her whether she should remain in the village, or seek a place of safety at some distance . . . [but], as she pronounced the last words, a cannon-shot passed through the lower part of the house upon which she uttered a piercing shriek and ran from the window. Having waited a few moments without seeing

---

2.   It is unfortunately the case that rape was a crime much associated with French troops: this is not to say that troops from other armies were not guilty of similar crimes, but in Napoleon's forces in particular a cult of masculinity was encouraged which laid much emphasis on sexual prowess, the problem being intensified by the fact that the soldiers were encouraged to believe, first, that, as Frenchmen, they were irresistible to foreign women, and, second, that women were a legitimate spoil of war. For all this, see M.J. Hughes, *Forging Napoleon's Grande Armée: Motivation, Military Culture and Masculinity in the French Army, 1800–1808* (New York, 2012). Meanwhile, in the original Landsmann attempted to capture the woman's thick Irish accent by altering the orthography, but such is the stereotyping involved in this that the passage has been rendered in standard English.

3.   The 'reserve guns' mentioned here consisted of a scratch force of three 6-pounder guns and three 9-pounder guns that had been held back rather than being allocated to Wellington's infantry brigades as was the case with the rest of the artillery. N. Lipscombe, *Wellington's Guns: the Untold Story of Wellington and his Artillery in the Peninsula and Waterloo* (Oxford, 2013), p. 43.

her again, I rode off to the reserve guns, and never heard any further details of this event, for in the afternoon I found the house quite abandoned.

[p. 202][Arriving at the reserve guns] in vain I enquired after Sir Arthur Wellesley as I was very desirous of joining him, but no-one could give me any information as to where I should be likely to meet with him, [and] I therefore remained with the reserve guns, thinking that would be the place to which he would most probably direct his attention.

I was much pleased and surprised at the readiness with which my horse's nerves had been reconciled to the violent explosions of artillery, for, after a few shots had been fired, he became perfectly steady. [However], as soon as the Fiftieth Regiment, behind which I happened to be in conversation with its commandant, Colonel G. Walker, began a running fire, the poor animal was deeply agitated and made various attempts to run off with me towards the rear.

The Fiftieth were in line on the right of the reserve guns and just sufficiently retired from the crest of the hill to be out of sight of the enemy, and, instead of advancing in line, or by divisions and companies, to fire on the enemy, each man advanced singly when he had loaded so as to see into the valley, and fired on having taken his aim [whereupon] he then fell back into his place to reload. By this management the enemy, who were manoeuvring at long musket range on some hills much inferior in height to those we occupied and making their arrangements for the attack, concluded that the guns were supported by a small number of light infantry only.

At this time some circumstance drew my attention towards the rear, and at a short distance to the right, where I found the Ninth Regiment in column of companies at quarter distance with the left in front.[4] The musket shots were whistling over our heads in great abundance, [and], as I was walking my horse along the right of that regiment . . . a shot having tickled the feather of one of the men about the centre of a division, he stooped or, as [it] is usually called, bobbed. The officer on the right, who was standing a pace or two in advance, and whose vigilant eye was directed along the front of his division, was greatly offended at this involuntary movement, and called out in a stern voice and great severity of aspect, 'Who is that I see bobbing there? What [p. 204] are you bobbing about, sir? Let me see you bob

---

4.   Although British infantry habitually fought in line, they used column for manoeuvre. In this case, the precise formation consisted of each of the battalion's ten companies being formed up in line one behind the other with sufficient space between them for each company to about face and wheel to the right – as the battalion was 'left in front', to do otherwise would have reversed the normal arrangement of the companies when the battalion was deployed in line and in the process offended against precedence – and then wheel left into line.

again, sir, and I'll . . .'⁵ This severe rebuke was exceedingly proper and would have
had its desired effect, had not a cannon shot or howitzer shell, I know not which, at
this most critical moment, just as he had commenced his threat . . . whizzed over
the officer's head. The noise made by such a missile when passing within a yard
or two of a person's head is, to say the least of it, exceedingly disagreeable, and the
strongest nerves would not always save the individual from this most reprehensible
bobbing, so down went my officer a yard at least . . . In an instant he had recovered
his original erect position having looked neither to the right nor to the left, his face
the colour of his coat . . . By the rapidity with which he had recovered his position,
he may [p. 205] at the instant have entertained a hope his bob had not been noticed;
if so, how keenly must he have felt his disappointment, for the whole of the front
rank of the division in his rear had seen it and also many of the men in his own
company, which was instantly manifested by each of them muttering, 'Who is that
I see bobbing there? What are you bobbing about, sir?' and then adding 'Who bobs
now?'

Having returned to the vicinity of the Fiftieth Regiment and the reserve artillery,
and being without any fixed pursuit, Brigadier-General Anstruther observing my
want of occupation, and his aide-de-camp's horse having been killed, called me
to attend him to supply his place . . . [p. 206] I did not hesitate for a moment and
immediately followed him . . . [p. 207] The first order I received in my new staff
situation as aide-de-camp was to watch the movements of some of the enemy's
cavalry on our right . . . As they were at a considerable distance, I found it necessary
to use my glass, but, the wind being very strong, I dismounted with a view to
obtain a rest to steady my hand. I first tried to support my hand on my saddle, but
my horse was too unsteady, [so] I then went to a windmill close-by, where a drum-
major and all his little fry were . . . crowded together . . . in hope of protecting
themselves from shots. I could not behold these poor little fellows, pale and with
looks manifesting extreme anxiety, without experiencing many painful feelings.

I found it, however, impossible to rest my glass against the mill without disturbing
the drum-major, who could not be persuaded to move more than his head and
body . . . by which my object was defeated. Upon this, in a rather pettish manner,
I said to him, 'Keep your skulking place, you coward: I shall not disturb you!' I
[then] retired a [p. 208] few steps, endeavouring, under the shelter of the mill from
the wind, to hold up my glass. I had not withdrawn from the spot occupied by the
drum-major more than half a minute when I heard a sharp slap accompanied by a
deep groan. I turned round and observed the unfortunate drum-major with hand

---

5. As used here, 'division' does not refer to the normal collection of 8–12 infantry
    battalions with some supporting artillery – a force perhaps 5,000-strong – but a
    fraction of an individual battalion (usually 2 companies).

on his breast, and nearly bent double, suffering severe pain. I thought he had been shot through the body, but, on removing his hand, I found a musket ball which had struck his cross-belt [and] made a deep dent in it without passing through. The poor fellow was led away and I think I was afterwards informed that he had died in a few days in consequence of this contusion.

At length I got a sergeant's halberd to support and steady my hand, and I soon perceived the head of a column of cavalry winding round the end of a hill as if endeavouring to turn our right flank and so cut in between the first and second lines: the latter was on a ridge of high ground commanded by General Hill. Just at this time a few nine-pounders loaded with spherical case [i.e. shrapnell shells] fired by Captain [p. 209] Elliott from the right of the second line . . . about 2,000 yards distant from the cavalry were so perfectly directed, and the fuses cut with so much accuracy, that the cavalry turned round and effected a hasty retreat.[6]

[p. 210] I now reported this event to Anstruther whom I found near the Fiftieth Regiment and the reserve guns and my attention was quickly drawn to the formation of a large column of [p. 211] attack at a short distance to the left of our direct front. The column was in close order and appeared to consist of about 5,000 grenadiers and was advancing upon the reserve guns in double-quick time covered by a swarm of *voltigeurs*, the latter running up in the most daring manner to within twenty yards of the guns.

During the whole progress of this column, the artillery kept up a most destructive fire, each of the guns being loaded with a round-shot and, over that, a canister, and I could most distinctly perceive at every discharge that a complete lane was cut through the column from front to rear by the round-shot whilst the canister was committing dreadful havoc on the forward ranks. At this period, Lieutenant-Colonel Robe, commanding the artillery, and near whom I happened to be, turned to me, and observed, 'You're a lucky fellow to be mounted, for, by God, if something be not very quickly done, the enemy will, in a few minutes, have our guns, and we shall be all bayoneted!'[7] [p. 212] 'Then', said I, 'order up your

---

6.   The battle of Vimeiro was the first occasion on which the British army used the shrapnel shell. Properly known as spherical case, this was a recent innovation developed by a Major Shrapnell, and consisted of a standard artillery shell to which was added a large number of musket balls. As a result, the British were provided with an extremely effective anti-personnel weapon which replicated the devastating effects of ordinary canister at far greater ranges than would otherwise have been attainable. Lipscombe, *Wellington's Guns*, p. 26.

7.   The officer mentioned here is Lieutenant Colonel William Robe, a highly experienced artillery officer who played an important role in many actions of the Peninsular War until being severely wounded in the autumn of 1812 and forced to retire from active service. His youngest daughter was to be named Vimiera [*sic*] in honour of the battle.

horse and be ready for the worst!' 'No, no', exclaimed the gallant Robe. 'I'll neither leave my guns nor my gunners: I'll share the fate of my brave boys, be it what it may!' The words here recorded are *verbatim* those used by Robe in expressing his entire devotion to the service.

The enemy's column was now in advancing in the most gallant style, the drum . . . marking the double-quick time of the *pas-de-charge*. I could distinctly hear the officers in the ranks exhorting their men to persevere in the attack . . . and I could also distinguish the animated looks and gestures of the mounted officers who, with raised swords, waving forwards, strongly manifested their impatience at the slowness of their advance to which they also loudly added every expression of sentiments which they thought best calculated to urge their men to be firm in their attack and irresistible in their charge.

In this way, the enemy having very quickly [p. 213] approached the guns to within sixty or seventy yards, they halted and endeavoured to form their line under the protection of the *voltigeurs*.[8] I was then by the side of Anstruther to whom I said, 'Sir, something must be done or the position will be carried.' [At this] the general replied, 'You are right', and, without a moment's delay, he raised his hat as one about to cheer, and called out to the Forty-Third and Fiftieth Regiments, 'Remember, my lads, the glorious 21st of March in Egypt! This must be another glorious 21st!'

---

8.   This is a particularly interesting remark. For a century or more, there has been intense debate about the practices adopted by the French infantry when on the attack. Thus, while all commentators are agreed that the normal formation used on such occasions was various forms of the column, there is no consensus as to what happened when units reached close range. On one side a largely French and American school insists that, as laid down in the army's tactical regulations, troops were supposed to deploy into line and open fire, on the other a largely British school is convinced that the aim was rather the proverbial *attaque à l'outrance*, the aim being rather for the columns to keep going and, in effect, terrify the defenders into running away. This argument is far from easy to resolve as the evidence is contradictory. If this is an example of French infantry forming line on reaching close range, the battles of Albuera and Waterloo, to name but two, provide clear examples of columns only trying to deploy into line after they discovered that the troops facing them refused to budge in the face of their advance. Given that changing formation close to the enemy was always an extremely risky business in that any unit that attempted such a move was wide open to a sudden counter-attack, and given, too, that allowing the men to open fire in the course of an advance was tantamount to abandoning any further movement on account of the fact that loading and firing became a de facto substitute for the offensive action that was the only way of carrying the day, the editor's view is that most French officers favoured the bayonet, and that the incident described by Landmann is therefore something of an exception.

I have no doubt that this appeal had its effect. Walker immediately advanced his gallant Fiftieth to the crest of the hill, where he gave the words, 'Ready, present, and let every man fire when he has taken his aim!' This order was most strictly obeyed and produced a . . . destruction and carnage which the enemy had not anticipated. Then, raising his drawn sword and waving it high over his head, Walker called out, 'Three cheers and charge, my fine fellows!' and away went this gallant regiment, huzzahing all the time of their charge down the hill, before the French had recovered from discovering [p. 214] that the guns were not unprotected, as I afterwards was informed that they had up to that instant fully believed.

This rush forward was awfully grand: the enemy remained firm and almost motionless till our men were within ten or twenty yards from them [and] then discharged a confused and ill-directed fire from some of the front ranks, for the line had not yet been formed to its full extent and the rear was already breaking up and partially running off. The whole now turned round and started off, every man throwing away his arms and accoutrements as also his knapsack, a cap and, in short, everything that could have obstructed his utmost speed, and thus a gallant column, which but a very few moments before had numbered 5,000, at least, of the stoutest hearts in the army was repulsed, scattered and completely thrown out of action. The complete dispersion of this column presented a most interesting and curious sight: the whole of [its members] being dressed in white linen greatcoats gave them, whilst in confusion and running for their lives, exactly the appearance of an immense [p. 215] flock of sheep scampering away from the much-dreaded shepherd's dog.

The charge of the Fiftieth had been followed by the charge of the Forty-Third Regiment, and, I believe, another, and, after pursuing the fugitives to the distance of 300 to 400 yards, we gave up the chase, our people perceiving that they were losing ground . . . Some of the regiments on the right of the Fiftieth after the charge of the latter, or simultaneously with it, having also charged or advanced in pursuit of the flying and broken remnants of the column, which, but five minutes [p. 216] before had presented so imposing a front, having gone on to a very imprudent distance in advance of the line, Anstruther ordered me to go with all possible speed, halt them and bring them back.

The order I had just received was very important and . . . I started accordingly with as much speed as my horse could make down a steep hill and over a very broken gravelly surface . . . for, with regret, I perceived the regiment I was endeavouring to overtake was pushing on after the flying enemy without reflecting on the risk to which they were exposed by extending their distance from the main line. This regiment had advanced half a mile or more when I came up with them in a wood . . . [p. 218] I found it no easy task to enforce a halt . . . Seeing the importance of the case and quickly discovering the difficulty which the commanding officer had to contend with . . . I offered to assist him . . . and it was not before we had ridden up and down the lines several times . . . that the pursuit was abandoned. The regiment was at that time much broken as to line and almost intermixed with the enemy . . .⁹

Having succeeded in carrying my orders into effect . . . [p. 219], I made off to report to Anstruther, and on my way I found a regiment in line in the valley, which I believe was the Fifty-Second, midway betwixt us and the position which we had occupied from the commencement. Upon going up to the officer in command, who was dismounted, I observed he had a white handkerchief wound round his hand, and, on my expressing a hope that he was not severely hurt, he stated that he had received a shot through the palm of his hand as he raised it over his head, huzzaing at the moment of charging the enemy. This regiment had been sent forward to occupy the ground and prevent the (French) light infantry from cutting off the retreat of the regiment I had just before succeeded in halting . . .

[p. 229] The firing had now almost totally ceased and the enemy was actively engaged in collecting his scattered troops, and in reforming [p. 230] them into line in order to make as formidable appearance as the general disaster which he had suffered at all points could enable him to accomplish. In this way, Junot . . . contrived to show us a line drawn up on a range of hills parallel to our position and at the distance of a mile or more with a view, no doubt, to being regulated in his movements by those we might adopt. The ground between us was variously scattered over with killed, wounded, arms, drums, caps, knapsacks, canteens, dead horses . . . ammunition wagons and . . . cannon, but the track which the before-mentioned column of attack had followed, was conspicuously marked, to a great distance, by the number of killed and wounded who had fallen under our artillery fire in its progress towards us and which regularly increased in numbers as the column had approached. At the extreme point of its advance, where an attempt had been made to deploy and form the line, the dead and dying were in some places absolutely lying in heaps, three or four men in height. The wounds of [p. 232] nearly the whole of these being inflicted by cannon shot, were, it may be supposed, truly horrible, and of every possible variety . . . [p. 233] Having returned towards the top of the hill, where Robe's reserve guns had experienced [p. 234] such a

---

9.   The identity of this unit is unclear, but it may well have been the Ninety-Seventh Foot: known as the Queens' Germans, this was a unit that had originally been recruited from sometime Hapsburg soldiers who had been induced to enlist in the Spanish army after being captured by the French in the Italian campaigns of 1796–7 and had then been taken prisoner a second time by the British when they had occupied Menorca in 1798. The regiment had fought well enough in Egypt in 1801, but by 1807 it had become 'a repository of foreigners of all sorts' and in consequence may well have been prone to indiscipline. See M. Wishon, *German Forces and the British Army: Interactions and Perceptions, 1742–1815* (Houndmills, 2013), p. 142.

narrow escape, I there observed my friend Captain Morrison of the Royal Artillery, and I believe that I was the first who noticed to him that his cocked hat had been shot through just over the back of his head . . . which had torn it much more than was sufficient for the passage of a grapeshot, which I suppose it was which has so nearly killed him, and at the same moment he was the first to acquaint me with my having received a shot . . . through my hat and exactly in the same part of it.

Appendix 4

The Battle of Vimeiro as Recounted by Adam Neale[1]

[p. 11] The whole French army, commanded by Junot in person, was yesterday completely routed in the neighbourhood of this village . . . [p. 12] The troops, as usual, turned out under arms an hour before daybreak, and no alarm took place till about eight o'clock when it was announced that our pickets on the Lourinha road were attacked. However, as no great bustle ensued, I breakfasted quietly with a few friends, and then walked out with the intention of purchasing a mule, an animal here of some importance. Passing along the streets of the village, I heard several officers assert that the French were advancing in great force to attack the position, while others thought it would be just an affair of pickets. Still, the noise of the musketry fire seemed to approach and several movements to be taking place among the troops on the heights. At length the discharge of artillery commenced when I determined to get on the heights where our left wing was posted and to which they had just removed from the valley the heavy artillery. On crossing the valley in which were placed the wagons, oxen and commissariat stores. Having reached the spot where the brigade of guns was posted, I had a complete view of the whole scene, a scene the grandest and most picturesque you can well imagine. [p. 13] The valley, village and extent of [their] beautiful and romantic surroundings were stretched beneath my eye as on a plan. The atmosphere was serene; the sun blazed forth from a blue and silvery sky, streaked with fleecy clouds, and I could distinctly perceive every movement of the contending armies.

The French were at this moment advancing in several columns from the eastward under cover of some pine woods, driving in our pickets and riflemen who retreated to a height to the southward of Vimeiro on which [was] posted the centre or advanced guard of our army. It was composed of Brigadier-General Fane's brigade of riflemen, Brigadier-General Anstruther's brigade and the Fiftieth Regiment.

On these columns of French a tremendous fire was kept up by the artillery belonging to the centre which was placed in front of two white windmills on the height. The fire was returned by the guns of the enemy with great spirit, but it was evident that our artillery was much better served than theirs and that the carnage

---

1. Extracted from Neale, *Letters from Portugal and Spain*, pp. 11–21.

caused by the lately invented shrapnell shells was prodigious. Nevertheless, they continued to advance with great intrepidity, But they were charged in a most gallant manner by [p. 14] the Fiftieth Regiment, on which they turned their backs and fled to the woods in all directions.

At this time another party who were advancing into the road which enters Vimeiro from the northward were met and repulsed with great loss by the Second Battalion of the Forty-Third. This battalion had been stationed near the church in order to prevent the enemy from entering the village as it appeared to be their design, in attacking our centre, to penetrate through Vimeiro and possess themselves of our baggage and commissariat stores.

On the right of the centre the enemy were checked by the bayonets of the Ninety-Second Regiment and [the] Second Battalion [of] the Fifty-Second, and in these operations Brigadier-General Acland's brigade, which had only landed at Maceira during the night, and was passing along the valley to arrive at the heights, lent a very well-timed, effectual assistance, and the heavy artillery, lately brought up from the valley, did immense execution, the shrapnell shells making considerable gaps in the enemy's columns.

On giving way, the enemy were pursued by the gallant Lieutenant-Colonel Taylor, who charged them with his small body of horse in the most daring style, and cut them [p. 15] down in great numbers. Sorry I am to add that in performing this service, he lost his valuable life. A great proportion of his men fell with him.[2]

While these things were going on in the centre, I had advanced considerably to the left, and got in the rear of . . . the brigade commanded by Major-General Ferguson which was the left of our army. Here the enemy came up with great impetuosity. They were opposed in the front by our riflemen, whom they drove in. Coming up, however, with Major-General Ferguson's brigade, they received a tremendous volley and were shortly afterward brought to a charge. This was an operation their nerves could not stand and they immediately gave way. Our troops

---

2.   This episode was less glorious than Neale suggests. Initially, the unit concerned, the Twentieth Light Dragoons, the only British cavalry unit that had thus far reached Portugal, did well, breaking through a squadron of dragoons that had been sent forward to protect the fleeing infantry and sabreing or forcing to surrender many of the unfortunate fugitives. However, as was so often to occur with British cavalry in the years that followed, Taylor then either lost control of the situation or was himself overtaken by a fit of passion, for the tiny unit – it had just 240 men on the field – proceeded to go out of control and rode deep into the French positions where it was soon overwhelmed at the cost, apart from Taylor himself, of twenty rank and file dead, another twenty-four wounded and eleven prisoners. Oman, *Peninsular War*, I, p. 257.

pursued them with eagerness, killed or wounded an immense number and took several pieces of cannon . . .

Close to the spot where Major-General Ferguson's brigade received the attack of the French stood a small farm house into which it had been determined to carry the wounded. Thither I [p. 16] repaired and witnessed a scene the most distressing. Around the building, whose interior was crowded with the wounded, lay a number of poor fellows in the greatest agony, not only from the anguish of their wounds, many of which were deplorable, but from the intense heat of the sun, which increased the parching fever induced by pain and loss of blood. Two fig trees afforded the scanty blessing of a sort of shade to the few who were huddled together beneath their almost leafless branches. Over the surrounding field lay scattered the fragments of arms and military equipments of every description – caps, muskets, swords, bayonets, belts and cartouche boxes covered the ground, on which were also stretched in many an awful group, the friend and foe, the dying and the dead . . . On entering the cottage to survey the sadly interesting group within, I recognised . . . [p. 17] I could be useful . . . to a great many who, but for my interference . . . might have remained for many hours in excessive pain. To several, [however,] a simple inspection of their wounds, with a few words of consolation, or perhaps a little opium, was all that could be done or recommended. Of these brave men, the balls had pierced organs essentially connected with life, and in such cases prudence equally forbids the rash interposition of unavailing art and the useless indulgence of delusive hope . . . [p. 19] A hospital mate was . . . left in charge of them till the morning, and . . . [at] eleven o'clock at [night] I left them to proceed towards [p. 20] [Vimeiro] accompanied by Staff Surgeon F_____. The night was so dark that it was necessary to have recourse to a Portuguese guide . . . On crossing the fields to get to the . . . road, I shuddered as we involuntarily stumbled over many an unburied corpse of man and horse. We found the road almost impassable from the number of tumbrils and artillery wagons of the enemy which were broken down in every direction. Our ears were saluted on passing the [p. 21] church yard by the heavy moaning and exclamations of the wounded French, with whom the church and the cemetery were crowded. 'Ah, mon Dieu, mon Dieu! Le sang coule: je meurs, je meurs!' ['My God! My God! The blood is flowing. I am dying! I am dying!'] At length, with a great deal of difficulty, we reached Vimeiro. The streets . . . were choked up by the long line of ox wains bearing in from the fields the wounded, whose haggard countenances appeared more wretched from the glare of the torches which blazed around them and increased the horrors of the impressive scene.

Appendix 5

The Action at Cacabelos as Recounted by Robert Blakeney[1]

[p. 54] Early on the morning of the third [of January] the Reserve marched up towards the crown of a low hill in front of Cacabelos [p. 55] on the Bembibre side. Here we halted, leaving so much of it above us as to screen us from the view of an approaching foe. No enemy having as yet advanced, the general of division ordered a hollow square to be formed facing inwards. A drumhead court-martial sat in rear of every regiment, and within the square were placed the triangles. The culprits seized in the town, as soon as tried and sentenced, and a general punishment took place along the four faces of the square; this took place for several hours.[2]

During this time our vedettes came in frequently to report to the general that the enemy was advancing. His only reply was 'Very well.' The punishment went on . . . Two culprits . . . seized in the act of committing a robbery stood with ropes around their necks. Being conducted to an angle of the square, the ropes were fastened to the branches of a tree which stood there, and at the same time the delinquents were lifted up and held on the shoulders of persons attached to the provost-marshal. In this situation they remained, awaiting the awful signal for execution which would instantly be carried into effect by a mere movement from the tree of the men from whose shoulders they were supported. At this time (between twelve and one o'clock as well as I can remember), a cavalry officer of high regimental rank galloped into the square and reported to General Paget that the pickets were engaged and retiring. 'I am sorry for it, Sir', said the general, 'but this information is of a nature which would induce me to expect a report rather by

---

1.   Extracted from Sturgis (ed.), *Boy in the Peninsular War*, pp. 54–62.
2.   The town concerned was Bembibre. As already recounted (see note 138, p. 124), this place had been the scene of serious disorders the previous day, and, as commander of the Reserve, Paget was furious: not only were the strictest orders issued against pillaging, then, but patrols were sent into the town and many men arrested. With respect to the two men sentenced to be hung, Blakeney recounts that they were taken in the act of robbing an individual, this being a crime that was always punished much more heavily than mere larceny.

a private dragoon than from you. You had better go back to your fighting pickets, Sir, and animate your men to a full discharge of their duty.'

General Paget was then silent for a few moments, and, apparently suffering under great excitement. [p. 56] He at length addressed the square by saying, 'My God! Is it not lamentable to think that, instead of preparing the troops confided to my command to receive the enemies of their country, I am preparing to hang two robbers? But though *that* angle of the square should be attacked, I shall execute these villains in *this* angle.' The general again became silent for a moment and our pickets were heard retiring up the opposite side of the hill and along the road which flanked it on our left. After a moment's pause, he addressed the men a second time in these words, 'If I spare the lives of these two men, will you promise to reform?' Not the slightest sound, not even breathing was heard within the square. The question was repeated: 'If I spare the lives of these two men, will you give me your word of honour as soldiers that you will reform?' The same awful silence continued until some of the officers whispered to the men to say 'Yes' when that word loudly and rapidly flew through the square. The culprits were then hastily taken away from the fatal tree by a suspension from which they but a moment before expected to have terminated their existence. The triangles were now ordered to be taken down and carried away.

Indeed, the whole affair had the appearance of stage management for, even as the men gave the cheers customary when condemned criminals are reprieved, our pickets appeared on the summit of the hill above us intermixed with the enemy's advanced guard. The square was immediately reduced, formed into columns at quarter-distance and retired, preceded by the Fifty-Second Regiment who started forward at double quick time and, crossing the River Cua, lined its opposite bank. The division, coming up, passed over the bridge, with the exception of the Twenty-Eighth's light company, who were left behind with orders to [p. 57] remain until the whole of the Reserve should have crossed, and then to follow.

General Paget now moved forward and took up a strong position on the side of a sloping hill immediately in front of Cacabelos. His extreme right somewhat outflanked the village [and] his left rested on the road to Villafranca. The whole line was protected by a chain of hedges and stone walls which ran close in front. Our battery of six guns was pushed some way down the road leading to the bridge to take advantage of a small bay by which they were protected and concealed from the enemy. The light company of the Twenty-Eighth, as soon as they retired from the bridge, were to be posted immediately under the guns, which were to fire over our heads, the declivity of the road allowing that arrangement. The left wing of the Twenty-Eighth Regiment [was] pushed forward immediately in rear of the guns . . . for their protection. The right wing of the Twenty-Eighth now formed the extreme left of the line.[3] Further in advance, and extended to the left along the bank of the stream, their right close to the bridge, the Fifty-Second were placed.[4]

The Cua, an insignificant stream but at this season rising in its bed, runs along the base of the sloping hill upon which Cacabelos is situated at the distance of from four to five hundred yards. At this bridge, the light company, as has been said, were posed until everything belonging to the reserve should pass over, and, before this was entirely accomplished, our cavalry (at first preceded by the Ninety-Fifth, whom they passed through) came galloping down to the bridge, followed closely by the enemy's dragoons. The enemy's advance being seen from [p. 58] the high

---

3.   At first glance this statement is extremely confusing. However, by 'right wing' Blakeney does not mean the extreme right-hand end of the Twenty-Eighth's line, but rather a sub-unit of the single battalion it had on the field, namely the more senior of the two wings of five companies apiece into which battalions were divided and could, on occasion be split.

4.   There is some confusion about the site of this action. Most accounts state the bridge defended by the Reserve was that across the River Cua which flows from north to south just west of the village of Cacabelos itself, but this does not seem to fit with Blakeney's otherwise very detailed account of the battle, while the sketch map of the action prepared by Captain Alexander Gordon of the Fifteenth Hussars shows the Fifty-Second, Twentieth and Twenty-Eighth posted at the eastern edge of a village along the line of what looks very like a potential watercourse that runs down at an angle to join the Cua (by no means, incidentally, 'an insignificant stream') a few hundred yards to the south. Admittedly no stream is shown on Gordon's map, but reference to Google Maps suggests that there is indeed such a feature at that point. Also noteworthy is the fact that Blakeney makes no mention of buildings but does talk a lot about walls and hedges. On balance, then, reading Blakeney, it looks as if the action took place at the foot of the slopes to the east of the village. Yet consider this alternative version that comes to us from the pen of Captain Charles Cadell of the same unit: 'The Fifty-Second Regiment under Colonel Barclay, went through the village in double-quick time and in the most beautiful fashion took possession of the vineyards on the opposite side of the river, while the rest of the Reserve crossed the bridge under cover of the Ninety-Fifth and formed on the hill behind the Fifty-Second. By this time the enemy were upon us in great force and attacked the Ninety-Fifth, the cavalry joining in the onset. They were terribly galled by the rifles as they advanced through the village. The Ninety-Fifth then retired up the road to the right and left, the French being at the same time exposed to a murderous fire from the Fifty-Second in the vineyards which completely checked them. The Fifty-Second then retired up the road when the enemy were again most gallantly repulsed. The French in this affair lost the general officer commanding the advanced guard and many men. A column of them was also severely handled by Captain Carthew's guns and stopped [from] descending the hill on the other side of the river.' C. Cadell, *Narrative of the Campaigns of the Twenty-Eighth Regiment since their Return from Egypt in 1802* (London, 1835), pp. 51–2.

ground in our rear, the battalion bugles sounded our recall, but it was impossible to obey for at that moment out cavalry and the Rifles completely choked up the bridge.

The situation of the light company was now very embarrassing[: it was] in danger of being trampled by our own cavalry, who rode over everything which came in their way, and crowded by the Ninety-Fifth and liable to be shot by them, for in their confusion they were firing in every direction. Some of them were a little worse for liquor . . . and we were so mixed up with them and with our own cavalry that we could offer no formation to receive the enemy who threatened to cut us down. At length, the crowd dissipating, we were plainly seen by the French, who, probably taking us for the head of an infantry column, retired. We sent them a few shots.

As soon as the Ninety-Fifth, who had lost between thirty and forty prisoners on this occasion, had crossed over and lined the hedges on the opposite side, and our cavalry, taking retrograde precedence more through horse-play than military etiquette, had cleared the bridge, the light company followed. It was mortifying to reflect that, after such an uninterrupted series of brilliant achievements, their farewell encounter with their opponents should thus terminate, even although they may have been slightly outnumbered, but neither of their two gallant leaders were present.[5]

The light company now occupied their destined post under the guns and accounted for not having obeyed the battalion bugles which had continued to sound the recall during the whole time of our advance.[6] The cavalry rode on without a halt to join the main body, than on the march for Lugo.

[p. 59] Shortly after we had gained our position, either supposing that the bridge was abandoned by the retirement of the light company, or because their courage was wound up to proper fighting pitch, the French cavalry advanced at a quick trot down the hill. Our guns instantly wheeled out upon the road and played upon their column until they became screened by the dip in the road as they approached the bridge. Here they were warmly received by the Fifty-Second Regiment, now freed from our own dragoons, and the Ninety-Fifth, and upon this they made

---

5.   The import of this remark is not quite clear, not least because the identity of the two leaders concerned is never revealed. In theory, Blakeney could mean Paget and the brigade commander, Disney, but it seems more likely that he is referring to the light company's captain and lieutenant. If this last is the case, then the implication is that Blakeney, who was the light company's ensign, was in command.

6.   This, too, is rather puzzling, as Blakeney specifically says that the light company retired as soon as the bugles were sounded. Perhaps what he means as the fault that had to be accounted for is rather the delay in getting back across the bridge. In this case 'advance' could be taken as shorthand for 'time that light company remained on the far side of the stream'.

a most furious charge at full speed over the bridge and up the road towards our position. During this onset they were severely galled by the Ninety-Fifth who by this time had lined the hedges on either side of the road within a few yards of its flanks, and by the light company immediately in their front, whom it was evidently their intention to break through as they rode close to our bayonets. But their ranks being much thinned by the destructive fire of the Rifles and of the standing ranks of the light company, their charge was in vain and their gallant leader having fallen close under our bayonets, they wheeled about and underwent the same ordeal in retiring so that but few escaped to tell the tragic tale. One alone among the slain was severely regretted, [namely] their gallant leader, General Colbert: his martial appearance, noble figure, manly gesture and, above all, his daring bravery called forth the admiration of all. I say that one only [of the slain] was to be regretted, for the wanton cruelties committed against the women and children on the previous day were too recent to be either forgiven or forgotten.[7]

This attack of the French cavalry was most ill-advised, ill-judged and seemingly without final object in view. [p. 60] It is true that their bravery was too obvious

---

7.   As the rearguard of the army cleared Bembibre, the French cavalry had got in amongst the last fugitives and inflicted many casualties. Thus, 'We had a great deal of trouble with the stragglers, numbers of whom were so drunk that all our efforts to drive them on were fruitless, and we were obliged to abandon them to their fate. They were soon overtaken by the French chasseurs who treated them most unmercifully, cutting to their right and left and sparing none who came within reach of their swords. They were even accused of wounding the sick men whom they overtook in the hospital wagons.' Wylly (ed.), *Cavalry Officer in the Corunna Campaign*, p. 154. Of all this, Blakeney was an eyewitness: 'We had proceeded but a short distance when the enemy's horsemen . . . approached the place, and then it was that the apparently lifeless stragglers, whom no exertion of ours was sufficient to rouse from their torpor, startled at the immediate approach of danger, found the partial use of their limbs. The road instantly became thronged by them: they reeled and staggered and, screaming, threw down their arms. Frantic women held forth their babies, suing for mercy by the cries of defenceless innocence, but all to no purpose: the dragoons . . . advanced and cut right and left, regardless of intoxication, age or sex. Drunkards, women and children were indiscriminately hewn down – a dastardly revenge for their defeat at Benevente.' Sturgis (ed.), *Boy in the Peninsular War*, p. 51. Here, too, is Cadell: 'One of the handsomest men of the grenadier company of the name of McGee was coming along the road, lame from an accident, his firelock and pack having been taken by his mess-mates to enable him to keep up; he was, however, overtaken by two French dragoons, and, although unarmed and helpless, inhumanly cut to pieces almost within our sight. The exasperation of the grenadier company was terrible: they longed to have an opportunity to avenge the death of their comrade.' Cadell, *Narrative*, p. 48. Finally, what is odd about Blakeney's account of the fight at Cacabelos is that he makes no mention of the generally accepted story that Colbert was shot at exceptionally

to be doubted, but they rushed on reckless of all opposition whether actual or probable, and had they succeeded in cutting through the light company, which they would have found some difficulty in doing . . . they would have been in a worse position than before: when they had passed beyond the light company a hundred yards, they would have encountered the left wing of the Twenty-Eighth Regiment, supported, if necessary, by the right wing directly on their flank . . . and, had their number, which was but from four to five hundred men, been quadrupled, every man must have been shot, bayoneted or taken prisoner . . .

[p. 61] Not long after the failure of the charge headed by General Colbert, some French dragoons together with their light troops crossed the Cua under the high ground occupied by our right and centre. They were opposed by the Ninety-Fifth, who moved from the hedges which flanked the road to meet them, and a severe skirmish ensued. The enemy's cavalry, who on this occasion mixed with their skirmishers, were fast gaining ground on the right of the Rifles, [and so] the bugles from the position sounded the retreat, but were very imperfectly obeyed. Some of the Fifty-Second Regiment who could no longer restrain their feelings at seeing the critical situation in which their old friends were placed, darted forward from their position above to their assistance, and the Twenty-Eighth's light company, making a partial extension along the hedge which flanked the road upon which they were stationed, sent many an effectual shot in their aid.[8]

The fight now became confused and the enemy's numbers increased with every instant. Cavalry, *tirailleurs*, *voltigeurs*, Ninety-Fifth and those of the Fifty-Second

---

long range by a rifleman named Tom Plunkett, not to mention the fact that he implies that the general perished in fairly close proximity to the men holding the bridge. This cannot but add to the many doubts which have been raised about the story, not least the fact that there is no first-hand account of the incident, the only sources of the story being the memoirs of three veterans of the regiment (Kincaid, Surtees and Costello) who were not at Cacabelos, and in at least one case offer details which do not seem particularly plausible. That Plunkett got the credit for bringing down Colbert is established fact, but the reason why will probably forever remain unclear: judging from the secondary accounts, which all emphasise not that Plunkett fired at very long range but rather that he ran forward towards the enemy to take his shot, the most likely explanation is that he was seen to bring down Colbert after having taken up a very exposed position so as to attain a better field of fire. For all this, see G. Caldwell, *Thomas Plunkett of the Ninety-Fifth Rifles: Hero, Villain, Fact or Fiction* (Godmanchester, 2010), pp. 18–23, and S. Haddaway, 'Rifleman Thomas Plunkett: a pattern for the battalion', http://www.napoleon-series.org/research/biographies/c_plunkett.html, accessed 7 August 2017.

8.   The Ninety-Fifth cannot be said to come out well from this account, and it may therefore be the case that the story of Tom Plunkett was deliberately 'talked up' so as to divert attention from a day in the regiment's annals that was less than glorious.

Regiment who flew to the aid of their friends, now formed one indiscriminate mass, and the light company . . . could no longer fire except at the dragoons' heads . . . It stung us to the heart to see our gallant comrades so maltreated with aid so near, for, had we of the light [p. 61] company crossed the hedge under which we were drawn up and advanced a short way in regular order so as to form a *point d'appui*, all would have been put to rights, but we durst not move an inch, being posted close to our guns for our protection and every moment expecting to encounter another charge of cavalry.

At this time General Merle's division appeared on the hills in front of the position and moved forward. The Reserve now showed themselves, probably with a view of inducing the enemy to delay their attack until the morning. A heavy column of the enemy were pushed forward toward the left of our position in front of where the Fifty-Second Regiment had been posted. Their intention was evidently to cross the stream, but, their column soon becoming unveiled, our guns again wheeled out on to the road and opened such a destructive fire that, although close to the Cua, they hastily retired, after having sustained considerable loss. Had the fifty-Second remained as first posted, the carnage in the column must have been immense, but it is probable that the enemy were aware of that regiment having shifted their ground, for they sent no skirmishers in advance of their column. The skirmish, hitherto sharply maintained by the Ninety-Fifth and Fifty-Second against their opponents, now slackened and shortly ceased. The French *tirailleurs* and cavalry, perceiving the failure of their infantry attack on our left and that they were fast retiring, retired also down to the banks of the Cua.

Select Bibliography

Memoirs, Journals, Contemporary Accounts and Collections of Correspondence

Anon., *Journal of a Soldier of the Seventy-First, or Glasgow Regiment, Highland Light Infantry, from 1806 to 1815* (Edinburgh, 1819)

Cadell, C., *Narrative of the Campaigns of the Twenty-Eighth Regiment since their Return from Egypt in 1802* (London, 1835)

Clinton, H., *A Few Remarks explanatory of the Motives which guided the Operations of the British Army during the late Campaign in Spain* (London, 1809)

Dobbs, J., *Recollections of an Old Fifty-Second Man* (Waterford, 1863)

Forster, J. (ed.), *The Works and Life of Walter Savage Landor* (London, 1876)

Frere, W.E. and H.B.E. (eds), *The Works of John Hookham Frere in Verse and Prose* (London, 1872)

Gleig, G.R., *Lives of the Most Eminent British Military Commanders* (London, 1832)

Glover, G. (ed.), *'A Hellish Business': the Letters of Captain Charles Kinloch, Fifty-Second Light Infantry, 1806–1816* (Godmanchester, 2007)

Glover, G. (ed.), *From Corunna to Waterloo: the Letters and Journals of two Napoleonic Hussars, 1806–1816* (London, 2007)

Glover, G. (ed.), *The Diary of William Gavin: Ensign and Quarter-Master of the Seventy-First Highland Regiment, 1806–1815* (Godmanchester, 2013)

Glover, G. (ed.), *The Letters of Lieutenant-Colonel Sir John Cameron, First Battalion, Ninth Regiment of Foot, 1808–14* (Godmanchester, 2013)

Gurwood, J. (ed.), *The Dispatches of Field Marshal Lord Wellington during his Various Campaigns in India, Denmark, Portugal, Spain, the Low Countries and France* (new and enlarged edn, London, 1852)

Hamilton, A., *Hamilton's Campaign with Moore and Wellington during the Peninsular War* (Troy, New York, 1847)

Hibbert, C. (ed.), *The Recollections of Rifleman Harris* (London, 1970)

Ilchester, Earl of (ed.), *The Spanish Journal of Elizabeth, Lady Holland* (London, 1910)

Jackson, Lady (ed.), *The Diaries and Letters of Sir George Jackson* (London, 1872)

Landsmann, G., *Recollections of my Military Life* (London, 1854)

Leach, J., *Rough Sketches in the Life of an Old Soldier* (London, 1831)

Leith-Hay, A., *A Narrative of the Peninsular War* (London, 1831)

Lewis, M., *A Monody on the Death of Lieutenant-General Sir John Moore with Notes Historical and Political by Robert T. Paine, Esquire* (Boston, 1811)

Londonderry, Marquess of, *Narrative of the Peninsular War from 1808 to 1813* (London, 1828)

Ludovici, E., *On the Road with Wellington: the Diary of a War Commissary* (London, 1924)

Maurice, J.F. (ed.), *The Diary of Sir John Moore* (London, 1904)

Moore, J.C., *A Narrative of the Campaign of the British Army in Spain commanded by His Excellency, Lieutenant-General Sir John Moore, K.B., etc., etc., etc., authenticated by Official Papers and Original Letters* (London, 1809)

Moore, J.C., *The Life of Lieutenant-General Sir John Moore, K.B.* (London, 1833–4)

Morley, S., *Memoirs of a Sergeant of the Fifth Regiment of Foot containing an Account of his Service in Hanover, South America and the Peninsula* (Ashford, 1842)

Napier, W., *History of the War in the Peninsula and in the South of France from the Year 1807 to the Year 1814* (new edn, rev. by C.J. Esdaile; London, 1880)

Neale, A., *Letters from Portugal and Spain comprising an Account of the Operations of the Armies under their Excellencies Sir Arthur Wellesley and Sir John Moore from the Landing of the Troops in Mondego Bay to the Battle of Corunna* (London, 1809)

Ormsby, J.W., *An Account of the Operations of the British Army and of the State and Sentiments of the People of Portugal and Spain during the Campaigns of the Years 1808 and 1809* (London, 1809)

Paget, E. (ed.), *Letters and Memorials of General Sir Edward Paget, G.C.B., collected and arranged by his Daughter, Harriet Mary Paget* (London, 1898)

Patterson, J., *The Adventures of Captain John Patterson, with Notices of the Officers, etc., of the Fiftieth or Queen's Regiment, from 1807 to 1831* (London, 1837)

Porter, R.K., *Letters from Portugal and Spain written during the March of the British Troops under Sir John Moore* (London, 1809)

Russell, J., *Recollections and Suggestions, 1813–1873* (London, 1875)

Southey, C.C. (ed.), *The Life and Correspondence of Robert Southey* (London, 1849–50)

Southey, R.W., *A History of the Peninsular War* (London, 1823–32)

Stapleton, A., *George Canning and his Times* (London, 1859)

Steevens, C., *Reminiscences of my Military Life from 1795 to 1818*, ed. H. Steevens (Winchester, 1878)

Sturgis, J. (ed.), *A Boy in the Peninsular War: the Services, Adventures and Experiences of Robert Blakeney, Subaltern in the Twenty-Eighth Regiment* (London, 1899)

Toreno, Conde de, *Historia del levantamiento, guerra y revolución de España*, ed. R. Hocquellet (Pamplona, 2008)

Venault de Charmilly, P.F., *To the British Nation is presented by Colonel Venault de Charmilly, Knight of the Royal and Military Order of Saint Louis, the Narrative of his Transactions with the Right Honourable John Hookham Frere, His Britannic Majesty's Minister Plenitpotentiary and Lieutenant-General Sir John Moore, K.B., with the Suppressed Correspondence of Sir J. Moore, being a Refutation of the Calumnies invented against Him and proving that He was never acquainted with General Morla* (London, 1810)

Wylly, H. (ed.), *A Cavalry Officer in the Corunna Campaign, 1808–1809: the Journal of Captain Gordon of the Fifteenth Hussars* (London, 1913)

Secondary Sources

Anglesey, Marquess of, *One-Leg: the Life and Letters of Henry William Paget, First Marquess of Anglesey, K.G., 1768–1854* (London, 1961)

Brownrigg, B., *The Life and Letters of Sir John Moore* (Oxford, 1922)

Bruce, H.A., *Life of Sir William Napier, K.C.B., Author of the History of the Peninsular War* (London, 1864)

Caldwell, G., *Thomas Plunkett of the Ninety-Fifth Rifles: Hero, Villain, Fact or Fiction* (Godmanchester, 2010)

Davies, D.W., *Sir John Moore's Peninsular Campaign, 1808–1809* (The Hague, 1974)

Day, R., *The Life of Sir John Moore: Not a Drum was Heard* (Barnsley, 2001)

Esdaile, C.J., *The Peninsular War: a New History* (London, 2002)

Esdaile, C.J., *Women in the Peninsular War* (Norman, Oklahoma, 2014)

Esdaile, C.J. and Muir, R., 'Strategic planning in a time of small government: the war against Revolutionary and Napoleonic France, 1793–1815', in C.W. Woolgar (ed.), *Wellington Studies* (Southampton, 1996), pp. 48–71

Fortescue, J.W., *A History of the British Army* (London, 1899–1930)

Haythornthwaite, P., *Corunna, 1809: Sir John Moore's Fighting Retreat* (Oxford, 2001)

Hibbert, C., *Corunna* (London, 1967)

Macdonald, J., *Sir John Moore: the Making of a Controversial Hero* (Barnsley, 2016)

Oman, C., *A History of the Peninsular War* (Oxford, 1902–30)

Oman, C.M.A., *Sir John Moore* (London, 1953)

Summerville, C., *March of Death: Sir John Moore's Retreat to Corunna, 1808–1809* (London, 2003)

Wilkin, W.H., *The Life of Sir David Baird* (London, 1912)